Moral Imagination in the Twenty-first Century

What role could or should moral imagination play in managerial and corporate decision-making? This book focuses on three simple questions: Why do ordinary, decent managers engage in questionable behavior? Why do successful companies ignore the ethical dimensions of their processes, decisions, and actions? And what motivates a successful company such as McDonald's, which closed its 800 restaurants in Russia, to depart from a large and very profitable market? Working from the assumption that all human experience is socially constructed and incomplete, this book argues that a critical missing element in many instances of alleged managerial or corporate wrongdoing is a simple phenomenon: moral imagination. In this fully updated edition, three new chapters and topical case studies, such as Boeing and Google, allow readers to bring process philosophy and systems insights into organizational and managerial thinking. A valuable resource for scholars, students, and corporate decision-makers.

PATRICIA H. WERHANE is Professor Emerita in the Darden School of Business at the University of Virginia and DePaul University, and the author or editor of 36 books and 150 articles and book chapters. She was the founding editor of *Business Ethics Quarterly* and the executive producer of two video series on poverty alleviation and on founding thinkers in business ethics and corporate responsibility. She was a Rockefeller Fellow at Dartmouth College, Andersen Fellow at Cambridge University, and Fulbright Scholar at All Hollows Collage, Dublin.

DAVID J. BEVAN directs postgraduate courses in action learning at St. Martin's Institute of Higher Education, Malta, and is author of more than fifty articles in critical management and business ethics. He is a visiting professor at King's College London where he obtained a PhD in social accounting with a background in philosophy and higher education. He has served on the management faculties of international universities, currently serves the editorial boards of several management and ethics journals, and edits two book series for Springer.

Moral Imagination in the Twenty-first Century
Individuals and Organizations

PATRICIA H. WERHANE
University of Virginia

DAVID J. BEVAN
Saint Martin's Institute of Higher Education

CAMBRIDGE
UNIVERSITY PRESS

Shaftesbury Road, Cambridge CB2 8EA, United Kingdom

One Liberty Plaza, 20th Floor, New York, NY 10006, USA

477 Williamstown Road, Port Melbourne, VIC 3207, Australia

314–321, 3rd Floor, Plot 3, Splendor Forum, Jasola District Centre, New Delhi – 110025, India

103 Penang Road, #05–06/07, Visioncrest Commercial, Singapore 238467

Cambridge University Press is part of Cambridge University Press & Assessment, a department of the University of Cambridge.

We share the University's mission to contribute to society through the pursuit of education, learning and research at the highest international levels of excellence.

www.cambridge.org
Information on this title: www.cambridge.org/9781009565851

DOI: 10.1017/9781009565875

© Patricia H. Werhane and David J. Bevan 2026

This publication is in copyright. Subject to statutory exception and to the provisions of relevant collective licensing agreements, no reproduction of any part may take place without the written permission of Cambridge University Press & Assessment.

When citing this work, please include a reference to the DOI 10.1017/9781009565875

Original version published as *Moral Imagination and Management Decision Making* © 1999 Oxford University Press

Revised edition published 2026

A catalogue record for this publication is available from the British Library

Library of Congress Cataloging-in-Publication Data
Names: Werhane, Patricia Hogue author | Bevan, David, 1948– author | Werhane, Patricia Hogue. Moral imagination and management decision-making
Title: Moral imagination in the twenty-first century : individuals and organizations / Patricia H. Werhane, University of Virginia, David J. Bevan, Saint Martin's Institute of Higher Education.
Other titles: Moral imagination and management decision-making
Description: Cambridge, United Kingdom : Cambridge University Press, New York, NY, 2026. | Includes bibliographical references and index.
Identifiers: LCCN 2025018080 | ISBN 9781009565851 hardback | ISBN 9781009565844 paperback | ISBN 9781009565875 ebook
Subjects: LCSH: Decision making – Moral and ethical aspects | Management – Moral and ethical aspects | Business ethics
Classification: LCC HD30.23 .W467 2026 | DDC 658.4/08–dc23/eng/20250814
LC record available at https://lccn.loc.gov/2025018080

ISBN 978-1-009-56585-1 Hardback
ISBN 978-1-009-56584-4 Paperback

Cambridge University Press & Assessment has no responsibility for the persistence or accuracy of URLs for external or third-party internet websites referred to in this publication and does not guarantee that any content on such websites is, or will remain, accurate or appropriate.

For EU product safety concerns, contact us at Calle de José Abascal, 56, 1°, 28003 Madrid, Spain, or email eugpsr@cambridge.org

Contents

Acknowledgments	*page* vi
1 Introduction	1
2 Why Do Good People and Great Organizations Do Bad Things?	15
3 Social Constructivism and the Very Idea of a Conceptual Scheme	56
4 The *Rashomon* Effect	84
5 Moral Imagination	97
6 Moral Reasoning and Moral Imagination	124
7 Systems Thinking, Process Philosophy, and Moral Imagination	140
8 Next Stages: Reformulating the Paradigm of Western Industrial Global Capitalism through Moral Imagination	157
9 Moral Imagination in Technological Development AMANDA MCCROSKERY AND BEN ZEVENBERGEN	173
References	196
Index	216

Acknowledgments

In Chapter 2 this version of the Boeing 737 MAX case was extracted with edits from Englehardt, Elaine, Werhane, Patricia, and Newton, Lisa, 2021, "Leadership, Engineering and Ethical Clashes at Boeing," *Science and Engineering Ethics*, 27: 11–17. Reprinted by permission of the authors.

In Chapter 3, "The Volkswagen Emissions Scandal," Darden Business Publishing Case UVA S-267. Charlottesville Virginia. 2018. Edited and reproduced by permission from Luann Lynch, Elizabeth Bird, and Cameron Curto. Reprinted by permission of Darden Publishing, Charlottesville, VA.

An earlier version of Chapter 7 was published in Patricia H. Werhane, 2002. "Moral Imagination and Systems Thinking," *Journal of Business Ethics*, 38: 33–42. Reprinted by permission of Springer Nature.

An earlier version of Chapter 8 was published in Bevan, D. and Werhane P., 2024. "Reformulating the Western Paradigm of Global Capitalism" in Pava and Dion, *Justifying Next Stage Capitalism*. Dortrecht: Springer. Reprinted by permission of the editors and publisher.

Chapter 9 was written by two managers at Google who use the framework of Werhane's moral imagination in their management workshops. Included by release from Google.

I Introduction

> I have used the word "attention" which I borrow from Simone Weil, to express the idea of a just and loving gaze directed upon an individual reality. I believe this to be the characteristic and proper mark of the moral agent.
>
> (Murdoch, 1971, p. 34)

Let us open with a context. In 1990 the giant American-based fast-food chain McDonald's opened its first restaurant in Russia, on Pushkin Square in Moscow. The company quickly expanded its operations, eventually opening 850 restaurants, of which 84 percent were proprietarily owned by McDonald's. The restaurants employed a total of around 62,000 employees. But in 2022, because of the Russian invasion and war in Ukraine, McDonald's decided to close all its restaurants, selling most of them to Russian owners and removing their name. Shortly following this action, almost 1,000 other foreign companies closed or curtailed their Russian operations. McDonald's decision was not without challenges, since most of these restaurants were very popular and profitable. A number of other American-based companies withdrew from the Russian market as well.

> "This is a complicated issue that's without precedent and with profound consequences," said McDonald's chief executive Chris Kempczinski in a message to staff and suppliers.
>
> "Some might argue that providing access to food and continuing to employ tens of thousands of ordinary citizens, is surely the right thing to do," he added.
>
> "But it is impossible to ignore the humanitarian crisis caused by the war in Ukraine. And it is impossible to imagine the Golden Arches representing the same hope and promise that led us to enter the Russian market 32 years ago."
>
> *(Morton, 2022)*

This book, like its predecessor *Moral Imagination and Management Decision-Making* (1999), explores the role of moral imagination in managerial and corporate decision-making. The aim here is to progressively develop some fresh process philosophy and systems insights into organizational and managerial thinking on three simple questions: Why do ordinary, decent managers engage in questionable behavior? Why do successful companies ignore the ethical dimensions of their processes, decisions, and actions? And what motivates a successful company such as McDonald's to withdraw from a large and very profitable market?

Working from the assumption that all human experience is socially constructed and incomplete, we will then argue that a critical missing element in many instances of alleged managerial or corporate wrongdoing is a simple phenomenon: moral imagination.

> Moral imagination refers to the ability to perceive that a web of competing economic relationships is, at the same time, a web of moral relationships. Developing moral imagination means becoming sensitive to ethical issues in business decision making, but it also means searching out places where people are likely to be hurt by decision making or behavior of organizations or managers. Moral imagination is a necessary first step, but because of prevailing methods of evaluating managers on bottom-line results, it is extremely challenging. It is essential, however, before anything else can happen.
> (Carroll, 1987, 13)

By "moral imagination" we include the awareness of various dimensions of a particular context as well as its operative framework and narratives. Moral imagination entails the ability to understand that context or set of activities from a number of different perspectives, the actualizing of new possibilities that are not context dependent, and the instigation of the process of evaluating those possibilities from a rational and moral point of view. It is the latter that distinguishes moral imagination. Thus, we shall argue, moral imagination, together with moral reasoning, are necessary ingredients in management decision-making.

Otherwise, one often gets trapped in a particular "schema" or narrative that fails to take into account important dimensions of one's activities, or one's imagination fails to take into account the moral dimensions of any human decision-making. McDonald's withdrawal from the lucrative Russia market illustrates such decision-making.

If ethics involved simply a process of evaluating questionable people or questionable institutions engaged in bad behavior, there would be many fewer ethical *issues*. However, most ethical issues in business are not a result of clear-cut misbehavior. They usually involve smart managers and reputable companies that somehow, in some ways strayed in their behavior. For example, recent Boeing 737 MAX disasters and other Boeing headaches we will outline in Chapter 2 are not results of pure evildoing. Rather, and reminiscent of the features of "Postmodern Ethics" (Bauman, 1993), it is a processual distancing of administration from engineering, the preoccupation with profitability rather than quality control and a number of other seemingly simple factors contributed to these tragedies. (See Englehardt et al., 2021 and Chapter 2 of this book.)

Another recent incident was the BP Deepwater Horizon disaster, one of the largest environmental catastrophes in history (Averill et al., 2022): a massive oil spill that occurred in April 2010 in the Gulf of Mexico and which gives us an opportunity to consider the processes involved. An explosion on the Deepwater Horizon oil rig, operated by Transocean and leased by BP, led to the deaths of eleven workers and triggered an oil spill that lasted for eighty-seven days, releasing around 4.9 million barrels of oil into the sea. Key causes of this accident were complex and can be seen as arising from a number of overlapping processes:

- Well design failures – the well design for the BP Macondo Prospect well was complex and lacked the adequate redundancy measures that might have prevented a blowout. The operator chose a less expensive, "long string" well casing, that was more susceptible to leaks, rather than selecting a liner system that would have provided additional safety barriers.
- Structural failures – Halliburton, the contractor responsible for cementing the well, used a nitrogen-foamed cement that was intended to create a seal around the well. In fact, this cement seal failed to hold. Laboratory tests, to

which BP had access, had indicated that this cement mix could be unstable, but they went ahead without taking any extra precautions.
- Equipment failures – the blowout preventer (BOP), manufactured by Cameron, was a final line of defense to prevent oil from flowing uncontrollably. It was found later that this BOP had a depleted battery and it failed to function, making it redundant when the blowout actually occurred.
- Safety culture lapses – BP and its contractors demonstrated historic safety lapses and cost-cutting measures. In a drive to reduce expenses, BP often compromised on safety. Investigations later showed there were clear warning signs of the risk of an impending blowout, but both BP and Transocean supervisors either ignored these or downplayed their severity to stay on a less expensive maintenance schedule.
- Failures in attention to routine – just before this blowout, there were inconsistencies in the pressure tests conducted to check the integrity of the well. However, these test results were misinterpreted by both BP's and Transocean's crew, and operations continued despite signs of pressure imbalances, which should have been taken as a clear indication that gas was seeping into the well.

Even worse, the disaster was also the result of multiple incidents of compounding poor decisions made in pursuit of economic efficiency, and a lack of regulatory oversight and safety protocols further amplified the risk. United States government investigations later found that the regulatory agencies involved actually lacked the resources and authority to enforce the highest safety standards, and that BP and its partners had not been held strictly held accountable.[1] This case illustrates how a whole system can go awry because of simple neglect of procedures and obvious signs of weaknesses in the operations.

Why do these tragic events occur? The former Federal Reserve chairperson Paul Volcker argues that the common thread in these scenarios is "good, old-fashioned greed" (quoted in Bacon and Salwen, 1991, A10). But that explanation, while probably partially

---

[1] The BP Deepwater Horizon disaster underscores the risks of high-pressure deepwater drilling and the need for rigorous safety measures in offshore oil production. It led to new regulations and reforms in offshore drilling operations with a view to preventing similar incidents in the future.

true, is not altogether satisfactory. No one at Boeing nor its subcontractors had any wish or anything to gain with the explosions of the 727 MAX. Nor has BP profited from their failure. Yet, as we shall see, these incidents were caused by human and organizational failures.

These cases raise seemingly simple questions with which we began this book. Ethical issues in business, like those in personal life, are troublesome, the more so because most managers in today's open and competitive economy are smart, well-intentioned people, and the companies they manage ordinarily intentionally try to avoid egregious behavior. Why is it, then, that some become involved in questionable activities or produce harm while others do not? Is merely human fallibility the cause, or is something more at stake?

A second set of questions derives from other cases. Most managers and most companies are not without ethical difficulties. Indeed, it would be strange if they were, because neither the people nor the companies they constitute are infallible. But the problem is not merely a one-time weakness of will but what we would call moral amnesia or moral blindness, an inability to remember or learn from one's own and others' past mistakes and to transfer that knowledge when fresh challenges arise. As a result, as we saw at Boeing, after the two tragic crashes of their newly reconstituted 737 MAX, when a door from one of their 737 planes fell off while in flight (Gelles, 2019). Fortunately, no one was killed, but it was a close call. And there were further questions and mishaps, caused in part by organizational failure. Are these failures merely due to sloppy quality control or can they be traced to managerial decision-making that pressured the company to produce more planes, putting production ahead of quality.

These cases, and others, tell a story about business, and it is not a positive story. None of these incidents need to have occurred, nor should they have been repeated. They create a false impression that business is not a morally worthwhile enterprise, although, as we will contend, this is not true, as the McDonald's and other companies' withdrawals from the very profitable Russian market illustrate, withdrawals based primarily on principle, not profit. This is not to conclude that McDonald's or any other company is perfect. Companies are created by human beings, and we are each, in different ways, imperfect; so, too, are the organizations we create and manage. But the conclusion that free enterprise commerce is evil is troublesome if not false. In order to tell a positive story about business, we have to figure out how to avoid these needless negative outcomes.

There is a third set of issues we will investigate in this book: cases that illustrate how a certain set of beliefs or a narrative becomes so dominant that we begin to believe that narrative without verifying its truth. We organize our experience through a nexus of mental models that create a series of stories or narratives. When one narrative becomes widely accepted, it can affect one's judgment and bias the ways one deals with other facts even to the extent of excluding from consideration or even falsifying verifiable data.

The role of narratives is important, for example, in following the adventures of Sam Bankman-Fried (SBF) in his creation of enormous very profitable cryptocurrency trading firms, through which he became the darling of Wall Street and was admired by politicians whom he wooed and supported. Despite this myth of a successful trader, SBF's firms eventually went bankrupt because they "lost" (i.e., they could not find) $7 billion of depositors' assets. Perhaps SBF thought he was playing a game with these currencies. He thus created a narrative, an interpretation of reality that cryptocurrency trading was a game like chess, and one explanation of his behavior is that others as well as SBF bought into that narrative despite its fantasy.[2] Similarly, according to at least two commentators, after numerous successful launches, NASA officials began to think that the agency was invincible and that the space shuttle was a perfect, even risk-free vehicle (Feynman, 1989, 179–183; Schwartz, 1987, 56–67).

The consequences of accepting these sorts of narratives are obvious. The more than 20-year-old and still ongoing series of cases

[2] Note that after SBF was proven guilty of fraud and imprisoned, the successor companies made good on almost all of the "lost" $7 billion. Bankman-Fried, however, remains in prison (Rowe, 2024).

of alleged fraud involving over 600 sub-postmasters in the British Post Office system was due primarily to a managerial belief system that assumed all software was infallible (Flinders, 2024). The software the Post Office organization employed turned out to be faulty, but it took at least fifteen years to unearth this faulty belief system that perpetuated wrong convictions of these sub-postmasters.

Chapter 2 begins with an exploration of a number of tempting ways to approach these complex issues of intentionality and moral accountability. If "good, old-fashioned greed" is a factor, we need to investigate the role of self-interest in managerial decision-making. It will turn out, however, that self-interests are complex matters, that people are motivated by other interests including genuine interests in other people, and that egoism, alone, is a defective mechanism for explaining human and organizational behavior.

According to the moral development literature, a second option is to speculate that managers at Boeing, for instance, operated on the lowest level of moral development, gauging their moral judgments on what Lawrence Kohlberg and other psychologists call the preconventional level, using self-interest and personal gain as the only goal of their activities, and basing their actions simply on whether they would be caught. This analysis might be plausible to describe some behaviors, although there is independent evidence of his strong moral upbringing, but it hardly describes most managerial decision-making. It is true that most managers act for the self-interest of their companies, and one can safely conclude that no one wants to get caught engaged in wrongdoing. Yet evidence from a number of studies suggests that most managers operate at least on the conventional moral development level; they care a great deal about interrelationships and appeal to conventions, social mores, and the law to guide their actions (Derry, 1989).

Alternately, one could conclude that managers of companies in trouble are of weak moral character, that they do not exhibit the virtues of excellence, honor, and respect for community (Solomon, 1992). This, too, is a difficult contention to verify, and again, there is contrary evidence that Boeing's engineers were basically decent, even personally virtuous people.

There is still another set of explanations of moral amnesia or moral blindness. Each of us, as a member of a particular society embedded in family, religious, social, and political relationships and as a professional, a manager, or an employee, has, or acquires, a number of social roles. These roles are defined by the social institutions in which one finds oneself or is a member. Sometimes these roles and their concomitant responsibilities overwhelmingly shape one's worldview and strongly influence one's judgments. We find, for example, religious zealots so committed to a cause or, on a smaller scale, employees so committed to their company and its survival, that they will perform activities unconscionable or even absurd to the ordinary outsider. In the Volkswagen (VW) diesel engine scandal, the numerous managers and engineers who participated in this fraud had to know that this was illegal as well as opaque to its customers. Their perceived commitment to keep VW as the world's largest car manufacturer and their obedience to managerial authority of VW overrode ordinary role expectations and the universal code of safety all engineers are expected to adhere to. It overrode moral considerations and legal requirements. That this behavior was a conflict of interest for an engineer did not deter their commitment to the company as the first priority.

Moral philosophers offer another set of reasons. Few managers have had serious training in moral philosophy, nor do many of them understand the nuances of deontology, utilitarianism, rights theory, and theories of virtue or justice. There is a set of arguments that develops the thesis that training in moral reasoning might increase moral awareness, facilitate moral decision-making, and, it is proposed, prevent many of the problems from occurring. Moral education, if complete, would prevent many of the incidents we have cited, according to this thesis. It will turn out, however, that the simple teaching and application of moral principles or rules may not alleviate all problems. It is not always lack of logic or ignorance of moral principles that causes these problems but the principles' general character that fails in the specificity of its application. This specificity has not so much to do with the particular situation at issue, per se, but rather with how the situation is perceived and framed by its protagonists. What is evident, however, in many cases, is not weak moral development: neither a failure of moral character, nor a lack of understanding what is right or wrong, but rather a setting aside of moral considerations in the pace or fog of business activities. So simply learning about moral reasoning or moral theory, in the abstract, by itself, does not appear to be enough unless one somehow and with attention integrates those reasoning skills into actual practice.

We shall argue that most individual managers are not without moral sensibilities or values, nor are they motivated merely by greed or even self-interest, nor are most of these managers at a low level of moral development. Companies, too, are not without moral sensibilities, and many corporations such as Boeing have a values statement and an ethics program for managers. Nevertheless, in many situations and in the course of many processes, managers have an unduly narrow perspective on their situation and little in the way of moral imagination. As SBF illustrates, some managers confuse reality with what they want it to be. Others lack a sense of the variety of possibilities and moral consequences of their decisions, as well as the ability to imagine a wide range of possible issues, consequences, and solutions. Some individuals and institutions are trapped in the framework of history, organization, corporate culture, and/or tradition of which they are only at best vaguely aware, a framework that often drives their decision-making to preclude taking into account moral concerns, a framework that sometimes even allows or encourages managers to overestimate their powers and abilities. Still other managers are so focused on their roles and role responsibilities to a particular organization that they fail to consider simple norms of morality.

To account for these phenomena, we shall defend a simple point. All reality is socially structured. All experience is interpreted or constituted by a conceptual scheme and an overlapping set of incomplete mental models through which we selectively frame, order, organize, and interpret the data of experience. Each of us functions through a set of mental models that are socially learned, culturally inculcated, educationally reinforced, and experientially altered. These mental models are necessarily incomplete and volatile; that is, they can be relearned and changed. They are neither universally, socially, institutionally, nor culturally the same in every individual, although they overlap and are socially, institutionally, and culturally shared or shareable with others. In some settings certain mental models function as scripts that focus our attention on a particular set of habits for dealing with that set of events in that context. In those cases these mental models serve as focusing mechanisms to bracket out other points of view or other schema. Thus, the kinds of mental models operative in any setting create decision-making habits that may preclude the taking into account of some important data. For example, as we shall argue in more detail, Boeing's long-term successes in the aerospace industry may have led to lethargy: to a failure to reinvigorate safety and quality measures.

Moreover, all human experiences are embedded in a set of narratives, many of which are not of one's own making. We are born into a particular historical tradition, and we find ourselves part of religious, social, and cultural traditions embedded in a language. We do not choose these traditions and narratives, nor can we always escape them. Sometimes these narratives can be distorting, as the SBF case illustrates. Still, we shall argue further, none of us is merely defined by our background narratives. Each of us is an author of, as well as a participant in, our own history and narratives.

Therefore, even though all experience is interpreted, reality is socially constituted, and our experiences are embedded in series of narratives, we shall argue that who we are, what we do, and how we behave are not merely narrative driven or conceptually constrained. There are at least two reasons why this is so. First, we shall argue, the self cannot be merely equated with its roles and social relationships, despite the impossibility of getting at the self apart from those roles and relationships. Thus, the existence of some narrow-minded decision-making, or the dominance of strongly differentiated role responsibilities, does not morally excuse misbehavior or the occurrence of untoward consequences that could have been avoided. Second, because mental models and narratives are incomplete and overlap, human choices are not merely context determined. Underlying all human activity is what Donald Davidson calls a "common coordinate system" (Davidson, 1974, 5) that accounts for human understanding and communication and for the fact that any particular mental model can be examined and revised.

One of the primary reasons for the undesirable outcomes in the cases we have cited is a paucity of moral imagination. Most managers and their institutions do not lack moral principles. Rather, they sometimes have a narrow perspective on their situation. They lack a sense of the variety of possibilities and moral consequences of their decisions and the ability to imagine a wide range of issues, consequences, and solutions. Some individuals are trapped in an organizational framework and tradition of which they are only vaguely aware, a framework that often drives their decision-making and excludes considerations of moral concerns. Managers do not always remember and thus learn from their mistakes, because they do not realize they have made mistakes. Sometimes, too, a dominant narrative creates a story that, while plausible, distorts and narrows the frame of decision-making.

A developed moral imagination gives managers means to disengage themselves from a particular situation, from its narrative, from one's roles, and from a dominating conceptual scheme. Moral imagination enables one to assess one's situation, to evaluate present and new possibilities, and to create decisions that are not parochially embedded in a restricted context or confined by a certain point of view. Without moral imagination, mistakes are reiterated.

However, one should not confuse moral imagination with practical moral reasoning. As we outline in Chapter 6, moral imagination is a necessary but not a sufficient condition for creative moral managerial decision-making. Without moral imagination one can easily be drawn into a particular mindset that does not take into account other critical perspectives. On the other hand, imagination alone can create fantasies that, too, become dominating and falsifying narratives, as the British Post Office cases demonstrate. Moral reasoning is a crucial element in management decision-making, an element that nevertheless depends on moral imagination as its driving force and on moral standards as its "bottom line." Practical moral reasoning takes into account ethical theory but not abstractly. Moral reasoning begins with the particular – a specific scenario. This is because in the first instance ethics has to do with human relationships and human activities, not with abstract formal principles. It generates conclusions from that particular set of events, taking into account not merely the situation but its narrative and the set of mental models or conceptual schemes that frames these events. Moral imagination is essential to get one from a particular situation to a more disengaged perspective. At the same time, moral reasoning helps to challenge any event with stipulative principles or minimum moral standards that are not context dependent or merely forms of role morality. Management decision-making, then, must be contextual, imaginative, and rational. It must begin with the particular, but go beyond that, in order to avoid obvious errors in judgment. Moral imagination and moral reasoning provide concrete managerial and organizational decision-making skills with which to avoid questionable activities, prevent unseemly consequences, and enable a manager or a company to create decision models that contribute positively to corporate and societal well-being.

There is one more dimension of moral imagination: reminding ourselves that decision-making, and indeed all human activities are embedded in systems and subsystems that entail ongoing ever-changing processes. This dimension of analysis will be outlined in Chapter 7.

To conclude the body of this work in Chapter 8 we step back from our analyses of individual, managerial, and organizational moral imagination to look more broadly at the role of moral imagination in analyzing and critiquing contemporary global capitalism and multinational corporations (MNCS), which seemingly have ubiquitous roles in expanding this phenomenon. We will engage in morally imaginative thinking to disengage from a Western capitalist mindset to look more broadly at the various cultures and "social imaginaries" that inhabit our world. While conceding that various forms of capitalism dominate economic thinking, we conclude that, given the cultural and ethnic diversities existing throughout the planet, an approach or set of approaches that acknowledges diverse social imaginaries might better serve these localized points of view. In the long run the goal of poverty alleviation, if not economic development, might better be achieved.

Throughout the book we have cited cases in which imaginative decision-making has enabled or even driven managers to be creative, profitable, and morally exemplary. Companies such as McDonald's and others that withdrew from Russia, have, in certain circumstances, gone beyond what is expected in the processes of ordinary managerial decision-making. These managers and their companies knowingly and creatively exhibited moral imagination, an imagination "disciplined by respect for the real" (Tuan, 1989, 10). They took moral risks, and they exhibited exemplary moral leadership while continuing to be profitable.

We end the book with an example of moral imagination in practice. This chapter is written by two managers at Google who conduct workshops using moral imagination as the template for managerial ethical decision-making. Their narrative illustrates how moral imagination and moral reasoning are not merely theoretical ideas but can be employed in practice to raise awareness of the many dimensions of corporate decision-making and action and strengthen managerial decision-making so that questionable behavior is alleviated if not avoid altogether. With their moral imaginations fully at work, decision-makers become, in Henry James's words, "finely aware and richly responsible" (James, 1934, 62, cited in Nussbaum, 1990, 111).

Or, to take an idea from Iris Murdoch (1919–1999) whose text appears as an epigraph to this chapter, managers and executives are giving their fuller attention to what they are doing and to the possible outcomes along the way. In Murdoch's philosophical and literary work, "attending" is a central concept that refers to a form of moral perception and a disciplined, compassionate attention to reality. Murdoch was influenced by philosophers such as Simone Weil (1909–1943), who had written about "attention" as a form of profound, selfless focus on the other, beyond personal desires or prejudices. Murdoch proposes that moral growth requires overcoming the ego's impulses and focusing on the true nature of others and the world. In this sense, attending involves cultivating a clear-sighted, loving gaze toward others, unclouded by selfish desires, which Murdoch saw as central to the development of virtue (Murdoch, 1971). Her novels (see for example Murdoch, 1969) illustrate this idea through characters who struggle to see each other clearly among an array of personal illusions, demonstrating how attending is both difficult and transformative. For Murdoch, this attending to the reality of others' is closely linked with love and compassion. In our genuinely attending to someone, we acknowledge their complexity, allowing for deeper empathy. Murdoch believed (and expressed in a more secular way) that attending to others would help dissolve self-centered patterns that often distort human relationships (Weil, [1947] 1952).

2   Why Do Good People and Great Organizations Do Bad Things?

BOEING AND THE 737 MAX

> At the Boeing Company, our first commitment is to the people and customers who rely on our products and services to protect, connect, and explore our world and beyond. We are each personally responsible for honoring that commitment and for serving as stewards of our company's legacy of aerospace excellence and innovation. We do that by committing to our values, and by holding ourselves to the highest standards of conduct in how we do our work, and how we treat one another. We understand that observing the highest ethical business standards is not only the right thing to do but is critical to our long-term success as a company.
>
> (Boeing, 2024)
>
> ... [what] we had in the two downed airplanes was a textbook failure of airmanship.
>
> (Langewiesche, 2019, 66)[1]

Boeing is one of America's largest defense contractors and is also one of the world's two largest aircraft manufacturers. It is known for reliable aircraft, and the 737 models that have been the workhorse for short flights and for small airlines all over the world for more than thirty years. Recently Boeing upgraded this plane with the 737 MAX models, and because of its stellar reputation and the reliability of the 737, it had orders for thousands of planes. Unfortunately, in 2018, Boeing 737 MAX malfunctions were the causes of two fatal air crashes in Indonesia and Ethiopia with the total loss of 346 lives. Subsequently the Federal Aviation Administration (FAA) grounded all 737 MAX flights. Obviously, the crashes and the subsequent

---

[1]   This version of the Boeing 737 MAX case was extracted with edits from Elaine Englehardt, Werhane, Patricia and Newton, Lisa, 2021, "Leadership, Engineering and Ethical Clashes at Boeing," *Science and Engineering Ethics*. 27: 11–17. Reprinted by permission.

grounding of these aircraft is a financial blow to Boeing and a great loss to those airlines relying on these new aircraft.

Most of the blame for the crashes has fallen squarely on the aircraft's malfunctioning software. A recent article about the 737 MAX describes the problem as follows:

> The immediate culprit (of both accidents) was a sensor failure tied to a new and obscure control function that was unique to the 737 MAX ... The Augmentation System [MCAS], an automated flight-control feature, applies double-speed impulses of nose-down trim, but only under circumstances so narrow that no regular airline pilot will ever experience its activation – unless a sensor fails. Boeing believed the system so innocuous, even if it malfunctioned, that the company did not inform pilots of its existence or include a description of it in the airplane's flight manuals.
>
> *(Langewiesche, 2019, 40. See also Pasztor et al., 2019)*

While there is no question about the occurrences of malfunctions, the case is more complicated. Langewiesche (2019) writes that "it was the decisions of the four pilots [in the two airplanes] more than the failure of a single obscure component, that led to the 346 deaths" (41). He argues persuasively that a well-trained pilot educated not merely on the mechanics and control panels of the aircraft but also a pilot experienced in what he calls "airmanship," learning how to react to unpredictable circumstances, could have flown these aircraft to safety, despite the malfunction. So then is the 737 MAX's flawed design only partly to blame?

To answer that question, we have to examine Boeing's corporate culture and the efficacy of its dominant logic. Boeing has long advocated pilot-centric designs that depend as much on pilots' skills as on cockpit technology. Perhaps, as Langewiesche argues, skilled pilots could have dealt with the 737 MAX's difficulties simply by turning off a few switches. Boeing's rival, Airbus, on the other hand, has created planes with technologies that allow the aircraft to fly almost by themselves. According to Airbus's CEO, this technology dramatically reduced the accidents resulting from pilot error (Langewiesche, 2019, 41). Despite this competition, however, Boeing continues with its pilot-centric design approach.

That pilot-controlled approach works well when pilots are well trained and are familiar with the specific aircraft. Unfortunately, the careful pilot training that is conducted in almost all developed nations is not well replicated in many emerging economies. The desire for air transportation, and stiff competition between airlines, often results in the hurried and rote training of pilots throughout the developing world. Such pilots can respond to routine instrument flying but are not always prepared for adverse flying conditions. Indeed, Lion Air has such a terrible safety record that in 2007 the European Union and the United States permanently banned all Indonesian airlines from flying in or over their air space (Langewiesche, 2019, 42). Even the Indonesian government acknowledges that pilot error contributed to the Lion Air 737 MAX crash (Pasztor et al., 2019, 1). More specifically it attributes the insufficient training to Boeing's failure to inform them of important changes to the 737 MAX's avionics software.

Boeing and Airbus have both been aware of the imperfect training and poor air safety records in many developing countries. They have engaged in pilot retraining, very successfully in China, which now has an impressive safety record. In other countries, however, Boeing's efforts were unsuccessful. Despite Boeing's awareness of its failed efforts with Indonesia's Lion Air pilot training, Boeing continued selling its planes to Lion Air, in 2011 accepting an order for 201,737 MAX planes (Langewiesche, 2019, 45).

Like the NASA disasters we will analyze in a following chapter, this scenario illustrates silo mentalities at Boeing and a stale corporate culture or dominant logic. Boeing's expertise is in pilot-centric aircraft. They have not changed that view despite fierce competition from Airbus and even though many of their foreign customers' pilot training programs are not pilot-centric. This model resulted from a siloed engineering approach and assumption that their planes are the best. Given the longevity of Boeing's success and excellence of its aircraft there was good reason to for holding this view. But we would suggest that this siloed thinking coupled with a dominant logic that Boeing is "the best" has created a twenty-first-century blind spot. Boeing depends on foreign orders to survive. But not all countries have the same commitment to excellence in pilot training and safety. Therefore, as Pasztor writes, "the plane maker and the FAA [need to] pay more attention to interaction between humans and cockpit computers ... average pilots who typically have less experience ... The pilots [of the Indonesian and Ethiopian planes that crashed] did not react in the ways that Boeing and the FAA assumed" (Pasztor et al., 2019, 1).

The pilot errors in Ethiopia and Indonesia were not only the result of insufficient training but also had a cultural component. In the iPhone age, the internet and cell phones are nearly ubiquitous. This breeds a misplaced complacency about technology. Overreliance on seemingly reliable technology gives rise to expectations that automation is the norm and that machines are self-correcting. Long before the 737 MAX crashes, these pilots were unprepared for unanticipated malfunctions. Their complacency had conditioned them to think that malfunctions would rarely require human intervention. This was not what pilots expected from aircraft manufactured in America. Boeing's incongruity with its more automated rival in Europe exacerbated the problem. But rather than adjusting to its diverse customer base abroad and/or, like Airbus, building an airplane that could essentially fly itself, Boeing continued with a twentieth-century engineering approach that would cost more than 300 lives.

Another problem was a specific design choice that undermined safety. In the early 2000s, Boeing engineers developed the MCAS for use in their military tanker. That design had multiple redundant sensors serving as safeguards in case one malfunctioned. Another set of Boeing engineers designed the 737 MAX and adapted the MCAS system, but with only one set of sensors. Whatever the reason, evidence shows that installing multiple sensors at least increases the price of the MAX. Sadly, leaving out this duplication was likely critical because the original design afforded pilots and the airplane itself a better chance of reacting to and correcting malfunctions (Sider and Tangel, 2019, 1–2).

Maureen Tkacik identified a third problem. She contends that the problem lies in the managerial structure at Boeing. Originally an engineering company with a focus on engineering excellence and safety, Boeing has now become preoccupied with profitability. Airplanes are considered commodities and safety is secondary to efficiency of production and sales (Tkacik, 2019, 1, 9). The division of engineering from managerial roles (as we saw at NASA) may have created silos and a corporate culture or dominant logic aimed at profitability and beating Airbus. Moreover, as difficulties surrounding the three-year late release of the 787 demonstrated, Boeing reduced its engineering staff by half, opting instead to outsource many components. This may have affected quality control and thus affected the design of the 737 MAX.

According to an engineer at Boeing commenting on the 777 jet in the 1990s, "One of the things that we do in the basic design in the pilot always has the ultimate authority of control. There is no computer on the airplane that he cannot override or turn off" (Tkacik, 2019, 1, 9). This was forgotten in the design of the 737 MAX, since it was difficult, at best, to turn off the MCAS. Whether this was an oversight, an effort not to overburden the pilots with unnecessary information, or a budget issue remains to be seen. (Tkacik argues it is the latter, but the jury is still out on that question.)

Finally, there is the difficult question of corporate culture. Recently Boeing released what were a plethora of internal emails, internal communications between engineers, between managers, and sometimes, between engineers and managers many of which complained about the corporate culture at Boeing. This culture, according to these perceptions, was driven by cost-cutting and profitability, all of which often overrode high engineering quality and safety. Accordingly, one email expressed the opinion that he would not let his family fly in a MAX (Pasztor, 2020, 1–2). Another email described the MAX as "designed by clowns who in turn are supervised by monkeys" (Gelles, 2020). Still another wrote, "I don't know how to fix these things . . . its systemic. It's culture. It's the fact that we have a senior leadership team that understand very little about the business and yet are driving us to certain objectives" (Pasztor, 2020, 2).

WHY DO GOOD PEOPLE AND DECENT ORGANIZATIONS DO BAD THINGS?

Since the time of Aristotle – to refer to the earliest records 2,500 years ago – people have been debating why good people engage in questionable moral behavior, and even repeat their mistakes. Why do these incidents continue to occur in a company as highly reputed as Boeing? Why do they sometimes reoccur? In this chapter we explore a number of explanations for these phenomena.

It is often argued that human beings are motivated primarily by self-interest; in business, managerial or corporate self-interest, sometimes even greed, accounts for questionable and even egregious behavior. Moreover, none of us is perfect, and so in large companies such as Boeing there are bound to be errors of judgment. From the psychology of moral development literature, one might conclude that some of these people have a low level of moral development; hence, they act without much regard either for the social or legal networks of relationships or for the consequences of their actions to themselves, to other people, or to their company.

Other explanations also attempt to account for these events and their perpetrators. Each of the cases cited in Chapter 1 occurs in a sociocultural and legal framework. It is then sometimes argued that social, political, and legal institutions, along with the corporate culture and the particular roles and role responsibilities of the managers and companies in question, create a causal nexus that constrains what we as outsiders might consider morally appropriate behavior and often precludes the consequential avoidance of harm.

> Moral blindness is characterized by conformity and dependency on the business corporation, institution, or administrative system ... Moral blindness implies that the administrator or manager has no

capacity of moral thinking. They only follow orders and justify their actions by reference to the technical goal-rationality of the organizational system. ... This attachment includes an abstraction from concrete human needs and concerns.. Where members of the system identify with their role and position in the organization ... An element of this moral indifference is the cooperative role of the victims of evil ... This instrumentalization implies
a dehumanization of the victims that are considered not as human beings but as elements, things or functions of the system.

(Rendtorff, 2020, 20–21)

Finally, both on the individual and corporate level, it is sometimes argued that many companies and their managers either are unaware of the moral dimensions of their activities or lack skills in moral reasoning. According to this argument, proper moral education could raise the level of individual and institutional moral awareness, enhance moral development, and give managers theoretical tools from moral theory with which to deal with ethical issues. These managers, then, fully trained in moral reasoning and moral theory, would apply such training to their decision processes with more positive results.

In what follows, we examine these explanations and approaches. Each of them, it will turn out, focuses on a part of what is important in managerial and corporate moral decision-making; each will aid my analysis of these questions throughout the book. However, none of the approaches we outline in what follows exhaustively answers these questions: Why do ordinarily decent managers or reputable companies get into trouble? Why do they sometimes repeat their mistakes? None of these explanations deals with the role of moral imagination in ethical decision-making.

HUMAN NATURE AND SELF-INTEREST

All companies are social organizations. They consist of people, and people are rarely morally perfect by almost any normative measure of morality. It thus follows that companies, like individuals, will be likely to make moral errors. This may seem obvious, and it is equally obvious that many of us continue to repeat our mistakes at least some of the time. But it is not obvious why managers, faced with issues similar to those they have faced in the past, when those former issues were public incidents that received media, regulatory, and public attention, repeat similar mistakes.

If it is correct that a motive for corporate misconduct is "good, old-fashioned greed," one could conclude that Boeing and other companies simply acted in their own self-interest, trying to accumulate as much wealth for themselves as possible by manipulating the system. Such an assessment is surely partly accurate. But what do we mean when we say that a company or a manager acted in its own self-interest, or that Boeing's aberrations are all a matter of old-fashioned greed. It may turn out that acting in one's own self-interest is a complex matter indeed.

To think through the role of self-interest as a motivating force, let us turn to the philosophy of Adam Smith. We go back to Smith because he and Thomas Hobbes are both often cited, along with Bernard Mandeville, as the fathers of psychological egoism, the view that human beings "naturally" and primarily act in their own self-interest. At least in the case of Smith, this is simply a misreading. The Nobel Prize economist George Stigler asserts that Smith's well-known work *The Wealth of Nations* "is a stupendous palace erected upon the granite of self-interest" (Stigler 1971, 265). According to Stigler, Smith argued that businesspeople, acting in their own interest in the marketplace of commerce and trade, will, even unwittingly, create wealth and economic growth for the political economy in which they operate and even create well-being for those who do not participate directly in commerce. This interpretation of Smith's famous invisible hand argument is well known and need not be rehearsed again here. However, it may be helpful to trace the roots of Smith's alleged point of view, a view we have developed elsewhere, that belies what he says in his earlier work, *The Theory of Moral Sentiments*

(TMS), and is contrary to his full analysis in *The Wealth of Nations* (Bevan & Werhane, 2015; 2022; Werhane, 1991a).

In the TMS, Smith makes some interesting observations about the nature of self-interest. The idea of any state of nature, even a hypothetical one such as Hobbes proposes, where each of us is an isolated independent being, is alien to Smith's description of human nature. Smith says, "It is thus that man, who can subsist only in society, was fitted by nature to that situation for which he was made" (Smith, [1759] 1976, II.ii.3.1). As a social being dependent on and interacting with others, we are each the subject of our own interests, so there is a trivial sense in which all our interests are "self-interests." That is, they are the interests of the self. But we are not always ourselves the object of those interests. Human beings "by nature" are endowed with at least three kinds of drives, each having different objects directed to the self (the selfish passions), to others (the social passions), or in reaction to others (the unsocial passions). Each of the first two drives or passions has its virtues and vices: the virtue of the selfish passions is prudence; their vice is selfishness; the virtues of the social passions are benevolence and justice; their voices are malevolence and injustice. Thus, according to Smith, each of us is the subject of and motivated by our passions and interests, but many of our passions and interests are other-directed. Acting altruistically or dispassionately is as natural as acting in one's own self-interest, or even selfishly. This does not mean that all of us are alike; some of us are more selfish or more generous or have a stronger commitment to fairness than others. But no one of these passions is more "natural" than any other, and the interests of the self are more or less equally directed to the self and to others (Smith, [1759] 1976, I, II).

The statement that some person or some company acted in its own self-interest presents a series of complex considerations. One would want to be able to distinguish first what sort of self-interest the individual or company was acting in and then determine whether the individual or the company was both the subject and the object of that self-interest. For example, as we recounted in Chapter 1,

McDonald's, which had over 850 franchises in Russia, along with a few other American companies, withdrew from Russia and the Russian fast-food market. The fast-food giant said it made the decision because of the "humanitarian crisis" and "unpredictable operating environment" caused by the Ukraine war (Morton, 2022). In this case, McDonald's franchises in Russia were the subjects of the company's interests. But the object of the decision to withdraw, even when that decision threatened McDonald's own self-reflective interests to be profitable and to continue a well-known and popular line of fast-food businesses in Russia, cannot be beneficial to these interests. One might argue that this decision was in McDonald's long-term self-interest to preserve its reputation. That would be true. But one cannot predict how this will affect McDonald's reputation or profitability.

Second, acting in one's own interest where one's well-being is both the object as well as the subject of action does not necessarily exclude taking into account the interests of others, for those interests are almost always necessary to achieve success. Indeed, if Smith is right about the social nature of human beings (Smith, [1759] 1976, III.ii.3), it is impossible not to take others into account, if only negatively. So even if one is cynical about McDonald's decision in the Russian case, even if it was only trying to save its reputation, the result may have hurt long-time Russian consumers of its food, so it was not necessarily beneficial for those stakeholders, nor for McDonald's shareholders. But McDonald's seemingly was acting on principle, the defiant statement about the evils of the Ukrainian war and Russia's instigation and involvement in it.

Third, acting in one's own self interests in either sense is not necessarily evil. One must be careful to distinguish not only the quality of the action itself and its object, for example, oneself or one's company, but also the motivation, for example, greed, self-interest, or the well-being of certain stakeholders, and what in fact that action produces. Many self-interested, even greedy, actions do not harm others. If, for example Boeing's engineers became engineers in order to amass a fortune, they would not be alone in that motivation, nor necessarily bad people. But when self-interest overwhelms propriety, morality, or law, such actions become unconscionable. The fact that no one blew the whistle at Boeing until after the 737 MAX flaws were discovered, is evidence that most of Boeing's engineers were to some extent protecting their own interest not to be fired. This was selfish. Was this evil?

While one considers famous insider trader, Ivan Boesky's alleged statement that "greed is good" (Boesky, 1986, as repeated by Gordon Gekko in the film *Wall Street*), one must nevertheless be careful not to equate all self-interest with greed nor to proclaim that acting in one's own self-interest is always morally questionable. Interestingly, in the case of Boeing, failure to redesign the 737 MAX carefully and inform and train all pilots of the plane from every country of its complex new mechanisms was not in their self-interest, and had both little to gain, and much to lose by not doing so. So, analyzing corporate or managerial wrongdoing or unintentional harm from the perspective of self-interest or greed does not always get us very far. Something else is at stake.

THE CASE FOR MORAL DEVELOPMENT

Still, it is tempting to conclude that the top management at Boeing gauged their judgments mostly by focusing on their own personal gain as the object of their self-interest and based their actions on whether they would be caught. According to moral psychologists such as Lawrence Kohlberg (1981), who pioneered a scale of moral development, if that were true, these executives at Boeing would be operating at a low level of moral development in his hierarchy.

Kohlberg and his followers have argued that in growing up human beings go through stages of moral development, just as they go through stages of cognitive development, and that each stage depends on the preceding one. It has been well documented that we do develop cognitively, grounding more complex learning experiences on simpler ones. Similarly, Kohlberg argued, people go through stages of moral learning. As small children, we focus primarily on ourselves.

In what Kohlberg labeled two preconventional stages of development, children focus on rewards and punishments for their own behavior; they are obedient precisely because they are afraid of getting caught and being punished, and they focus on satisfying their own needs, gauging their relationships with others in terms of what others can do for them. According to Kohlberg, in these two early stages each of us is both egocentric and naively consequentialist, seeking primarily to avoid punishment and to achieve personal gains. In his studies of human behavior Kohlberg found, interestingly, that many criminals function primarily at these two low stages of moral development.

If we follow the path of normal development, Kohlberg argued, as teenagers and then as adults we reach two conventional stages of development. In the third stage we are highly socialized conformists; we look to peers and other groups for behavioral expectations, approval, or disapproval. At the fourth stage we become law abiding; we follow rules, respect authority, and develop a sense of duty in relation to the law or society (Kohlberg, 1969; 1981).

Kohlberg also posited two postconventional stages of moral development wherein we are able to identify and apply more universal moral values or rules. At these stages, as free and autonomous selves, we judge both our own behavior and that of social groups, cultures, and communities to which we and others belong. As we develop to these highest stages, we first make moral judgments on the basis of utility and social contracts and then on the basis of universal principles of justice and the equality of human rights (Kohlberg, 1969). Given these postconventional stages, Kohlberg and his students and followers tested people to find out at what stage they operated. Later psychologists, such as James Rest, have devised educational methodologies and forms of moral education that allegedly advance students' level of moral development, and thus, ultimately, they conclude, improve behavior (Rest, 1988; 1994).

Kohlberg's theory of moral development is, however, controversial. The alleged universal existence and the content of moral stages as depicted by Kohlberg have come under extensive scrutiny. One of the best-known critiques was formulated by one of Kohlberg's former students, Carol Gilligan. Gilligan questioned what she initially found to be gender differences between male and female stages of moral development. Although the relationship between gender difference and types of moral development is also controversial, her work has shown that not all of us experience Kohlberg's stages of moral development, particularly the conventional and postconventional stages, as he described them. Gilligan and others depict Kohlberg's description of moral development as too formal and abstract. They find that it focuses on the primacy of the individual in all stages of moral development, as distinct from the individual in the context of social relationships, and that it imagines that one could achieve complete autonomy when developing universally acceptable and applicable principles of fairness without consideration of context or particular social situation (Gilligan, 1982; Kohlberg et al., 1983).

While agreeing with Kohlberg that the preconventional stages are egoistic ones, Gilligan describes moral development as the development from simple to more complex social relationships, where one becomes attached to others and responsible for oneself and others in these relationships. Gilligan describes the conventional stages as a development of interrelationships and caring for others. At the highest stages of moral development, one has both a strong sense of self and of others in a network of interrelationships that are, at the same time, caring, attached, and interdependent (Gilligan, 1982).

Much can be learned from the work of Kohlberg, Gilligan, and their followers. From their studies one can conclude that people deal with moral issues differently, some of us more naively than others, some of us primarily from self-interest, some of us depending on law, convention, and social relationships, and others seeking more ideal or universal principles through which to ground and evaluate moral decisions. At the same time, Gilligan is surely correct that one cannot extricate oneself from all human social relationships; indeed, that extrication itself would be a social act. Human relationships play central roles in moral decision-making at every level. None of us lives in a human vacuum. We are born into and affected by human relationships, even in acts of solitude and rejection, and these relationships are part of being moral or immoral (Friedman, 1993; Smith, [1759] 1976). Kohlberg's highest stage of moral development, the postconventional levels, postulates abstract moral principles, and standards that are independent of particular situations and social relationships. If, however, we cannot achieve total independence or autonomy that is not in some way connected to, and an outcome of, social relationships, then the status of these abstract principles comes into question. Moreover, it is impossible to verify universal absolute moral principles. Nevertheless, Kohlberg pointed to a human tendency to set out certain principles as ideals or as candidates for universal principles.

One could speculate that in the highest stages of moral development people have a good sense of the self in relationship with others. They relate to, respect, and even care about each other, and set out stipulative candidates for moral principles as possible evaluative and judgmental ideals. Moreover, whether or not each of us goes through stages of moral development in ways Kohlberg or Gilligan describes, still, part of the ability to be morally imaginative depends on the ability to evaluate moral stances critically and even the reasoning processes of oneself, one's company, and one's community. Boeing executives appeared to have an inability to make such critical evaluations; thus, they may not have developed to this stage of critical moral reasoning and moral imagination. Moreover, lest we neglect and forgive them, engineers at the Boeing plant in Seattle, in particular, who spotted the flaws in the 737 MAX failed, nevertheless, to blow the whistle to anyone either within the company or more publicly. Were they morally blind to this possibility? Were they afraid of being fired? Or did they simply perceive their jobs as engineering without any managerial responsibility for decision-making, even when lives were at risk?

Most advocates of moral development argue that ethics can be taught to adults – that one can improve the moral development, and thus the character and ultimately the behavior, of adults. According to Rest,

> dramatic and extensive changes occur in young adulthood (the 20s and 30s) in the basic problem solving strategies used by the person in dealing with ethical issues. That is, the basic assumptions and perspectives by which people define what is morally right or wrong change in this period, and the change is just as dramatic and fundamental as change in the years before puberty.
>
> *(Rest 1988, 23)*

How this is to be achieved is also subject to some agreement. Researchers such as Rest and Muriel Bebeau, each of whom has experimented with moral education over many years, suggest that the moral education of adults is best achieved by presenting them with real case studies or scenarios relevant to adult experiences. In developing morally, adults learn to move from the particular, from specific instances of moral conflicts to more general situations, seeking guidelines applicable to those and similar relationships. One begins by raising awareness of the existence of ethical issues, although raising awareness is not enough, by itself, to improve behavior. Additionally, Rest and Bebeau argue, one must provide students with moral reasoning skills to discuss, think through, and try to resolve the ethical issues illustrated in the cases. Through practice one becomes adept at analyzing particular cases and formulating more general decision procedures and principles to apply to new scenarios. Conversely, one could start from a general principle and apply it to a particular application. We shall argue that beginning with general moral principles is usually not as successful as starting with particular cases, and we shall argue that the success of either sort of moral decision-making depends, in great part, on a well-functioning imagination (Bebeau, 1994; Rest, 1994; Rest and Naváez, 1994).

These movements, from the particular to the general and the converse, are illustrated differently in decisions of different companies. Earlier we mentioned the McDonald's case. Notice that in this instance the principle of questioning harm to Ukrainian people outweighed the fact that McDonald's remaining in Russia would probably cause no harm to Ukraine and provide inexpensive fast food for many Russians. So, one might argue that from the point of view of customer relations and shareholder value, McDonald's decision was a questionable one. Nevertheless, it was surely not made on the basis of its selfish interests.

The discussion of theories of moral development and education helps us to understand the decision-making processes in this case. This was a principled ethical decision surely taken after a great deal of thought. Nevertheless, McDonald's tried to operate from a high stage of moral development, although this decision came with challenges. The fact of Russia's human rights violations conflicted with a very large Russian market. We shall argue later that it takes imagination, moral imagination, to make decisions such as this, because they go beyond apparent conventional demands of morality, of the market, or of the business in question.

In summary, moral development theories describe human cognitive and moral development. At least in part, they account for moral error and reiteration of mistakes, attributing these phenomena to lower stages of moral development. But theories of moral development have more difficulty explaining why an intelligent, well-educated person such as most Boeing engineers and executives, could get so involved with marketing new airplanes that they would have forgotten that planes are complex machines and that even a small error can affect their performances and those who fly in them. For the McDonald's decision, there is no self-interested "payoff," either in the short run or long run, and little in the way of conventional explanation to account for this decision.

DESCRIPTIVE EXPLANATIONS

In every incident or set of events there are a number of related common causes of the incident, of factors that influence managerial and corporate behavior; any or all of which can cause the abdication of individual moral responsibility in corporate and other organizational settings. We shall discuss three: (1) the conflation of what is legal with what is expected morally; (2) a misidentification of professional responsibility with organizational responsibility; and (3) the identification of moral responsibility with role responsibility. We shall argue that each of these factors (and there are others) is important and necessary, indeed crucial, to explain these phenomena.

Turning first, to the possible conflation of legal with moral choices, it is questionable whether the two 737 MAX crashes involved anything illegal in either Indonesia or Ethiopia, since Boeing followed albeit weak pilot training protocols of Indonesia and Ethiopia. Yet surely letting their new planes fly by pilots untrained in the new technology was, at best, unethical.

Moreover, US Federal prosecutors alleged Boeing committed conspiracy to defraud the government by misleading regulators about a flight-control system that was implicated in the crashes, which occurred in Indonesia in October 2018 and in Ethiopia less five months later (AP News, 2021).

Connected to the conflation of legal and moral issues is a second factor that may affect managerial moral judgments. In making moral judgments, those managers who are also members of professional organizations, for example engineers, must weigh their organizational responsibilities against their professional responsibilities. Engineers everywhere of every ilk have an implicit code. This code proscribes the actions of engineering professionals just because they are members of those professions, and at least this code is meant to override both personal inclinations and nonprofessional organizational or corporate demands. As professionals, engineers have strongly differentiated roles; that is, in cases of conflict, the demands of the professional role and its code of conduct override organizational and personal demands.[2]

---

[2] The first of the Fundamental Canons of the code of the National Society of Professional Engineers (NSPE) says that engineers shall "hold paramount the safety, health, and welfare of the public" (Harris et al., 2019, 6):

Given such a professional mandate, it is clear that not blowing the whistle on the 737 MAX when they were certain of its flaws, according to evidence from many inside emails, was scarcely in the best interest of passenger customers. Not to change the design, evidence suggests that engineers at Boeing were afraid of being fired. They may have not realized the possibility of a conflict of interest between the demands of their professional code and those of their roles in the 737 MAX production team. They appeared to allow organizational demands to dominate.

Let us qualify these arguments. It would certainly be a gross exaggeration and downright incorrect to say that all engineers and managers merely do as they are told and do not think for themselves as independent, morally responsible individuals. However, Boeing, like other organizations, harbors some practices that neither encourage independent managerial decision-making nor provide avenues for questioning what might, by standards outside the institution, be unacceptable activities. Sometimes, too, managers become so involved in their roles and accompanying expectations that their judgments reflect what they perceive to be their role responsibilities.

ROLES AND ROLE RESPONSIBILITIES

We have used the Boeing case to dramatize two simple and common phenomena: the confusion of role responsibilities to do one's job well with the role responsibility to follow management orders; and, second, the subordination of concern with more general moral responsibilities

> Engineers are obligated not only to abide by code prohibitions, thereby refraining from causing harm, but also, under some circumstances, to actively prevent harms caused by technology or other engineers. Prevention of harm usually involved (1) identifying and disclosing potential harms and (2) attempting to prevent them ... If their professional judgment is overruled, under circumstances where the safety, health, property, or welfare of the public are endangered, they shall notify their employer or client and other such authority as may be appropriate.
>
> (Section II.1.a of the NSPE Code, page 10, reprinted in Harris et al., 2019, 6, 9)

to those of one's role. Each of us functions within a political system, within social and economic institutions, in a culture, under law, and connected to a set of religious, cultural, and social mores. Sometimes, even if one grasps the right action, one is prevented, or appears to be prevented, from executing that action by regulation, law, custom, sanctions, or other pressures. This factor works on a number of levels. A corporate culture, a set of regulations, a government, law, religious convictions, peer pressures, or even personal habits can entrap individuals or groups of individuals in a perspective that is either ultimately self-defeating or self-deceptive. The managers' contentions that they were "just following orders," or "doing their job," both illustrate in a dramatic way that entrapment.

> Let us step back from these examples to define "role" and role morality. Role refer[s] to constellations of institutionally specified rights and duties organized around an institutionally specified social function ... [where] an institution [is any public system or social arrangement that] includes rules that define offices and positions which can be occupied by different individuals at different times.
>
> *(Hardimon, 1994, 334–335)*

Families (however defined), professions, trades and trade unions, corporations, churches, and states are all institutions. Not all social arrangements entail roles. For example, friendships may not involve role differentiation, and, depending on the cultural context, characteristics such as race and gender may or may not have social role dimensions. Everyone in every society has a number of roles that define various relationships between individuals, between individuals and institutions, and between institutions themselves. Each of us as an individual has a large number of interacting and overlapping cultural, professional, religious, and social roles, and these change. For example, one of the authors of this book is of Irish background, a mother, a daughter, a professor, a writer, a student, a consultant, an employee, an employer, a Protestant, an

American, a member of the world community, an environmentalist, a liberal, a humanist, and so on. All of these adjectives describe intricate social relationships, and some of them refer to specifically defined social roles.

Roles have an impersonal quality. They are general descriptions or refer to a social status, such as motherhood, that apply to all occupants of that role, or at least, occupants of that role within a particular culture, ethnic group, or profession. Roles carry with them certain expectations, rights and duties, norms, and ideals that are either implicit or explicit, even sometimes legally or contractually defined. There is an impersonal, socially defined collection of expectations and demands that comes with each role, and when we take on a role we assume certain rights and duties as we "play the role." Connected, for example, with the role of an engineer are certain technical expectations connected with that role, job expectations depending on the engineer's position, and as a member of a profession, certain professional normative demands. In addition, most roles are usually associated with ideals, norms that define, for example, the perfect mother or the ideal firefighter (Downie, 1971; Emmet, 1966; Hardimon, 1994; Luban, 1988; Werhane, 1985). Thus, along with each role are moral demands as spelled out by that role, and these define what David Luban has called "role morality" (Andre, 1991; Luban, 1988, chapter 6).

That we have roles, that there are certain expectations in occupying these roles that most of us adhere to most of the time, and that we make moral judgments about role behavior are each crucial elements of human experience and social interrelationships. The existence of roles permits a predictability of human behavior and a stability in social relationships. Ordinarily there are good moral reasons for acting according to role demands and ideals. A mother who ignores her children or a manager who does not take seriously his fiduciary responsibilities to his company under most circumstances is judged to be immoral both by the standards of role morality and by judgment of a commonsense perspective (Andre, 1991).

The difficulty is that each of us is enmeshed in a collection of overlapping social, professional, cultural, and religious roles, each of which makes moral demands. This condition becomes problematic when the demands of a particular role become confused, when these demands come into conflict with those of another role, or when role demands clash with what we might call common morality. The lawyer who protects a known repeated murderer, the psychologist or priest who honors the confidentiality of a criminal's confession, or the reporter who witnesses a spouse committing a crime faces role conflicts. They are pulled in different directions by their professions, their personal ties, perhaps the company where they work or the partnership to which they belong, and commonly held societal moral norms. In business, as both the Boeing and BP cases illustrate, albeit with different consequences, the managerial role pressure to be competitive, efficient, and profitable can often conflict with the claims of common morality.

Sometimes we adopt two or more contradictory roles simultaneously without perceiving possible conflicts of interest. The most obvious examples are members of the US crime syndicate who are often exemplary church members and good family persons, and yet use a decision model in business dealings that contradicts the values of church and family. "Mafia mentality," as we could crudely label this phenomenon, is the ability to function in such contradictory roles simultaneously.

Ordinarily we reserve the notion of a strongly differentiated role to describe professionals such as doctors, nurses, lawyers, or engineers whose autonomous professional codes dictate certain forms of behavior that take precedence when one faces choices that invite ignoring the professional code in question. Managers are thought to have weakly differentiated roles because there is no independent professional managerial code that sets standards for professional managerial behavior.

There is another kind of problem with role morality. Acting within the normative expectations of one's role cannot always be guaranteed to produce the best outcomes. As we shall see when examining the Volkswagen diesel emission scandal, engineers and managers were acing within their role responsibilities at Volkswagen, but the outcome was not positive. Individuals are identified in a nexus of social roles and social relationships. By analogy, organizations such as corporations define themselves in terms of their roles as spelled out in their objectives. The roles of corporations are related to their function, their mission, and their goals. Along with individuals, we also hold corporations and other organizations morally responsible for carrying out their role responsibilities and we hold organizations responsible for untoward consequences of their actions even when at first sight they appear not to be within their role responsibilities.

What is to be learned from the discussion of roles and role morality? First, and most obviously, roles function normatively, and we react to their responsibilities and demands. In each of these incidents, managers faced conflicting role responsibilities – to be good managers or good professionals, or to be obedient managers and disobedient professionals. To settle these conflicts, one cannot appeal merely to role morality, because it is the moral demands of each role that are at issue.

There is a second shortcoming of role morality. While role responsibilities account for much of what we do, and role morality is important in judging accountability for role responsibilities, not all moral responsibility can be reduced to role responsibility or even to the question of conflicting role responsibilities.

We tend to judge people in their roles not merely by the demands of that role or by conflicting demands but also by the demands of common morality. Our evaluation of Adolph Eichmann is one very strong example. Eichmann was an exemplary clerk for the Nazi regime, and a law-abiding citizen. The trains he scheduled ran on time and were full. No space was wasted, and he kept detailed records of the contents. But that is not enough, in itself, to excuse his behavior. The trains were filled with primarily Jewish people and their destinations were extermination camps in Germany, Poland and

Austria. We do not want to let him "off the moral hook," so to speak, despite his role-defined "proper" behavior, his efficiency, and patriotic commitment. We want to say that what he did was evil *because* he so completely identified with his role, his station, and its duties, and because of the terrible consequences of his role actions (Arendt, 1963; Rendtorff, 2020).

The Eichmann example brings up the most dangerous difficulty with role adaptation and role morality, that of unquestioned obedience to one's role demands, and particularly when those demands are defined by a person or an institution in authority. Beginning in 1964, Stanley Milgram, a psychologist, carried out a set of experiments that demonstrated how individuals, when given a set of instructions by a person in authority, will often carry out those instructions, even when they are absurd, dangerous, or life-threatening. In the Milgram experiments the subject was asked to give an electric shock to what he or she was told was an innocent learner if the learner did not respond correctly to some fairly innocuous questions. With each mistake the learner received an increasingly intense shock, up to 450 volts. If a subject questioned the experiment or expressed concern about inflicting electric shock on the learner, who was a stranger to the subject, an authority figure in a white coat, often Milgram himself, assured the subject that he or she was following a documented scientific procedure, and that "the experiment must go on." Some subjects simply quit in the middle of the process, yet in experiment after experiment, Milgram and his students were surprised to discover that over 50 percent of all subjects carried out the shock level to the 450 volts. Although the experiment was set up so that the learner did not actually receive real shocks, the subjects did not know that until after the experiment was completed (Milgram, 1969).[3]

In a subsequent experiment, Philip Zimbardo (1973) conducted an experiment with college students, many of whom had read Milgram's work. In Zimbardo's experiments students were to act out

---

[3] Later experiments produced similar results despite changes in venues and narratives. And women of all professions did equally as badly as men.

prison roles as wardens, guards, or prisoners over a period of two weeks. Prison-like cells were created and role-playing student "prisoners" were "arrested" and brought to the "prison." After a few days most of the prisoners became subservient to the "guards," and the guards in turn became aggressive, dominating, and in some cases inflicted arbitrary punishment. Zimbardo had to abort the experiment after six days because of the inhumane treatment of prisoners by the guards. Playing a role or acting under conditions that are defined and shaped by an authority figure, then, Milgram and Zimbardo concluded, can produce unthinkable consequences.

While less dramatic, many Boeing engineers followed the whims of management or what they perceived to be their directives even when their inactions threatened passenger lives. Thus, in certain circumstances role demands can override ordinary, common sense moral sensitivity or smother individual conscience (Arendt, 1963; Wicks and Freeman, 1990).

How do we account for moral blameworthiness in these examples so that moral judgments about role behavior are not confined to whether an agent is fulfilling his or her role? In this context, it is tempting to conclude that the object of moral judgment is the self apart from its roles, the self as an independent moral agent, not merely the self as it is engaged in its roles, a self that is both free from identification with any particular role and is ultimately, because of its autonomy, morally responsible. It is that self we are holding morally responsible when we condemn Eichmann for following his role responsibilities and Boeing engineers for obeying what they feared was a job loss if they reported on the 737 MAX problems.

Because each of us has many roles and because we are capable of distancing ourselves from any one role, we need not be fully engaged in any one role so that it becomes overriding. Each of us has a variety of roles and role responsibilities; no one role completely defines the self. Moreover, no person is so mired in one role that he or she cannot be distant from its demands, even though we often fail to do so. Even as children we learn to play and play-act various roles. We learn early on about distancing ourselves from identifying completely with anyone's particular role. Each of us can compare and contrast various roles and role responsibilities simply because no one role is complete and because we have so many of them (Goffman, 1961, 92–95).

But what is the nature of the non-role-defined self – the moral agent to whom we ascribe moral responsibilities as distinguished from role responsibilities? When one attempts to sort out the self apart from its roles, there is a further difficulty – the difficulty of getting at that self. When one eliminates all roles, say, of one of the authors – as professor, mother, daughter, sister, writer, citizen, environmentalist, humanist, Democrat – what is left? Who she is is created in large measure from these roles. Roles and role morality overlap with other social relationships so that the division is not always clear. This is evident in citizenship, for example, where duties are less well defined and where one's role could be sharply or vaguely differentiated. All she has left without roles are vague social relationships. She is now a friend without role duties, a distant relative, a nonvoting nonperson with no identity of Irish descent, a non-practicing Protestant, an observer, a reader, an appreciator but not a critic of art, and so on. Without any roles one becomes amorphous, undefined, and it is difficult to delineate one's responsibilities and obligations as a moral person.

Without roles we are left with the quandary of how to relate moral agency to moral responsibility. Moreover, a notion of the self, Michael Sandel and others argue, cannot be purely autonomous or devoid of all social relationships without being what Sandel has called "dispossessed," and indeed, altogether empty. In *A Theory of Justice* (1971), John Rawls argues that principles of justice are best constructed by rational persons behind a hypothetical "veil of ignorance" where individuals have no knowledge of their place in history; their cultural, ethnic, religious, or economic circumstances; their social status; or even their age, gender, intelligence, or natural abilities. From this position individuals have no knowledge of their own emotions, desires, value system, or of their place in history or society. Rawls argues that postulating this hypothetical position is necessary in order to draw up principles of justice that will be fair to people whatever their position, social or economic status, gender, religion, ethnic background, or historical position. Hypothetically we suggest, this would be the position of an ideal spectator, one who was totally disengaged from his or her community and life circumstances, an individual who, then, at least according to Rawls and others who hold this view, could make purely disinterested moral judgments and develop universal principles of justice and morality. Such a person additionally would be at Kohlberg's highest stage of moral development.

Michael Sandel persuasively claims, however, that individuals in such a position would be "wholly unencumbered subjects" (Sandel, 1982, 172) and thus devoid of character and the ability to make worthwhile choices. If one disengages oneself from all roles and social relationships, one becomes ahistorical, without family, gender, nationality, ethnicity, and cultural perspective. Thus, one becomes devoid of desires, values, and goals; one becomes psychologically empty. Having no background and no possibilities (or every possibility) from which to choose, individuals behind a veil of ignorance simply make blind choices on the basis of "arbitrarily-given preferences" (Sandel, 1982, 168). In that case the notion of autonomy makes no sense because as a purely autonomous self, one is without psychological resources to form choices, to accept or reject alternatives, or to make moral judgments. Such a self can be neither responsible nor irresponsible because it has no resources with which to make judgments at all, and principles it adapts would be equally arbitrary (Luban, 1988, 122–130; Sandel, 1982, 154–174).

On the other hand, if the self is merely determined by its various socially defined roles and social relationships, it is "radically situated" so that its actions merely result from the complex interrelationships between these roles. If this is the sum total of who we are, it is not easy to explain how we are self-reflective, self-critical, creative makers of history and authors of change. Nor can that description account fully for moral blame. As a result, we would be forced to conclude that

Eichmann was simply a product of the Third Reich and thus exempt from further moral condemnation. Most of us are uneasy with this conclusion, but without some notion of an autonomous self, it is difficult to formulate an explanation of what appears to be one's ability to choose, change, and deal with role conflicts, and thus be subject to moral judgment. What we want to say is that the moral agent we attempt to hold responsible for role behavior is always an engaged agent-self, not an abstract dispossessed entity, but one not merely determined by social relationships and roles – something more than one's engagements.

In defending the view that "the self is socially constructed," Larry May, following Charles Taylor, argues that what we call the self or personal identity of the self is a "web knit from various identifications and commitments that one makes with various social groups" (May, 1996, 13). A large part of such a web, we would argue, consists of one's roles. Out of this web, one develops a core, according to May, a sense of self-identity formed and made up from commitments and values integrated in this web of relationships. The uniqueness of each self is formed from the peculiar web of roles and relationships one develops out of social interactions. As we mature, one can develop a sense of stability and integrity that creates a temporary unity of the core self, but still, the core self is by and large a self-in-process.

May has carefully advanced the notion of a socially constructed self; still, if the core self is a nexus of roles and relationships, one is left with questions concerning the nature of the moral self that we hold responsible despite its roles and relationships, because how or whether the core self is something more than its web of commitments and relationships is unclear.

David Luban attempts to solve the problem of the moral self that is more than its roles and relationships by arguing that, in making moral judgments about role responsibilities, we acknowledge each other as persons subject to precepts of common morality. At the same time, individually and personally, we cannot get at the self within us that is an utterly independent autonomous agent except as a nexus of roles. Luban is mostly correct in the following remarks:

> Ultimately, we reserve our autonomy from our stations and their duties so that we have the freedom to respond to persons qua persons-to obey what one may call the morality of acknowledgment. The situation is curiously asymmetrical: we are bound to extend to others a courtesy we are bound to refuse to ourselves. It is a delusion to think of myself as just a person qua person, a "me" outside of my social station[s]; but when the chips are down, it is immoral to think of you as anything less.
>
> (Luban, 1988, 127)

There are, however, at least two problems with Luban's conclusion. First, Luban tends to assume that a human being is merely the sum of roles, or at least, that all human relationships are role relationships. However, there is more to be said about the person qua person who is "myself." Although it is true that we cannot divorce ourselves from our relationships, the fact that we can get at a distance from any particular role implies an act of a self not merely a sum of its roles and social relationships.

In his book *Thick and Thin* (Walzer, [1994] 2019), Michael Walzer tries to account for a notion of moral agency that avoids both the difficulties of proposing a radically situated social self and the metaphysical problems of postulating a purely autonomous or dispossessed self. To achieve this, Walzer distinguishes between the "thick" and "thin" aspects of the self. If we understand his position correctly, Walzer claims that all our experiences are socially derived, perspectival, and constructed from our particular social, historical situation and its accompanying narratives. In that socialization process, we develop a number of interests, roles, memberships, commitments, and values such that each individual is an historical, cultural, and social product, a pluralistic bundle of overlapping spheres of foci, a thick self or selves. In the first instance, there is no self as a precritical, transcendental subject, totally ideal spectator, or dispossessed subject. Self-reflection and self-criticism develop but only later out of the thick socialized self or bundle of selves. Who we are as subjects of these experiences is a late development from our socialization process. Self-reflection arises when there are inconsistencies, disagreements, or clashes between one's interests, roles, commitments, and values, clashes that jar one into taking another point of view, a "meta" point of view that is still one's own. This view develops when one judges and redirects one's interests, choices, and commitments, and when one sees oneself in historical/social continuity and as a unity of thick perspectives. Walzer calls this point of view the thin aspect of the self. The thin self accounts for the unity and continuity of overlapping, changing thick selves and for our ability to make choices and changes that are not merely outcomes of our roles and social situation. Walzer, borrowing from Lionel Trilling, claims that this thin self "perdures" (Trilling, 1972, 99; Walzer, [1994] 2019, 101) through time and change. Yet, although it perdures, thus accounting for self-identity, the self is no more than the unity of a bundle of social selves, the self-reflective locus of this vast array of experiences. The thin self, then, is socially derived but not merely socially determined. It accounts for one's ability to choose, manipulate, and even change events, and it explains our ability to get a perspective on our situation and its positive and negative features. The self that is the role-evaluator, and that same self that we hold morally responsible for its role behavior, is a thin self; that which is the locus of the thick self, the self that is engaged in, defined and changed by, and changing, its various roles (Walzer, 1994, 2019, chapter 5).

The second shortcoming of Luban's conclusion is his assumption that the morality of acknowledgment is asymmetrical. That is, according to Luban, we recognize that others are moral persons, but we cannot acknowledge that personhood of or in ourselves, because we cannot perceive or get at that self apart from its roles and relationships. Appealing to the work of Emmanuel Levinas (1979), however, one can develop from this concept of "the other" a viable response to Luban's conclusion. Even if we cannot get at the self apart from among these roles and relationships, the act of recognizing others as persons is a reciprocal experience. Levinas suggests that in the process of confronting – or coming face-to-face with – other people in moral dialogue where we acknowledge others as moral selves, we acknowledge others as more than their roles and relationships. This process of confrontation or series of confrontations is often reciprocal in the sense that we perceive that other people perceive or acknowledge us as more than our roles and relationships. That is to say, in Walzer's terms, that we both see others as thin as well as thick selves, and we recognize that others perceive us similarly. Although this reciprocal acknowledgement may not be as dramatic as Levinas depicts it, it is surely the case that when we recognize and treat others as persons qua persons, we expect and, indeed, demand, reciprocal respect. Those Levinasian exchanges between persons provide us each with an understanding of the self as a moral agent despite any inability to isolate that phenomenon, because we are seeing ourselves through a reflection. And in the way the other treats us we create expectations about our behavior that transcend role expectations. It is in those exchanges where we treat others as persons and where we recognize another person's consideration and judgment of oneself as a person that we become able to recognize oneself as a moral agent. In acknowledging others as moral agents, we realize that we are more than our roles, even though we cannot perceive and have difficulty getting at the "more" – the pure subject of self – without a loss of the sense of self altogether (Levinas, 1979; Werhane, 1997).

Returning to the question of role morality and moral responsibility, one may conclude from this discussion that (1) the identification of legal and moral responsibility, (2) the priority of institutional or managerial demands over professional codes and other moral demands, (3) the demands of obedience to one's role expectations, and (4) role morality explain, at least in part, why good managers and good companies engage in questionable behavior. But role morality does not explain all moral or immoral behavior or offer avenues for resolving conflicts of interest or settling professional or legal dilemmas.

Because as human beings we are not exhaustively defined by our roles, each of us can get at a distance from and evaluate our roles and role responsibilities. Tools for evaluation include appeals to the precepts of common morality, those rules or precepts that most of us, stepping out of our roles and judging others, would regard as guides for how we and others ought to behave (moral rules such as equal respect for persons, avoidance of harm, respect for rights and fairness, honoring contracts, and respect for property), however particularly defined. Moreover, as Luban carefully asserts, we can and should use those same tools of common morality for judging organizations and institutions, particularly one's own organizations. Just as we evaluate people, we can also assess organizations and institutions, their roles, and the ends they allegedly serve. According to Luban, then, we can evaluate any role, its role-defined obligations, the organization to which it is attached, and whatever acts the role, role duties, or organization seem to demand. At each step we evaluate the role, role obligations, and the organization or institution both in terms of what justifies the institution, role, obligation, or act, and what the organization, role, obligation, or act justifies (Luban, 1988, chapters 6 and 7).

Obviously, it is difficult to evaluate every action one takes in every role without becoming consumed with evaluation as a full-time activity, and, as we shall argue in Chapter 3, there are limits to one's impartiality and disengagement. But the act of stepping out of one's role and creating a distance from its obligations and the organization in which the role operates can put into perspective the relative importance of the organization and its role demands. Such steps of evaluation are crucial, we would conclude, to avoid problems such Boeing continues to experience. It is those very steps that McDonald's took in pulling out of the Russian market.

TRAINING IN MORAL REASONING

There is another temptation in trying to answer why good people or fine institutions engage in questionable behavior or why we repeat our mistakes. This temptation is to argue that the missing element in the

Boeing case is simply managerial skill in moral reasoning. Given the failure of descriptive pathologies to prevent moral aphasia, the limits of role morality, and complications in arguing that managers are primarily motivated by self-interest or even greed, one confronts a fourth temptation: to improve moral behavior through traditional moral education. Managers at Boeing are rational adults who are responsible, morally responsible, for the engineering, legal and marketing decisions, and production of their commercial and military airplanes. So, this argument continues, let us talk to the managers of these companies about professional and moral responsibilities through the introduction of moral theory, locate the managers who misbehaved, and begin moral education. We might then test their stage of moral development and give them workshops on moral reasoning. That is, are they egoists, conformists, rule followers, law abiders, precedent setters, or philosophers? We will discuss professional and organizational codes of ethics, demonstrate the limits of role responsibilities and role morality, present some ethical theories (e.g., utilitarianism, deontology, virtue theory), and some theories of justice, and engage these managers in a series of practice sessions that apply moral theories to cases studies.

Recalling our discussion of the self in the last section, one might be tempted to link a notion of the thin self to impartiality, and that in turn to rational moral decision-making, and then to argue that an impartial rational perspective from which one engages in a moral reasoning process will solve or avoid many of the problems we have cited. The Boeing scenarios, in particular, suggest that one needs to find distance from the organization and its decision-making habits. A less biased perspective is crucial, because unless a manager can disengage from the context of a specific problem and his or her role in that problem, and unless an organization can do so also, parochially embedded decisions will result in activities that invite repeated moral failure. Scenarios such as phantom trading repeat themselves when one is unable to view one's role, one's company, and their demands from a more general moral perspective.

Therein lies the problem. Engineers are bound by professional codes of ethics; still, questionable activities persist in these professions. Almost 60 percent of the Fortune 1000 companies in the United States have codes of ethics, credos, or mission statements (Deloitte, 2021) and some have ethics programs in place. Yet improprieties continue even in companies such as Boeing, with its strong code of ethics.

The difficulty is not that moral principles are wrongheaded or that morality reduces to role morality. The difficulty is that when one begins from the general, starting with moral theory or theories, and then applies these theories or generalities to particular cases, sometimes there is a disconnect between theory and practice. This move is analogous to beginning with a discussion of the thin self without recognizing that it is an outcome of a nexus of thick social relationships. If Sandel is right, this discussion would be, at best, brief, because one cannot get at the thin self except through the thickness of its relationships and social context. Thus, Rest and others assert that ethics teaching begins with the particular-with particular cases or scenarios that capture the imagination from which one then generalizes. Moral decision-making should begin with particular real cases and scenarios, because that is what engages our interest, emotions, and moral sentiments. We argue that the subject matter of morality is the real – particular, actual cases, characters, events, situations, and dilemmas – the "thick" of human experience. Moral theory is about those cases. To begin with abstract moral theory separates that theory from the particular in such a way as to create two apparently separate realms of discourse. The disconnect between theory and practice is created in part because moral theory is formal or general, not contextual. Applications make sense only after terms have been defined to fit the situation. For example, some formulations of the principle of utility state that the end of morality and the proper goal of all moral action is to create "the greatest happiness for the greatest number" (e.g., Bentham, [1789] 1948). But the term happiness is abstract. When one defines it, one uses particular illustrations relative to particular persons or contexts so that the allegedly universal utilitarian formula is no longer universally applicable. Even virtue theory, which sometimes claims to be more situational, has difficulty if one begins by discussing the virtues, say, of courage or excellence, outside of a context. Courage in war, for example, is (or should be) different from courage in business.

In the chapters to follow we shall argue that all experience is socially structured, all experience is interpreted, so, as Martha Nussbaum (1990) has noted, "moral experience is an interpretation of the seen" (130). Some moral theorists try to distance themselves from that conclusion, but formal moral principles themselves are interpretations or constructions that also serve as framing mechanisms for the phenomena of our experience. Hence, if we look at some cases, such as the 737 MAX sales to Indonesia, from a utilitarian perspective, we could plausibly conclude that the large number of planes sold was important the long-term benefit to the company and its employees and shareholders. If we look at the case from a more Kantian perspective, worrying about the question or Indonesian pilot lack of training and negative precedent-setting for sales in other countries we might well come to another conclusion. These different ethical theories frame the case in contrasting ways so as to create different and sometimes even contradictory conclusions. This does not happen in every scenario, but that it happens in a number of instances illustrates how a particular ethical theory itself frames our experiences and how different theory frames the same experience differently. This phenomenon gives cause to worry about the efficacy of beginning with ethical theory in working through issues in business ethics.

There is an attendant problem, a problem with "limited rationality." It is possible within a particular institutional or theoretical context to develop limited objectivity so as to create a closed loop of decision-making. Well-trained pilots used to challenge new technologies adjusted to the peculiarities of the 737 MAX. Marketing managers at Boeing seemingly transferred that logic to other countries where pilot training is not as acutely intricate.

From one perspective, given these facts it seems reasonable to take the same product, the same marketing plans, and the same communication techniques to market infant formula in new countries. From a utilitarian perspective, too, this approach seems to be the right thing to do, all things considered. So, using a Western mindset they sold the 737 MAX airplanes globally without thinking of the differences in countries' mores and technological opportunities for dealing with complex software, using textbook and tested general marketing principles that had been successful in a number of markets. The result has been the deaths of hundreds of passengers.

In these new environments Boeing failed to consider any non-Western context, a context in which most pilots are trained merely by textbooks and only on the old Boeing 737s. Thus, what appeared to be reasonable and indeed a proper marketing approach failed because Boeing did not take into account traditions of other cultures in its marketing scheme. This suggests that what appears to be a rational perspective, while crucial to moral decision-making, may create a disconnect between what appears in theory to be correct and what, in particular fact, is so. We are suggesting that what seems to be a rational perspective, simply applying some rules, for example, well-tested marketing principles and techniques, to a new situation may not be enough, by itself, to avoid moral disasters.

MORAL BLINDNESS: SAM BANKMAN-FRIED AND FTX

Finally, returning to the idea of moral blindness, a recent case in the financial sector illustrates this phenomenon is a frightening way: the rise and failure of Bankman-Fried (SBF) and the crypto exchange FTX.

Samuel Bankman-Fried, known as SBF, founder of FTX, once one of the largest cryptocurrency trading companies in the world, is the son of two Stanford professors and grew up on that campus. Even as a young adult he was considered a bit weird; as a child he had almost no friends (McHugh, 2023). He dressed mostly in cut-off shorts and

T-shirts, preferring to read and play videogames, of which he became an addict. He was a constant gamer, playing his way through high school and then at MIT. His favorite game was and perhaps still is, "League of Legends," which he played almost constantly before being incarcerated. According to one report he even played while trying to sell FTX to some investors from a venture capital firm (Nguyen, 2022). These eccentricities became part of the dominating narrative about SBF – the myth that became a conviction held by wealthy investors and even members of Congress that SBF was an eccentric genius who could do no wrong in the crypto markets where he traded.

At MIT he learned about "effective altruism" (EA), a doctrine that promotes the goal to do good in the most efficient way possible. Even in his first job he gave away half of his salary (Lewis, 2023b). Later he reinterpreted EA to advocate the idea that one should earn as much money as possible and *then* give a great deal of it away. He was not that generous but did contribute heavily to various charities and to some political campaigns even to the Super PAC (Political Action Committee) of Mitch McConnell (Allison, 2022).

After MIT, SBF went to work for Jane Street, a Wall Street firm engaged in arbitrage trading strategies. It was at Jane Street that he learned about cryptocurrencies.

> Crypto is a *digital currency*, meaning it runs on a virtual network and doesn't exist in physical form like paper money or coins. Cryptocurrencies are often built using blockchain technology, which provides a secure recordkeeping and processing system for all of their transactions ... they can typically be transferred without using a third party, such as a bank ... Second, they are designed to be decentralized, meaning they're generally not backed, controlled, or owned by any government, central bank, or corporation. Instead, decentralized cryptocurrencies operate according to computer software that anyone with internet access can download and use to monitor and verify transactions.
>
> *(Fidelity, 2024)*

In 2017 SBF left Jane Street and started his own crypto trading firm, Alameda Research, located in Berkeley, California. But to avoid what appeared to be pending US legislation governing cryptocurrencies, SBF moved the company to Hong Kong, which had not yet felt the oppression of the Chinese government in its currency markets. According to Michael Lewis in his biography of SBF, most of the people Alameda hired in its early days were EAs without experience trading in financial markets or, for that matter, interest in money. "Most [employees] neither knew nor cared about crypto; they had just bought into Sam's argument that it was this insanely inefficient market in which they might use his Jane Street-like approach to trading to extract billions" (Lewis, 2023b, 83). Moreover, evidence from various former managers at Alameda claimed that SBF was a terrible manager, that he really did not manage or lead well nor did he think that such leadership and management were important for a successful crypto company (Lewis, 2023b, 97).

Later, after FTX was declared bankrupt, in a *mea culpa* interview with *Financial Times* editor Joshua Oliver, SBF admitted some of his failures. The former mogul has freely admitted in several interviews to what he called "massive oversights", "huge fuckups" and a lack of "rigorous thinking ... And to be clear, at its core, I fucked up. I fucked up big and people got hurt. And you didn't need a conspiracy theory to get there" (Oliver, 2022). Bankman-Fried denied intentionally committing wrongdoing but admitted "Hugh management failures" as part of the cause of FTX's bankruptcy.

In 2019 SBF founded FTX, moving it to the Caribbean, but physically located in the Bahamas. These islands were friendlier places for crypto because there were virtually no regulations or rules for their activities. Indeed, China banned cryptocurrency in Hong Kong in 2019, although online trading continued for a couple of years until the Chinese government cracked down on that too. Like Alameda, FTX was a crypto exchange where customers could trade in various cryptocurrencies. To make that trading easier and to attract loyal customers FTX (like other exchanges) issued exchange tokens, FTTs. Exchange tokens, (FTTs) minted by exchanges like Binance and FTX, entitle holders to benefits on cryptocurrency exchanges. Such benefits often include trading fee discounts, rebates "and early access to token sales held on the platform" (Stevens, 2022).

Despite or perhaps because of all its publicity, fueled by stories of the genius of SBF, beginning in early 2022 customers and lenders became nervous about the future, and the market for crypto currencies began to slide. The original "darling" of investments began to be questioned by investors and many began to withdraw their sizable investments, and lenders to Alameda and other exchanges called in their loans. By the middle of 2022 FTX and its sister company Alameda were in serious financial trouble. By November they stopped all trading in these two exchanges, and although SBF had what appeared to be a "Big Name" in the crypto market, he could not find another crypto investor company to lend him money to bail out all his investors.

On November 10, the Bahamian regulators froze FTX's assets. FTX and 100 related entities, including FTX US and Alameda, filed for bankruptcy on November 11, 2022. Bankman-Fried resigned. It was soon discovered that FTX had more than one million creditors (FTX Trading, 2022).

John Ray, who has overseen the $23 billion bankruptcy following Enron's collapse in 2001, was appointed CEO and chief restructuring office of FTX. Ray claimed FTX was the biggest mess he had ever seen:

> Never in my career have I seen such a complete failure of corporate controls and such a complete absence of trustworthy financial information as occurred here. From compromised systems integrity and faulty regulatory oversight abroad, to the concentration of control in the hands of a very small group of inexperienced, unsophisticated and potentially compromised individuals, this situation is unprecedented. What was "lost" was over 7 billion dollars in investor assets that seem to have disappeared from FTX and Alameda accounts.
>
> *(Huang et al., 2023; Lewis, 2023a, 236, requoted in Shroff and Reavis, 2024)*

Both Michael Lewis, the biographer of SBF and SBF himself questioned the wisdom of Ray, who never asked for any information from SBF. Questioning Ray's findings, Lewis writes, "It is true, as Sam said, that people don't see what they're not looking for. It is also true that they have a talent for seeing whatever they expect to see" (Lewis, 2023b, 238). Was Ray influenced with his conviction that SBF was evil?

Also at the same time, in November 2022, the US Department of Justice charged SBF with eight counts of fraud, money laundering, and campaign finance offenses and arrested him. He was also charged with funneling billions of dollars of FTX customer funds to Alameda, which eventually "lost" the funds or was confiscated by SBE himself. In total SBF and his firm, FTX were accused of defrauding customers to over 14 billion dollars through various schemes. Bankman Fried was arrested in the Bahamas and extradited to the United State for trial, where eventually, despite pleading not guilty, in November 2023 he was convicted of seven counts of fraud. Today he is serving his sentence in a medium-security prison in New York State while the verdict is being appealed (Osipovich, 2024).

This case illustrates both the Rashomon effect we will discuss further in Chapter 5 and moral blindness. Note that SBF, Ray and Lewis each present their own version of the FTX story. Lewis, in his book, is very sympathetic to SBF. Ray is convinced of SBF's culpability almost before he began running and investigating FTX. And SBF, while admitting his management failures, is convinced of his innocence in this collapse. The financial world bought into the SBF myth, and few questioned his behavior or financial abilities – they were blind to the possibility that FTX was fraudulent, Michael Lewis, in his narrative on SBF, presents SBF as naïve as well as eccentric who had little idea of the harm he had created at FTX and the fiscal damage he created for his investors and for those who lent FTX and Alameda money. Is Lewis, too, blind to SBF's culpability, or is Ray himself blind to the possibility of SBF's naïve innocence and the importance of SBF's input in finding the "lost" funds?

SBF has continued to argue for his innocence.[4] Although there is no public evidence to explain his motives, we suspect that SBF's gaming addiction clouded or blinded him from grasping that trading cryptocurrencies is not merely a game. Perhaps SBF imagined trading, like "League of Legends," was an exciting game where currencies were to be won or lost without regard to those affected by these antics. Bankman-Fried was dealing with other people's money, which they had trusted him to handle with integrity. He was indeed morally blind, but he is an intelligent adult and thus not exempt from moral as well as legal culpability.

CONCLUSION

We have before us, then, several factors that may contribute to morally questionable behavior and to repeatability of that behavior in similar circumstances. Self-interest, greed, and retarded moral development may be contributing phenomena. A confusion of legal and moral demands, possible conflicts of interest between professional and institutional commitments, conflicts of role responsibilities, or the identification of moral responsibility with role responsibility may lead to the subsequent abdication of individual moral responsibility to organizational demands. Analyses such as these are helpful in pinpointing weaknesses in individual, managerial, and corporate decision-making. But such analyses do not successfully attack the problem of moral lapses or simply a failure to consider the ethical consequences of their actions.

Apparently at least two factors are missing at these companies. Many of these managers and their organizations appear to lack (1) the ability to step back from their situation, to look at their roles, decisions, and actions from another perspective to evaluate or reassess their activities, and (2) a modicum of moral imagination, that is, the ability to imagine a wider range of possible issues, consequences, and

---

[4] After FTX was taken over by another management team, the company made enough money to repay almost all of the $6 billion with interest to investors (Yaffe-Bellamny, 2024).

remedies (e.g., that new airplane software technology might be a problem or find out whether there might be another viable and profitable way forward). In Chapters 5 and 6 we will argue that the appeal to imagination and moral minimums helps to mitigate this narrow way of looking at one's thinking and behavior.

3 Social Constructivism and the Very Idea of a Conceptual Scheme

VOLKSWAGEN EMISSIONS SCANDAL (OR THE "DIESEL DUPE")[1]

> At Volkswagen we are committed to investing in America, in our communities, and most importantly, in our people, and we deliver on our promises.
>
> (Volkswagen, 2014)

Volkswagen (VW) was founded in Germany in 1937 under the Nazi regime by the labor unions with the help of Ferdinand Porsche, the inventor of the Beetle (the people's car). Tasked with making a car that was affordable for all consumers, VW's flagship car, the compact and iconic Beetle, first rolled off the manufacturing floor in 1945, and by 1949, half of all passenger cars produced in West Germany were built by VW. By 2014, VW was one of the biggest firms in the world. It had factories in thirty-one countries, employing almost 600,000 people worldwide. In 2014, it sold 10.2 million vehicles, with a total profit of over 11 billion euros.

The company's stated values included "customer focus, superior performance, creating value, renewability, respect, responsibility, and sustainability" (Volkswagen, 2016). These values were intended to guide decisions made by employees throughout the company and were accompanied by a twenty-five-page Code of Conduct on which every employee was trained after joining VW. This Code of Conduct was written in 2009 and systematically rolled out to

---

[1] Edited and reproduced by permission from Luann Lynch, Elizabeth Bird and Cameron Curto, "The Volkswagen Emissions Scandal," Darden Business Publishing Case UVA S-267. Charlottesville Virginia. 2018.

employees across the globe in 2010. It addressed topics such as management culture and collaboration, anticorruption, and fair competition, and it was intended to be a "guidepost that combines the essential basic principles of our activities and supports our employees in mastering the legal and ethical challenges in their daily work" (Volkswagen 2010, 2015). In addition, all VW employees received compliance training; 185,000 were trained on compliance in 2014 (Volkswagen, 2015).

In 2007 the leadership of VW was changed and was now led by Martin Winterkorn. Under the leadership of Winterkorn and his mentor, VW Chairman Ferdinand Piëch (a grandson of VW founder Porsche and himself VW CEO from 1993 until 2002), VW became a tightly controlled, highly centralized company. Its corporate culture was one of command-and-control, with leadership setting aggressive goals and senior executives involved in even relatively minor decisions. The company gained a reputation for being hard-charging and brutally competitive, and former employees described an environment in which subordinates were fearful of ever admitting failure or contradicting their superiors (Ewing and Bowley, 2015).

Both Piëch and Winterkorn came from engineering backgrounds and kept a close eye on product development. Piëch, who recruited Winterkorn to Audi in 1981, became his mentor for more than twenty-five years; Piëch would boast that managers would be "shaking in their boots" prior to presentations before him, knowing that, if he was displeased, they might be fired instantly. By the time he became CEO in 2007, Winterkorn was considered "a cold, distant figure ... known for obsessive attention to detail." Unlike other contemporary auto industry CEOs, who were experts in financial management and turnarounds, Winterkorn was considered a "classic car guy" (Mutter, 2013). He was known for carrying a gauge with him at all times to measure flaws in vehicles as they came off the production line and for publicly disparaging subordinates. An industry analyst said, "He doesn't like bad news. Before anyone reports to him, they make sure they have good news" (Levin, 2015).

In the mid-2000s, when Winterkorn began his tenure as CEO and announced VW's goal of becoming the world's largest automaker within the next decade, the auto industry in the United States and around the world was facing significant engineering challenges. Persistently high prices at the gas pump and toughening mileage standards put pressure on automakers to design more fuel-efficient vehicles, while growing concerns about climate change spurred increasingly stringent emissions regulations. In order to drive sales, automakers needed to find ways to optimize fuel efficiency and emissions while still designing the high-performing vehicles that Americans had become accustomed to driving. The market for hybrid-electric cars, notably Toyota's Prius, was growing rapidly (US Department of Energy, 2016).

Rather than compete with Toyota and other automakers in the hybrid market, VW had opted for a strategy of diesel, viewing it as a huge growth opportunity within the US car market and a viable eco-friendly alternative. While diesel made up almost half of new car sales in Europe, it held just 5 percent of the US auto market in 2007, and Winterkorn believed it was an opportune time to expand diesel sales in the United States. Diesel offered a cheaper, more powerful alternative to hybrid vehicles, promising high fuel efficiency without sacrificing powerful performance. But before it could market fuel-efficient diesel in the United States, VW had to overcome one major roadblock: diesel cars generated significantly more nitrogen oxide (NOx) than gasoline-powered engines, making it difficult for them to clear the stringent American emissions standards without sacrificing fuel efficiency or performance. In order to sell its cars in the US market, a critical part of the company's goal of becoming the world's largest car manufacturer, VW would have to engineer a way to strip its cars of these pollutants to meet US regulations (Environmental Protection Agency, 2014; Plungis, 2015).

Whatever solution was devised, software was likely to be at the center of it. Modern cars contained approximately 100 million lines of software code that controlled everything from basic operations to media to safety. Software could also help a car control the amount of pollutants it emitted, by monitoring carbon monoxide and NOx emissions and then diverting pollutants to special systems that converted them into less harmful substances. Around the time that VW engineers were struggling to determine the right solution, auto industry–supplier Bosch gave VW diesel engine-management software for use during testing. This software could detect when a vehicle was in a testing environment and activated emissions-controlling devices. Bosch believed VW was only using this software during its internal testing, and sold the software to VW with the understanding that utilizing the software in publicly sold vehicles was illegal (Sorokanich, 2015).

Nevertheless, VW engineers adapted the Bosch technology and installed it in all its new diesels, which now performed well to meet the US EPA standards (Lawrence et al., 2015). By 2008, it appeared that "the power of German engineering" had once again pulled through. Volkswagen announced the rollout of a new clean diesel technology called the Lean NOx Trap, which it claimed had solved the problem of delivering high fuel efficiency while still meeting emissions standards. The new technology garnered considerable attention for VW. Its 2009 clean diesel Jetta TDI won the Green Car of the Year award, beating out hybrids and electric vehicles. It hosted a multiweek "dissolution tour" to "change any outdated perceptions about diesel technology" and prove its environmental virtue. Some of its vehicles were reportedly getting almost 60 mpg, which was unheard of for a nonelectric or hybrid car. At a conference on diesel emissions the same year, a VW executive boasted that "you don't have to sacrifice power to be environmentally conscious." Clean diesel became the centerpiece of VW's US marketing strategy, and sales took off. By 2014, VW's diesel cars accounted for 21 percent of the company's US sales (Volkswagen, 2013, 2014).

By 2014, VW was well on its way to achieving all four Strategy 2018 goals. Worldwide sales grew steadily at approximately 7.2 percent compound annual growth rate (CAGR) from 2007, when Winterkorn took over, to 2014 (Bloomberg Intelligence, 2016). Most notably, the company reached its sales goal in 2014, selling more than 10 million vehicles and surpassing Toyota in sales volume, thereby becoming the world's largest automaker four years ahead of the deadline it had set for itself (Hakim et al., 2015).

But in 2013, a nonprofit group called the International Council on Clean Transportation (ICCT) noticed something strange: Diesel technologies appeared cleaner in the United States than in Europe. The ICCT hoped to identify what made diesel technologies superior in the United States in order to improve emissions in Europe. The traditional in-lab emissions tests had not provided any clues to the engineering differences, which were producing lower-emission vehicles in the United States, so the researchers proposed on-road (as opposed to in-lab) testing of diesel cars in order to better understand these differences. They partnered with West Virginia University's Center for Alternative Fuels, Engines, and Emissions and California environmental regulators to perform tests on several types of diesel vehicles, starting with a BMW X5, a VW Jetta, and a VW Passat (all three selected by chance; they were models conveniently available to the researchers). The researchers compared in-lab and on-road emissions and mileage performance (Hakim et al., 2015; Lawrence et al., 2015).

Almost immediately, the two VW vehicles stood out. They performed flawlessly in the lab, but once on the open road, their emissions were significantly higher. What the researchers unexpectedly uncovered was that these differences were perhaps not the result of superior engineering but rather the result of cars specifically designed to take advantage of testing environments (Lawrence et al., 2015).

In early 2014, the researchers turned over the surprising results of the study to the US EPA, which questioned VW about the findings. Volkswagen flatly denied any accusations of wrongdoing. The West Virginia University researcher who led the tests said VW "tried to poke holes in our study and its methods, saying we didn't know what we were doing." The researchers eventually conducted an in-depth examination of VW's software, reviewing millions of lines of code for something to explain the strange discrepancy in emissions. They discovered an unusual set of instructions that was sent to emissions controls whenever the vehicle was only utilizing two of its four wheels (as it would during in-lab testing). In essence, the vehicle recognized whether it was in a test lab or on the road. The defeat device limited emissions in the lab (therefore hindering performance), but once out on the road, emissions returned to levels far above federal regulations and performance did not suffer (Hakim et al., 2015).

Armed with this information, EPA officials threatened to withhold certification of VW and Audi's 2016 diesel models, which forced VW's hand. On September 18, 2015 – one week after being named the world's "most sustainable automaker" (Hardyment, 2015) – the company publicly admitted that it had installed defeat devices on nearly 500,000 diesel vehicles across 14 models sold in the United States since 2009, when the clean diesel technology launched. This number was later scaled up to 11 million vehicles worldwide. It was discovered that the vehicles were emitting up to 40 times the US legal limit of pollution into the atmosphere (Gates et al., 2016).

Volkswagen officials apologized but vehemently denied widespread knowledge of the defeat devices within the company, blaming a few engineers for the error and claiming that senior management had no knowledge of wrongdoing. They claimed that the millions of lines of software code made it impossible for anyone to know every line, particularly upper management, meaning that engineers could have included the emissions-defeating protocol without management knowing (Kedrosky, 2015).

Despite denying any wrongdoing, CEO Martin Winterkorn resigned five days after the scandal became public, stating that "I am stunned that misconduct on such a scale was possible in the Volkswagen Group. As CEO I accept responsibility for the irregularities that have been found in the diesel engines ... even though I am not aware of any wrongdoing on my part" (Ewing, 2016; Winterkorn, 2015).

The fallout of the scandal was swift and far-reaching. Regulators across the United States and across the globe opened investigations. In the United States, the EPA stated that VW could face up to USD18 billion in fines – USD37,500 per car for each of the estimated 500,000 cars impacted. The FBI opened a criminal probe, as did the attorneys general of all 50 states, and the Justice Department opened a civil lawsuit against the company over the deception. Outside of the United States, Germany and the European Union also opened criminal investigations, and German officials raided VW's headquarters days after the scandal came to light (National Public Radio, 2015).

In June 2016, VW agreed to a $14.7 billion settlement in the emissions scandal. The settlement was estimated to provide $10 billion to fund buybacks of vehicles from approximately 475,000 vehicle owners and additional cash compensation of $2.7 billion was to assist in environmental clean-up and $2 billion to fund programs by the EPA and California that focused on cleaner vehicles (Ewing and Tabuchi, 2016; Isidore and Goldman, 2016; Lynch et al., 2018).

CONCEPTUAL SCHEMES

In this chapter we outline a basic if sometimes misunderstood assumption. The assumption is that we all perceive, frame, and interact with the world through a conceptual scheme modified by a set of perspectives or mental models. Putting the point metaphorically, we each run the information from our "camera" of the world through certain selective mechanisms: intentions, interests, desires, points of view, or biases, all of which work as selective and restrictive filters. We each have what we shall call our own metaphysical movies of the world, which entail projections of individual's perspectives on the data provided from our experience.

These schemes are analogous to movies, because, like movies, each of our perspectives varies from stark realism to fantasy and even error, and because, like movies, this selective process leaves a great deal of the data of experience "on the cutting room floor." Sometimes some of us have one-track minds. We filter all experiences through a point of view, and it can be difficult to change that perspective. Ordinarily most of us will adopt a number of perspectives, depending on the subject matter and our interests, and these perspectives change or can be altered. Ordinarily, too, we can understand the perspectives of another, although one does not always make such an attempt.

Socialization, culture, upbringing, education, exposure to artworks, and, in our culture, the media, one's profession, and one's working milieu all contribute to ways in which we view and deal with the world. Feelings, emotions, and each person's idiosyncratic method for formulating ideas influence, in turn, new perceptions. So our movies are often reinforced by our own continuing projection of a certain perspective on whatever it is that we experience. Sometimes, though, the movies are influenced, changed, or even radically reformulated (Werhane, 1992, 1999).

Given that thesis, we suggest that the Volkswagen emissions scandal has resulted from the differing scripts of VW's managers and engineers from what was acceptable legally and morally concerning diesel emissions. These contrasting scripts, mental models, or "movies" created differing expectations, resulting in conflicting priorities that contributed significantly to the scandal. In the VW case, we suggest that the VW engineers who redesigned their diesel engines for export to the United States and VW managers and executives all were somehow "on the same page," acknowledging the fraud and going along with it, in contrast to a more general point of view, another "script" that argues that disobeying the law in the country where you are operating, and unnecessarily adding to air pollution are both illegally wrong, and deceptive, thus morally wrong as well. And, as in the Boeing cases, no engineer at VW, and there were apparently more than 100 involved in redesigning the diesel engine, blew the whistle outside the organization, despite the engineering codes of ethics that place human safety first.

Beginning with Immanuel Kant, philosophers now agree, although not universally, that "our conceptual scheme mediates even our most basic perceptual experiences" (Railton, 1986, 172). We learn from Kant that our minds do not mirror experience or reality. Rather, our minds project and reconstitute experience. In brief, Kant's reasoning is as follows.

Whereas the content of each of our experiences may vary dramatically, the ways in which we organize, order, and think about our experiences are universally the same. For example, Kant argued, we all experience the world in three dimensions, in a space-time continuum, and we engage in similar sorting mechanisms such as quantity, quality, same as, different, equal to, and so forth. Kant also claimed that all humans order the world causally; that is, when an event occurs, we assume it has a cause, and, alternately, all events are assumed to be causally related to other events. Yet we organize our experiences as formal concepts: They lack content and cannot be perceived. For example, one cannot perceive time; one merely experiences events temporally. "Cause" and "effect" are not observable phenomena but merely the ways in which we frame relationships between phenomena. Kant concluded that all human beings order and organize their experiences through an identical set of formal concepts. So, although the content of each of our experiences may be quite different, the ways in which we order these experiences are exactly the same. This would explain how we can imaginatively understand experiences that we have never encountered and communicate with people of cultures, ethnic backgrounds, or historical periods quite different from ours.

Do some basic, innate structures of the mind identically order all human experiences, as Kant contended? The subject is controversial. What we might glean from Kant is that the mind organizes, orders, and even censors experiences through a conceptual scheme or set of schemes. The idea of a conceptual scheme implies that the notion of reality as "something outside all schemes" (Rorty, 1993, 443) makes no sense.

Somewhat disapprovingly, Donald Davidson describes conceptual schemes as follows: "Conceptual schemes, we are told, are ways or organizing experience; they are systems of categories that give form to the data of sensation; they are points of view from which individuals, [institutions], cultures, or [historical] periods survey the passing scene" (Davidson, 1974, 5). Davidson's disapproval centers around whether conceptual schemes are commensurably distinct. If, as he suggests, they are not, then they are philosophically uninteresting. He concludes, "We have found no intelligible basis on which it can be said that schemes are different [even though] it would be equally wrong to announce ... that all speakers of language, at least, share a common scheme and ontology" (Davidson, 1974, 20).

Still, the idea of a conceptual scheme helps to examine the notion of differing belief systems or worldviews, because it is not inconceivable that there are, or have been, more than one belief system or worldview. But, as we shall argue later in the chapter, conceptual schemes are not, indeed, cannot be, logically incommensurable. In what follows we shall distinguish the idea of a conceptual scheme from what some scientists and social scientists call mental models, as well as from what Davidson calls a common coordinate system.

The pervasiveness of conceptual schemes implies that each of us perceives and experiences from an always contextually changing point of view, a perspective that serves as a selective organizing, filtering, and focusing mechanism. Our conceptual scheme frames our perceptions. It focuses, schematizes, and guides the ways in which we recognize, react, and organize the world. In fact, how we define the world is relative to that scheme and thus all reality is conceptually structured. A conceptual scheme is the means and mode through which we constitute our experiences, although, we shall argue, conceptual schemes may not be universally identical. Neither are they, as Kant thought, all formal concepts of understanding.

SOCIAL CONSTRUCTION AND CONCEPTUAL SCHEMES

> The seemingly objective social world is constructed by human action and interaction.
>
> (Berger and Luckmann, 1966, 1)

Given the idea of the ubiquitous nature conceptual schemes, we will take that idea and defend a social constructivist perspective, that is, the view that human beings deal with and interpret their experiences *only* through cognitive frames, mindsets, or mental models. These models represent intuitive and unconscious methods of sense-making (see Weick, 1995). In addition to receiving sensory data, our minds continually interact with others. Through such shared interactions, we selectively filter and frame data though social learning processes. In the process of organizing, ordering, and discussing what we experience, we mentally bracket or omit data simply because we cannot observe or absorb all that we encounter through perception. Each person's mental model or set of models is finite because no one has the capacity to take in all of the data of one's experiences; to the contrary, we selectively focus on some aspects and necessarily must ignore others. Our cognitive framing exercises can and often do ignore important data.

Social construction theory takes this idea one step further with the claim that our shared mental models or schemes frame *all* of our experiences in the sense that they guide the ways in which we recognize and organize what we then call the world. From this claim it follows that the categories that we apply to reality are socially structured (Gorman, 1992). Indeed, according to social constructionism, this is the only way in which human beings can understand *anything*. Notice this is not the claim that our minds construct reality or what we call experience or the data of experiences. Rather, it is the contention that the incomplete and disparate ways in which we present and distill experiences are socially constructed, and thus finite. As a result, because we cannot take in nor frame all the data of our experiences, in sorting out we often omit or ignore important data that does not fit into our expectations. This phenomenon, called "bounded awareness," is unavoidable and common, but it can create what Moberg, Bazerman, and Tenbrunsel have called "blind spots," where we miss or ignore essential data (Bazerman and Tenbrunsel, 2011; Moberg, 2000). And as we noted in Chapter 2, Rendtorff goes so far as to claim that some of us are morally blind, incapable of grasping any moral point of view whatsoever (Rendtorff, 2020).

Often, too, we create habits that are reinforced internally or externally through social interactions. In new situations, these habits can reinforce choices and behavior that do not take into account bizarre or new situations as just that – new, and we tend to interpret these situations through our habits.

> The most serious problem ... is not that we frame experiences, it is not that these mental models are incomplete, sometimes biased, and surely parochial. The larger problem is that most of us either individually or in organizations do not realize that we *are* framing, disregarding data, ignoring counterevidence, or not taking into account other points of view.
>
> *(Werhane, 2007, 401)*

This problem, wherein we do not recognize our framing and editing, is not merely descriptive. It raises ethical issues. Because as human beings, and by analogy as organizations, we *can* become aware of this set of activities, albeit ubiquitous in all human perception and experience. If we can become aware of these issues and have the capacity to overcome or mitigate them, then, arguably, we may have a moral obligation to do so. How is that awareness possible?

Adam Smith, the eighteenth-century philosopher and political economist, worked out why we need not be trapped in one point of view, habit, or one set of mental models. In *The Theory of Moral Sentiments*, he argued that as conscious beings we have unique capacities. Not only are we aware of our surroundings but we are also aware of ourselves as existing in these surroundings and of our capacity to change these circumstances and, if you like, redirect our lives and our histories. This self-conscious awareness comes from a uniquely human capacity Smith calls the "impartial spectator" (Smith, [1759] 1976). The impartial spectator describes our abilities to step back and study our surroundings, our friends and neighbors, our enemies and even our own and others' mindsets. It is, he argues, the source of conscience and moral judgment, whereby we can evaluate ourselves, our points of view, and others less subjectively. This capacity, he believes, explains how we can extricate ourselves from bad (or even good) habits, make choices, and revise our mental models, expectations, and lives. Smith claims that while we can never completely extricate ourselves to get a purely impartial "view from nowhere" (Nagel, 1986), by developing this capacity we can make better judgments and redirect our lives accordingly.

If Smith's account of how it is that we can make choices and control our destinies is accurate, then, it explains how we can step back from a particular point of view and reevaluate our focus and judgments. By analogy, organizations, too, can disengage from their dominant logics and evaluate those perspectives, although their capacity to do so may be limited by a corporate culture that is so ingrained as to block such inquiry. We shall return to these organizational challenges in Chapter 7.

LINGUISTIC FRAMING

Many philosophers argue that conceptual schemes are semantically based (e.g., Anscombe, 1976; Johnson, 1993; Putnam, 1990; Rorty, 1993; Wittgenstein, 1953). Whether human beings conceptualize or deal with the world nonlinguistically is a thesis for another essay, but as Hilary Putnam and Richard Rorty argue, "*Elements of what we call 'language' or 'mind' penetrate so deeply into what we call 'reality' that the very project of representing ourselves as being mappers of something 'language-independent' is fatally compromised from the start*" (Putnam, 1990, 28; cited with approval in Rorty, 1993, 443; emphasis Rorty's). Language shapes our perspectives in such deeply grounded ways that it is difficult to imagine how we would conceptualize or frame experience purely non-linguistically, because the very act of describing and explaining such concepts and frames uses language. The question of whether language and linguistic ability are innate "deep structures" (Chomsky, 1965), hardwired as part of what it is to be a human being, is also controversial and takes us far afield from this project. However, all evidence points to at least three basic facts.

First, no group of human beings has ever yet been discovered, even in what we might agree are the most primitive situations, that did not have a well-developed, complex spoken language that can generate an almost infinite number of ways of expression in that language. Second, language is socially learned in early childhood. In rare instances children who have been brought up in isolation from other human contact do not speak, and after a certain age, around five, they cannot learn language (Langer, [1942] 1951). Third, whereas the fact of language is universal, grammar and syntax vary dramatically in context, thus framing widely different conceptual schemes that, in turn, create different belief systems.

If languages are the most basic means through which we structure our experiences, they are, in some sense, "metaconceptual schemes" because our language or languages constitute the background framing mechanism for a conceptual scheme. Yet a particular language is often incomplete, because its syntax and grammar can preclude formulation of certain kinds of conceptual schemes. Still, the theoretical possibility of understanding languages whose grammar and syntax are alien to our own (and thus a new conceptual scheme) is not precluded. While specific languages and even dialects are quite different, so that the way they shape and express belief systems is distinct, there is no logically private language that is, in principle, untranslatable. As Ludwig Wittgenstein posits in *Philosophical Investigations*, the notion of a rule-based language assumes a consistency of use so that in principle a language cannot be private; that is, no language is logically and in principle incomprehensible to anyone because rules can be learned (Werhane, 1992; Wittgenstein, 1953). This conclusion does not imply, for instance, that a word such as "ennui" in French has a one-to-one translation in English. It does not. But it does imply that because the grammar of French follows consistent repeatable patterns that are understandable, we as English language speakers can also learn to speak and read French. French grammar rules are different from English grammar rules, but they both are consistently rule-based constructions that allow a speaker of one language to learn another. It also implies that when we learn to read and speak French, and learn about the French culture, we can understand the meaning of ennui and why it has no exact equivalent in English.

MENTAL MODELS

In *The Fifth Discipline* (1990), Peter Senge explains conceptual schemes in terms of mental models, a term that comes from cognitive science literature. Although the term is not always clearly defined, mental model connotes the idea that human beings have mental representations, cognitive frames, or mental pictures of their experiences – models of the stimuli or data with which they are interacting – and that these are frameworks that set up parameters though which experience, or a certain set of experiences, is organized or filtered (Gentner and Whitley, 1997, 210–211). "Mental models are the mechanisms whereby humans are able to generate descriptions of system purpose and form, explanations of system functioning and observed system states, and predictions of future system states" (Rouse and Morris, 1986, 351). And as George Box memorably reminds us "all models are wrong" (Box, 1976, 792). A more accurate of mental models is that they are, at best, all incomplete, and indeed some are wrong. Mental models may be construed as hypothetical constructs of the experience in question, or precise scientific theories; they might be the schema that frame the experience, and through which individuals process information, conduct experiments, and formulate theories; or mental models may simply refer to human knowledge about a particular set of events or a system. Mental models thus account for our ability to describe, explain, and predict and may function as protocols to account for human expectations often formulated in accordance with these models (Gorman, 1992; Rouse and Morris, 1986).

The notion of a mental model is connected with what Karl Weick and others call sensemaking (Starbuck and Milliken, 1988; Weick, 1995). Sensemaking is defined as "placing stimuli into frameworks (or schemata) that make sense of the stimuli" (Starbuck and Milliken, 1988b, 51). This is a process of filtering, categorizing, sorting, framing, extrapolating, and interpreting the stimuli or data. Starbuck and Milliken take a neo-Kantian view that sensemaking, in various forms, is the way we deal with the data of our experiences, as well as the means for understanding, predicting, and explaining human events. Weick uses the term to account for the ways in which we invent, construct, interpret, and even revise our experiences. According to Weick, "the process of sensemaking is intended to include the construction and bracketing of the text-like cues that are interpreted, as well as the revision of those interpretations based on action and its consequences" (Weick, 1995, 8). Sensemaking is an ongoing process of clarification and explanation of situations or events. Thus, according to Weick, sensemaking often occurs retrospectively. That is, we often retrospectively reframe a past event from another point of view in order to clarify or make sense of it. Often this process revises the meaning of the event, reinterprets or even omits data, and reframes its significance (Gioia, 1986; Weick, 1995, 4).

According to Paul Churchland, the sensemaking process begins early in small children:

> Children learn to recognize certain prototypical kinds of social situations, and they learn to produce or avoid the behaviors prototypically required or prohibited in each. Young children learn to recognize a distribution of scarce resources such as cookies or candies as a fair or unfair distribution. They learn to voice complaints in the latter case and to withhold complaints in the former.
> *(1989, rpt. in Johnson, 1993, 190–191)*

We would argue that almost all human activity is sensemaking in various forms and that the operative mechanisms in sensemaking are clear from our use of mental models. Senge argues that mental models are "deeply held internal images of how the world works, images that limit us to familiar ways of thinking and acting" (Senge, 1990, 174). Mental models constitute the basis for our assumptions and points of view. They are created by theories, myths, stories, and images that frame, focus, or revise the ways we experience the world.

Examples of mental models and how they function abound. The creation story in the Bible has generated a belief system about the foundation of humanity and reality. Similarly, but alternatively, the Big Bang theory in astrophysics proposes an explanatory model that shapes the belief system of those who accept it. Theories about whether human beings are psychological egoists shape our expectations about behavior, about behavioral control, and about rewards and punishments. If we accept a neoclassical economic model that we are all, in our rational moments, utility maximizers, we will think differently about the value of human activities from, say, those who argue that rationality includes altruism and fairness.

The media, film, art, fiction, myths, and stories, too, shape our mental models or conceptual schemes. For example, a film such as *Wall Street* can change not merely our perceptions but our whole point of view about Wall Street and markets through the model it projects of questioning whether "greed is good"? Mental models, then, are not merely formal or universal concepts; in fact, their differences cause us to form parochial points of view and to misunderstand each other.

A point of view can become indelibly etched in our brain even when it actually misrepresents experienced phenomena. The art historian E. H. Gombrich points out the sixteenth-century artist Albrecht Durer's famous woodcut of a rhinoceros, depicting the animal with a heavy coat of armor. This depiction served as a model for renderings of the animal in natural history books until the eighteenth century, even though, in fact, for those who are not rhinoceros experts, rhinos do not have armor. Similarly, an early 1598 engraving depicting a whale with ears served as a model for whale images, even though whales are earless (Gombrich, 1961, 80–82).

In framing our experiences, mental models also function as focusing projectors. Some aspects of the kinds of projectors we use relate directly to the VW case. To borrow a phrase from the philosopher Michael Davis, we often have "microscopic vision." That is, we focus on a narrow range of phenomena or data, or we focus on that data in a careful, insightful way. Microscopic vision is crucial for engineering, the sciences, medicine, and other professions for study in great detail (Starbuck and Milliken, 1988). But as we saw earlier in the VW emissions scandal, such microscopic vision of its engineers failed to consider the environmental and legal ramification of what they were designing and the myopic view that this redesign would never be noticed nor picked up.

Dennis Gioia defines a mental model, or what he calls a schema, as "a cognitive framework that people use to impose structure upon information, situations, and expectations to facilitate understanding" (Gioia, 1992, 385). Gioia distinguishes schemas from scripts: "A script is a specialized type of schema that retains knowledge of actions appropriate for specific situations and contexts.... Scripts ... provide a cognitive framework for understanding information and events as well as a guide to appropriate behavior to deal with the situation faced" (Gioia, 1992, 385). Mental models, then, can function as specific framing scripts or mini belief systems in specific kinds of situations, or within the culture of institutions such as corporations.

Because of the pervasiveness of mental models, "as human beings we cannot have a view of the world that does not reflect our interests and values" (Putnam, 1990, 178; Rorty, 1993, 443). One way we deal with experience is normatively, through such notions as what one ought to do, what is right or wrong, what is good or bad, useful or destructive, and so on. Moral theories, such as utilitarianism or deontology, give us prototypical mental models with which to deal with these notions. Moral theories are mental models, systemic ways or models for thinking about normative issues, which themselves are schematized. So when one applies an ethical theory (or theories) to a set of complex design projects such as VW's manufacture of the diesel engine for export to the US, one is layering another interpretation or schema on an already schematized situation. No wonder, then, that sometimes moral theories can fail to trigger new thinking or decision-making by their proponents.

Not all mental models are cognitive. According to a number of contemporary philosophers and psychologists, another form of social construction is our emotions. A great deal of evidence suggests that our emotions, like our belief structures, are not merely innate, inchoate, and brutal outbursts. Rather, they, too, are socially constructed and learned. One learns both what emotions are and how to feel just as one learns what is good or evil, true or false, red or green, and the meaning of emotions varies culturally just as language does (Harre, 1986; Nussbaum, 1990, 287–294; Rorty, 1980). So, for example, ancient Greek color words are not easily translatable because their emotional meanings are quite different from ours. To illustrate, consider that Euripides describes blood as "green" or "yellow green." From a contemporary English-speaking point of view, this is a curious expression. However, for the ancient Greeks green was associated with youth or fear. In that context "green blood" makes sense (Dancy, 1983; Irwin, 1974).

Our own idiosyncratic interests, feelings, desires, and points of view also affect our mental models. Each of us perceives and deals with experience through perspectives that include our interests, desires, points of view, or biases, as well as cognitive and emotional frames through which we selectively frame and filter experiences. Each of us has, or is capable of having, a number of overlapping schema that may function differently in different contexts. These mental models do not merely frame our experiences; indeed, they function as selective mechanisms and filters for dealing with experience. We also "color" our experiences through our passions, feelings, intentions, interests, and foci, so that we each have an idiosyncratic way of shaping our experiences. In selecting, focusing, framing, organizing, and ordering what we experience, conceptual schemes bracket and leave out data, and emotional and motivational foci taint or color experience. Nevertheless, because schema we employ are socially learned and altered through religion, socialization, culture, educational upbringing, and other experiences, they are shared ways of perceiving and organizing experience; through our common language we can understand and communicate conceptual differences of each of our mental models.

HOW MENTAL MODELS ARE LIMITING

Because of the variety and diversity of mental models, none is complete, and "there are multiple possible framings of any given situation"

(Johnson, 1993,9). With that understanding, each of us can frame any situation, event, or phenomenon in more than one way, and that same phenomenon can also be socially constructed in a variety of ways. The way one frames a situation is critical to its outcome, because "there are ... different moral consequences depending on the way we frame the situation" (Johnson, 1993, 9).

In the VW case, from what we can find out from very limited data that has escaped from this company even after the discovery of the diesel reengineering model, there seemed to be no thought as to whether or how anyone outside VW would discover this anomaly. They seemed to have forgotten the curiosity of other engineers and engineering students to pull apart designs and find out how they were designed and how they operate. There seemed to be no measurement of risk in this deceptive emissions design, or if there was, no one blew the whistle, no one, not one engineer, nor manager who were in on the scheme. This behavior might also explain why no engineer at VW blew the whistle. They were engineers with the roles of designing vehicles and simply obeying orders of managers – an example of Milgram's worry about blind obedience to authority.

There is a third limiting mental model in this scenario – which is the corporate culture in which the VW diesel emissions redesign was initiated and carried out. Again, students of the case find very little data from VW about the inner workings of this company. But the fact that, just as at Boeing, *no one* among the probably hundreds of engineers who were engaged in redesigning this diesel engine nor the many managers and perhaps even VW executives who were privy and signed off on this project ever leaked this to the public or the media is plausible secondary evidence that this was a closed corporate culture: where everyone did their jobs, and did them well, and followed the orders of management and executives. This culture, then, seemed to reflect a culture whose activities were to remain within the company even despite their ethics codes to the contrary.

What was missing in VW teams was the moral imagination to examine the consequences of the "defeat" technology, to realize how its discovery might affect the company. Volkswagen engineers and managers involved in this project (and note that VW is a huge company, so this diesel engine project for US export was a small minority of the company's operations) failed to examine their agency and its consequences from any perspective except their own. Taking another perspective is crucial, because unless one can disengage oneself from the context of specific decisions, from one's particular "movie," decisions become parochially embedded and result in business decisions that threaten public safety and thus invite moral and fiscal failure.

The VW emissions scandal clearly illustrates the limiting nature of mental models. A certain mental model develops or is adopted that frames the scenario in which one is operating so that often we fail to see the limitations and finite perspectives, even distortions, of our worldview. A mental model is just that – a model – one of several ways to frame a situation with a number of other possibilities. When we fail to recognize these limitations, the consequences are sometimes worse than painting ears on whales.

INCOMMENSURABILITY AND THE ALLEGED RELATIVISM OF CONCEPTUAL SCHEMES

Because "the very project of representing ourselves as being mappers of something 'language-independent' is fatally compromised," as Putnam and Rorty assent, it is sometimes argued that conceptual schemes are incommensurable with regard to one another so that no one can "translate" one scheme to another or understand the concepts embedded in a scheme other than one's own (Gioia and Pitre, 1990; Jackson and Carter, 1991). Some writers have argued that the issue is whether Westernized conceptual schemes (i.e., our belief systems and/or worldviews) are incommensurable with each other (e.g., Davidson, 1974; Kuhn, [1962] 1970). Other writers such as Gioia and Pitre – in an early paper that Gioia later questions in his work with Gary Weaver (Weaver and Gioia, 1994) – appear to be introducing the notion of incommensurability to apply, in a more restricted sense, to mental models or what Gioia calls schema. Although the distinction is blurry, the term "mental model" usually refers to incomplete, learned, and revisable schema. If such schema are individually incommensurable, then one is left with the problem of solipsism. If these schemas are institutionally, socially, culturally, or parochially theory-based, so as to be logically incommensurable with other mental models, one faces an issue Donald Davidson calls conceptual relativism. According to Davidson, conceptual relativism is the thesis that

> there may be no translating from one to another, in which case the beliefs, desires, hopes, and bits of knowledge that characterize one person have no true counterparts for the subscribed to another scheme. Reality itself is relative to a scheme; what counts as real in one system may not in another.
> *(Davidson, 1974, 5)*

Although Davidson is referring to conceptual schemes in this quotation, if mental models are incommensurable with each other, his conclusions apply to mental models as well. The question of solipsism is interesting, but we do not address it further in this book, because in Chapter 2 we have argued that human beings are intrinsically social: We survive, develop, and mature only in a social context with other beings like ourselves. Earlier in this chapter, we argued that a private language, that, by its structure, is incomprehensible to anyone other than its speaker, is practically unviable. If both these theses are correct, if a mental model is socially inculcated through language and through other cultural media, and if mental models are incomplete, then they are shared or shareable with others. So idiosyncratic differences in how each of us deals with experience, and differences between cultures, languages, historical periods, and religions can, at least in theory, be comprehended and understood, although certainly not always shared or agreed upon.

Conceptual relativism, in referring strictly to conceptual schemes, is a stickier issue. This type of relativism argues that certain worldviews or "constellation[s] of beliefs, values, techniques, and scientific structures" (Kuhn, [1962] 1970, 175) are incommensurable with each other; these mindsets are mutually exclusive or conflict on such basic grounds that one cannot hold any two such views simultaneously. One could argue further that some worldviews are strongly or "dramatically" incommensurable incomprehensible from one to another so that someone who functions within worldview A could not comprehend worldview B, nor communicate with those who held it. It would follow from this second form of incommensurability that reasoning (and by entailment any moral reasoning) would be solely scheme-dependent and that one's reasoning processes simply could not function as reasoning in a worldview incommensurable with one's own.

These two forms of conceptual relativism reach quite different conclusions. The first formulation claims that some worldviews are incommensurable with each other – so that one could not advocate both simultaneously without contradiction – illustrated by, say, the Ptolemaic versus the Copernican view of the universe. It is obviously impossible to hold both that the world is the center of the universe and that it is not, and the theory and data interpretations that support each view by and large contradict each other. One cannot simultaneously be thoroughly Ptolemaic and thoroughly Copernican. Nevertheless, one can understand both views and their theoretical baggage, and Ptolemains can communicate meaningfully with Copernicans; that is, these theories are not strongly incommensurable.

To change from a Ptolemaic to a Copernican view, one must change many of the mental models operating in one's worldview, if not the entire conceptual scheme. Still, there is a basic mode of communication underlying both views that remains unaffected by this paradigm shift and accounts for the fact that we can recognize, acknowledge, and label that shift. According to Davidson, "different points of view make sense but only if there is a common coordinate system on which to plot them; that the existence of a common system belies the claim of dramatic incomparability" (Davidson, 1974, 6). Thus, paradigmatic differences between conceptual schemes do not necessarily imply strong incommensurability.

What is meant by a "common coordinate system"? Wittgenstein, Rorty, Davidson, and Putnam all claim, in different ways, that the common system is semantics or the fact of language (Davidson, 1974; Putnam, 1990; Rorty, 1993; Wittgenstein, 1953). What is important for our purposes is the distinction between a common coordinate system and conceptual schemes. Social practices, histories, or rule-following activities including particular languages, are mental models, part of one's conceptual scheme, and neither system nor scheme is logically private or incomprehensible to each other. The common coordinate system that we share as human beings is a precondition for human activities that include language; it is a "bedrock" for a variety of languages and other conceptual schemes. The distinction between conceptual scheme and common coordinate system reveals how we share common perspectives and how we can understand the language and the perspectives, of historically or culturally distant people. Indeed, a conceptual scheme and the possibility of both being aware of a conceptual scheme and revising it makes sense only if we assume a common coordinate system that precludes strong incommensurability or what Davidson calls "dramatic incommensurability."

Dramatic or strong incommensurability, the view that two conceptual schemes or worldviews might be incomprehensible in principle to one another, such that a person operating within one belief system could not comprehend the belief system of a second, implies that certain languages, institutions, cultures, or scientific theses can be logically private on a macro level because they are incomprehensible to anyone other than their speaker, adherents, and believers. According to this thesis, languages, cultures, or schemes would exhibit ways of identifying, connecting, iterating, and repeating in patterns, with a kind of consistency unknown to the rest of us. That is, there would be different common coordinate systems; indeed, terms like "common," "coordinate," and "system" would have unrecognizable meanings. The connections and patterns of re-identification would be utterly different from the ways we understand these terms, so different that we could not conceive of how such a constellation of conceptual schemes could operate as a belief system.

It is approaching the impossible to imagine another possible worldview that does not exhibit some characteristics of consistency, repeatability, or identity, some rule-based characteristics that would bind it together as a worldview. Yet dramatic incommensurability demands that notions such as consistency, rule-following, identity or sameness would be utterly different in two conceptual schemes. This difference would bar our comprehension of the other worldview. Thus, what dramatic incommensurability seems oxymoronic.

There is still a third way to think of conceptual relativism, in particular the thesis that because we cannot view experience from "nowhere," that is, from a position that is not tainted by language or some mental model, "reality itself is relative to a scheme; what counts as real in one system may not in another" (Davidson, 1974, 5). If all our experience is shaped by a conceptual scheme, then what we mean by "reality," or the "world," or even "experience" is similarly shaped by a conceptual scheme, so what might be perceived as "real" in one scheme would not be so perceived in another. The result would be a form of linguistic idealism, the idea that "essence is created by grammar" (Anscombe, 1976, 188).

There is one sense in which this thesis is plausible. What counts as "fact" for example, is different for different peoples, depending on whether and how their particular belief system treats myth, story, and scientifically verifiable data. These differences in what is fact or "true" can be seen even within a particular societal belief system. For example, in the United States we might assume that everyone, or at least every reasonable adult, has adapted a belief system that accepts as true what scientists have called verifiable facts. Thus, notions of truth and factual evidence are not consistent even among intelligent Americans.

Nevertheless, there is a difference between claiming that one cannot get at reality, or the real world, or experience except through some conceptual scheme and concluding that reality or experience is itself merely created or solely socially constructed. Arguing that the incomplete, disparate ways in which we present and distill experience are socially constructed is different from arguing that experience or reality itself is socially created. We argue here that how we conceive the world is conceptually dependent, that is, "essence is expressed by grammar" (Wittgenstein, 1953, § 371, my italics). This is quite different from concluding that "essence is created by grammar." When essence is created by grammar, we call it lying, fantasy, storytelling, or mythmaking. Within any belief system we are careful to distinguish fantasy and myth from "the real," "the true," or "the facts," even though each is socially structured by grammar and context.

CONCLUSION

The Volkswagen emissions scandal case demands that we examine carefully not just the case but also our perspectives and our biases. It invites us to question our habits and models of dealing with the world, to look into ourselves to find out how we make choices, and sometimes to question our presuppositions. Scientists and engineers, in particular, who work with allegedly "hard" data, are often misled into thinking that data is purely objective, forgetting that such data has usually been filtered through constructs such as a particular scientific model. Seldom do we heed what Werner Heisenberg ([1932] 1959) taught us some sixty years ago, that even the most allegedly unbiased observations of an event affect that event. We need to develop more critically evaluative perspectives even in engineering and scientific analyses and most surely in the use of statistics. Otherwise, we live in a costly twilight zone of our own mental models dictated by job-related roles, institutional mores, or ingrained habits.

Given that all human activities are embedded in some or other conceptual scheme and framed by mental models, are such critically evaluative perspectives possible? We think so. We have just been engaged here in an examination of a number of perspectives and their limitations. Because no conceptual schemes are logically incommensurable, and because mental models are incomplete and alterable, we can perceive conceptual schemes, find out which mental models are operative, to change our modes of intention, projection, and perception, and even modify our definitions of "fact" and "fantasy" without succumbing to the conclusion that all our experiences are mere storytelling. Part of the activity of critical thinking is traceable to the thin aspect of the self as discussed in Chapter 2. The self is more than its thick social interconnections and relationships, and in its evaluative, critical mode it perceives different perspectives and questions some of its roles, relationships, and previous decisions. As we shall explore later (in Chapter 6), one may be happy not to ever achieve a totally objective point of view. One can never examine oneself or one's experiences divorced from any context or frame. On the other hand, since each mental model is only a partial perspective, one can often analyze the mental models at work, the "movies" playing, and the schemas that affect and even limit decision-making from a critical perspective of the thin or core self.

This process of engaging in a critical perspective on oneself, one's activities, one's behavior, and one's situation is what we call the development of moral imagination, which we treat in detail (in Chapter 6). It involves, at a minimum, asking difficult questions and attempting to place oneself in a different perspective so as to regard events from another point of view, individual, organizational, and social. There is no guarantee that one will always achieve a sufficient distance from a particular dilemma or derive the best decision because distancing oneself may also lead to moral distancing so that the moral implications of the dilemma are bracketed as well. Still, as we assert (in Chapter 6), a process of questioning and a critically distancing oneself to test one's decisions can be steps toward a more engaged moral decision-making process and, more importantly, to moral responsibility. This sort of approach was not taken by the engineers at VW. This sort of stance is what philosophers call a supererogatory act, an act that goes beyond ordinary expectations and one that requires courage and leadership, the kind of leadership we saw in the McDonald's case. Of course, there is always the possibility that engineers who designed the faulty diesel were afraid to speak out even though they had to know what they were doing and that it was deceptive to the US regulators. Moreover, such actions do not always turn out well, as evidenced by the history of whistleblowers, many of whom have been fired, or blackballed from their industry or profession, and suffered personal problems. This is one of the few counter-instances when a whistle-blower has been reinstated and promoted to an even more responsible position. Still, as an engineer with a code of ethics to protect human safety, the lack of courage of VW engineers is nevertheless still despicable.

4 The *Rashomon* Effect

The Academy Award-winning 1950 Japanese movie *Rashomon* depicts an incident involving an outlaw, a rape or seduction of a woman, and a murder or suicide of her husband. A passerby, who is also the narrator, explains how the story is told to officials from four different perspectives: that of the outlaw, the woman, the husband, and himself. The four narratives agree that the outlaw, wandering through the forest, came upon the woman on a horse led by her husband; the outlaw tied up the husband; the woman and the outlaw had intercourse in front of the bound husband; and the husband was found dead. The narratives do not agree on how these events occurred or who killed the husband. The outlaw contends that consensual intercourse occurred between him and the wife, and he claims to have killed the husband. The wife depicts the sexual act as rape and claims that because of her disgrace, she killed her husband. The husband, through a medium, says that the sexual act began as rape and ended as consent, and that, in shame after being untied by the outlaw, he killed himself. The passerby's story confirms the husband's account of the sexual contact but claims that the bandit was initially afraid to kill the husband. The passerby depicted both men as cowards, preferring to save their own lives rather than protect the wife. Eventually, however, the husband was killed by the bandit. Interestingly, because the passerby is also the narrator of the film, recounting to friends the strange contradictory reporting of this event, we tend to believe his version. But what actually took place is never resolved.

In the preceding chapters we used a series of cases or narratives that depicted incidents in corporate decision-making. In this chapter we examine the role of narratives and make the following claim: The ways we present or re-present a story, the narrative we employ, and the conceptual framing of that story affect its content, what we believe, its moral analysis, and the subsequent evaluation (Chambers, 1996, 25). Sometimes, the narratives of a particular set of events contradict each other. At other times, when one narrative becomes dominant and appears somehow more plausible or preferable, we appeal to that story for reinforcement of facts, assuming that it represents what actually happened, even though our selection may have distorting effects. The result in either case is a *Rashomon* effect. Yet we seldom carefully examine the narrative we use, often unaware of the "frame" or mental model at work. If my thesis is correct, it is important, morally important, to understand the constructive nature and limits of narratives.

In Chapter 3 we argued that all experience is framed and interpreted through a conceptual scheme and a set of mental models that function on the individual, institutional, societal, and cross-cultural levels. We can neither experience nor present any story except through a mental model. Depending on which models are assumed to be operative, interpretations of a situation or event by persons, groups, institutions, or societies may differ greatly. In Chapter 2 we argued that without social relationships, and undefined by social roles, we are, at best, amorphous, ill-defined subjects. Nevertheless, as we argued further, we are not merely the sum of, or identified with, these relationships and roles; we can evaluate and change our relationships, roles, and role obligations; and we are thus responsible for them. So, too, we can also create, evaluate, and change our mental models, although the process ordinarily demands a highly developed moral imagination, as we explain in Chapter 5.

We now want to add another dimension to the idea of a conceptual scheme and mental models. If humans are intrinsically social beings, who we are and how we develop depend on a network of cultural and social relationships into which we are born and grow up. As a number of philosophers have argued, we are born into and depend on a world that is historically situated; linguistically, socially, and culturally defined; and usually in some process of evolution or change. We are born in the middle of a particular set of historical, political, economic, and social narratives or stories that we neither created nor chose. These narratives define our early roles, as children, as women or men, as tribal members, as worshippers, as citizens (MacIntyre, 1981, 199, 201; Sartre, 1956). These narratives and the language in which they are embedded are the background for individual experiences. They provide the initial conditions for the conceptual schemes we adapt that frame all our experiences and they often direct, influence, or confine the range of mental models we learn and adapt. Nevertheless, if Davidson is correct, background narratives themselves function as revisable conceptual schemes that are neither static nor incommensurable with each other. Thus, none of us is identified with our socially constructed thick selves; neither are we merely determined by our historical background or social narratives. We are at once byproducts of, characters in, and authors of, our own stories (e.g., Johnson, 1993, 153; Sartre, 1956). Still, sometimes we become so embroiled in a particular set of narratives, of our own making or not, that we fail to compare it with other accounts or evaluate its implications.

In addition to background narratives, our reports of events are also in narrative form: "All stories are shaped by a particular teller for a particular purpose, for all narratives are infected by their situatedness. Consequently [any story], even though it may be based on a real-life event, is mediated and thereby interpreted through narrative discourse ... and a point of view adopted" (Chambers, 1996, 25). Sometimes these allegedly true stories, these narrative accounts of actual events, take on a life of their own, one narrative becomes dominant, and we look to that account for data about the event without questioning its perspective or the basis for its "facts." In other instances, we find two or more contradictory narratives functioning side by side in the same milieu. In still other cases, narratives of the event in question become explanatory stories without any independent data to support their claims.

To demonstrate, we will recount different narratives of a recent case: the British Post office frauds. Each of the sets of narratives at work in this case illustrates different forms of a *Rashomon* effect at work. This illustrates how narratives we create can become coherent, self-referential models that take on the role of explanatory truth, even without any evidence that they represent actual events or the intentions of the protagonists in the narrative. Each set of narratives illustrates, in different ways, that narratives can confuse, bias, and even create what we take to be data, or facts, or even truth.

The *Rashomon* effect is an excellent model for considering whatever might be the truth of complex cases. Zygmunt Bauman identifies in "Postmodern Ethics" (Bauman, 1993) the widely uncontrolled moral impact of bureaucratic arrangements in advanced, modern businesses in the following terms.

> All social organization consists therefore in neutralizing the disruptive and deregulating impact of moral impulse. This is achieved through a number of complementary arrangements: (1) assuring that there is a distance, not proximity between two poles of action – the "doing" and the "suffering" one; by the same token those on the receiving end are held beyond the reach of the actor's moral impulse; (2) exempting some "others" from the class of potential objects of moral responsibility, of potential "faces"; (3) dissembling other human objects of action into aggregates of functionally specific traits, and holding such traits separate – so that the occasion for reassembling the "face" out of disparate "items" does not arise, and the task set for each action can be exempt from moral evaluation.
>
> *(Bauman, 1993, p. 125)*

With Bauman in mind, let us apply a *Rashomon* lens to the still current example of the British Post Office "scandal" as a means of exploring how and where things somehow go wrong, and even perhaps if there is someone to hold to account for any wrongdoing. We shall do this by presenting an account from a series of alternate and varying perspectives.

THE BRITISH POST OFFICE FRAUDS

Between 1999 and 2015 the British Post Office pursued operators of sub-post offices across the UK for alleged theft, fraud and false accounting based on information from its Horizon IT system installed in the late 1990s. That was despite knowing that from at least 2010 onwards that there were problems with the centralized accounting technology.

In total, about 3,500 branch owner-operators were wrongly accused of taking money from their businesses, with more than 900 prosecuted by the Post Office despite protesting their innocence and raising issues with the software in their defence. The scandal is frequently described as the most widespread miscarriage of justice in UK history... Hundreds of sub-post office operators ended up with criminal records and punishments ranging from having to do community service and wear electronic tags to being jailed. Many were left struggling financially or even bankrupt following convictions. Even those who did not go to court had to drum up money to cover non-existent shortfalls... Victims and their families were severely hit by stress, and in many cases illness, with the scandal linked to at least four suicides.

For years the Post Office, which has the power to investigate and prosecute without the need for police involvement, continued to defend itself against accusations and press reports highlighting problems with the IT system, developed by Japan's Fujitsu, including through legal means.

In 2019, a group of post office operators won a high court case in which their convictions were ruled wrongful and the Horizon IT system was ruled to be at fault. In 2021, the ruling was upheld on appeal, quashing the convictions of some workers who were wrongly accused of committing crimes, paving the way for compensation. However, even since the computer system was found to be defective, the Post Office has still opposed a number of appeals by operators ...

By December 2023, 142 appeal case reviews had been completed out of 900 people convicted during the scandal, with 93 convictions overturned and 54 upheld, withdrawn or refused permission to appeal. A total of £24 m has been paid out in relation to overturned convictions. However, there has been widespread criticism that the Post Office has been dragging its feet with delays to payments. Dozens of victims have died before they could receive any compensation. Post Office has also come under fire for further blunders, such as tax being charged on compensation and offering bosses about £1.6 m in bonuses, with handling of the Horizon inquiry one of four "metrics" on which payments were awarded.

The overturned convictions process is one of three different compensation schemes that have been established as the scandal developed, and last September ministers promised that every branch owner-operator whose wrongful conviction had been overturned would receive £600,000 in compensation from the government.

More than £130 m has so far been paid out to about 2,500 Post Office workers across the three schemes. However, in January of 2024 it became clear that the Post Office had almost halved the amount set aside for payouts as fewer owner-operators than expected had won or brought appeals.... To date no Post Office staff have been punished for the scandal. On Friday, the Metropolitan police confirmed for the first time that the Post Office is under criminal investigation over "potential fraud offences" committed during the scandal. ... The Met is already investigating two former Fujitsu experts, who were witnesses in the trials, for perjury and perverting the course of justice. (interpolated and summarized from Flinders, K. 2024, Strong, 2024, and Sweney, 2024)

How did such injustices occur? In 1999 the British Post Office purchased what was supposed to be invincible software, Horizon, from the Japanese company Fujitsu, software that allegedly could detect fraud and misdemeanors that might be occurring in post offices. Soon after, the software began to detect fraudulent behavior among sub-postmasters all around the country. The Post Office executives, having absolute faith in the software, began a series of prosecutions of these allegedly guilty sub-postmasters, all of whom pleaded not guilty. The Post Office so unquestionably bought into the invincibility of the software, guaranteed by Fujitsu, that the software narrative dominated their thinking. They did not seem to wonder why so many sub-postmasters, people of the same rank in the system, were being convicted. Fujitsu itself did not question its product despite some evidence of flaws in that system as early as 2003.

That year:

> IT expert Jason Coyne was instructed to examine the Horizon system as a neutral expert witness in the Post Office's civil case involving the Cleveleys Post Office branch in Lancashire. Coyne told the Post Office and Fujitsu that there were defects with the software (McCulloch, 2024). He said the technology installed was "clearly defective" and the majority of errors could not be attributed to Cleveleys sub-postmaster Julie Wolstenholme. Fujitsu disputed Coyne's report at the time and said he had misunderstood and taken a "very one-sided view" based on incomplete figures ... Because Wolstenholme had claimed unfair dismissal and the case was settled out of court, Coyne's findings did not become widely known.
>
> *(McCulloch, 2024)*

Even after these findings, still, Fujitsu did not imagine that its technology could be defective. It bought into the narrative that backed up the belief system that their software could not be flawed despite questions to the contrary.

The third narrative is that of the accused and convicted sub-postmasters whose appeals of the convictions all within the Post Office system were in vain. This was in part because, "(i) As a private company, and not a statutory body, the Post Office is not subject to government oversight. Thus it was able to bring private prosecutions against sub-postmasters without the involvement of the CPS and police. (ii), the sub-postmasters did not have an effective membership body to defend their interests" (Flinders, 2024).

However, there was a fourth narrative creating a series of events that began in 2004. A dismissed sub-postmaster, Alan Bates, from the small town of Craig-y-Don in Wales, began questioning the software, which as a sub-postmaster he found to be faulty, and the scenarios of guilty verdicts of so many sub-postmasters, many of whom he knew. Mr. Bates, as he is called in various narratives of the case including the 2024 documentary *Mr Bates vs the Post Office* (Strong, 2024), a documentary that brought worldwide attention to this scandal, began questioning the software, and brought that to the attention of *Computer Weekly*. When more of these convictions emerged and Mr. Bates persisted in his accusations, that journal began to pay attention, and in 2009 *Computer Weekly* began publishing articles questioning the Horizon software system and the convictions of so many sub-postmasters (Flinders, 2024).

In the meantime, in 2004 Bates began to meet with and organize convicted sub-postmasters around the country, and eventually they hired a solicitor James Hartley from the Yorkshire firm Freeths and a team of barristers under Patrick Green of Henderson Chambers. Sub-postmasters obtained funding for their case against the Post Office from litigation funders Therium. Bates and forensic accountant Kay Linnell formed a steering group to lead 555 claimants in the case *Bates & Others v Post Office Ltd*, which was heard under a group litigation order (GLO). Judge Peter Fraser issued his first judgment in March 2019, finding that the Post Office contract was unfair on sub postmasters (Pooler and Croft, 2020).

With the media attention growing to this scandal, and despite objections by Post Office executives and Fujitsu, finally, in 2020, an official inquiry into this matter was organized by the British government. This is still ongoing and incompletely resolved as this book goes to press.

Bates gave evidence at the inquiry for the first time on April 9, 2024. He told the inquiry that his twenty-year campaign had been inspired by a sense of injustice aligned to his own stubbornness:

> Once I'd started my individual little campaign, we found others along the way, and eventually we all joined up. It has required dedication, but secondly, it is a cause. I mean, as you got to meet people, and realize it wasn't just yourself. And you saw the harm, the injustice that had been descended upon them, it was something that you felt you had to deal with.
>
> *(requoted in Boffey, 2024)*

In a BBC interview, Bates referred to Post Office officials as "thugs in suits" and said the government had been vindictive in offering him a derisory sum in compensation (Espiner, 2024).

This long scandal points to the difficulties with a dominant narrative if it is not questioned or challenged. No one story or explanation is ever perfect or complete; yet as we see in this case, certain narratives, when their challenges are not examined, can be dominating and damning. While it is impossible to find out every fact or innuendo in any situation, not to question one's own narratives, as in the cases of the British Post Office and Fujitsu, is a form of moral fogginess if not blindness.

We have now set out a number of narratives: As in *Rashomon*, the storytellers are believed, but the truth underlying this set of narratives remained for some time unresolved. *Rashomon* examples, and there are many others, illustrate how apparently contradictory narratives can both operate in a particular situation. It also illustrates the power of a narrative based on, or appealing to, alleged facts such as the invisibility of software, or the emotion of identifying with an allegedly very rich smart young man, so that various other phenomena are disregarded, because those dominating narratives function as versions of the truth.

Both interesting and frightening, each of these narratives "fits" as an explanation. Each of them presents a believable account; yet, while functioning as coherent explanatory models, their veracity is unknown. Thus, this example, unlike the others, shows the believability of a logically viable explanatory narrative or set of narratives, even where there is no evidence to justify the descriptions or allegations.

SOME LIMITS OF NARRATIVES

What can we say about the role of narratives? Conditioned, but not determined by background narratives, each of us orders, selects, structures, and even censors all our experiences. These shaping mechanisms are mental models through which we experience the world, and we never see the world except through points of view, models, or framing mechanisms, some of which shape background and other more specific narratives. Indeed, narratives that shape our experiences and influence how we think about the world are essential to the coherence of our experiences. As we have just illustrated, some narratives are more closely based on actual experiences; others are taken from the narratives of others that we have accepted as true; still others are closer to fiction. In any case, some narratives influence, dominate, or reshape our thinking about certain events. In these instances, "life imitates art," or the "grammar," the alleged data of the narrative, creates the essence of the story that becomes fact for a number of its participants, readers, listeners, or the media.

Does this mean that one can never arrive at facts or truths? Yes and no. A longer answer requires explanation. The thesis that experience is always framed by a perspective or point of view is closely related to another thesis discussed in the last chapter, that "essence is expressed by grammar" (Wittgenstein, 1953, §371). In short, as we argued in an earlier chapter, our experiences are framed, organized, and made meaningful only through language. To put the point in more Kantian terms, the "stuff" of our experience is not created or made up (although sometimes we can and do make up the content of our experiences when we envelop ourselves in fantasy). The distinction between reality and fantasy may be that we do not make up the content of our experience. Nevertheless, that stuff, or phenomena, is never pure – it is always constituted and contaminated by our perspective, narrative, point of view, or mental models. Are we, then, trapped in these narratives?

One way to think about narratives is to appeal to Amartya Sen's concept of positional objectivity. Because narratives represent a collection of congruent points of view that others share or can share, they are, or can be, "positionally objective":

> What we can observe depends on our position vis-a-vis the objects of observation. . . . Positionally dependent observations, beliefs, and actions are central to our knowledge and practical reason. The nature of objectivity in epistemology, decision theory and ethics has to take adequate note of the parametric dependence of observation and inference on the position of the observer.
>
> *(Sen, 1993, 126)*

Position-dependency defines the way in which the object appears "from a delineated somewhere." This delineated somewhere, however, is positionally objective. That is, any person in that position will make similar observations, according to Sen. Sen assumes that from a certain point of view we are able to observe and process the same data similarly. We would add that the parameters of positionality are not merely spatial but involve a shared mental model, used as positionally objective.

However, a positionally objective point of view could be mistaken if it did not account for all available information. Sen points out that in almost all cases no one need unconditionally accept a positionally objective view. Almost any position has alternatives; almost every position has its critics. We would qualify that further. Allegedly, positionally objective phenomena are still phenomena that have been filtered through the social sieve of a shared mental model or narrative, neither infallible nor complete.

According to Sen, in addition to taking positionally objective points of view, we are able to engage in "transpositional" assessments or what Sen has called a constructed view from nowhere. A transpositional view from nowhere is a constructed critique of a positionally objective phenomenon, and no positionally objective view is merely relative or immune from challenge. This assessment compares various positionally objective points of view to determine whether one can make coherent sense of them and develop some general theories about what is being observed. From a transpositional point of view, mental models themselves can be questioned on the basis of their coherence or their explanatory scope. Transpositional assessments are constructed views, because they, too, depend on the schemas of the assessors. Although the challenge could be conducted only from another mental model, the assessment could take into account a variety of points of view. Still, revisions of the schema in question might produce another mental model that more comprehensively explained a range of phenomena or incidents. In short, studying sets of perspectives can show how certain events are experienced and reported and even the mental models or narratives at work in shaping the narratives about these experiences. Although one can never begin with a pure tabula rasa, nevertheless one can, at least in principle, achieve a limited, dispassionate perspective.

But if a constructed view from somewhere is a possibility, why, then, do we observe so many instances when people have failed to critique their situation from a more dispassionate or alternate perspective? Just as some of us fail to evaluate our roles, role obligations, and the institutions to which these roles are attached, so too, we often fail to evaluate what we take to be an objective point of view, and seldom do we think about the mental model or movie with which we frame our situation. A constructed view from somewhere is a metaphysical possibility, realizable only when one has a sense of the shortcomings of one's situation, that is, when one has a very active moral imagination.

Near the end of *Rashomon*, the narrator of the tale, the passerby, laments society's lack of trust resulting from the impossibility of ascertaining truth. Our mental models and the narratives in which we embed our lives and our activities must be examined and evaluated often and with care. In coming into contact with others' narratives, one should not depend on a single set of alleged facts or data as presented in their stories. Rather, we need to examine how the facts are constituted to make a story or a case, and one realizes that some of those cases can become prototypical narratives that we imitate. The "classic cases" need to be revisited or they will become cliched prototypes. We need also to be wary of assumptions generated by these prototypes, such as the assumption that the software the Post Office bought and used was accurate because it was software. The Post Office belief system caused egregious harm to those who were innocent of the claims they acted fraudulently because they assumed without question that what software presents as adequate evidence tells the whole story. Although we cannot arrive at the Truth, we can at least approximate well-wounded beliefs and distinguish them from myth and fantasy. Otherwise, we will find ourselves in a postmodern world illustrated by the British Post Office (or Bankman-Fried crypto stories and others), where fantasizing takes over, and the narratives we create take on the guise of reality (Vargish, 1991). In the next two chapters we examine in detail this process of developing well-grounded beliefs in the context of moral imagination.

5 Moral Imagination

BAYER CROPSCIENCE

In 2002, Bayer, a German-based multinational corporation whose "Science for a Better Life" program had operated in India for almost 100 years, bought the Indian company CropScience. Bayer needed hybrid seeds for some of its chemical processes, and CropScience had these seeds available from its small farms located across northern India.

CropScience had engaged with more than 10,000 small farmers across parts of India for their seeds, because Indian farmers are experts in growing hybrid seeds of various sorts. Thus, CropScience was commercially a most desirable company, and Bayer purchased it.

What Bayer had not realized (or forgotten) was that child labor was a widespread practice in the cottonseed industry, and this was accepted as normal/usual by Indian farmers. Production of the hybrid seed was labor-intensive, complex, and time-consuming. Cottonseed hybrid farming required approximately ten times more labor days than ordinary commercial cotton production. It required approximately 2,200 labor days per acre. Cross-pollination, a crucial stage in the farming process, was done manually and it continued for a period of six months.

To help with the cross-pollination stage, farmers frequently contracted extra labor. Children were often preferred because their nimble fingers were useful in carrying out the emasculation and cross-pollination and their height matched the height of the cotton plant. Additionally, children were agile and cheap, and made fewer demands than adults. Thus most small farms used child labor, particularly for harvesting seeds. The bad news was that most children working on cottonseed farms had either dropped out of school (mandatory throughout India) or had never attended formal school in the first instance. Part of Bayer's global mission includes the statement that

"We follow a clear 'zero tolerance to child labor' policy in our business operations worldwide" (Bayer, 2024, 6).

Because of this principle that was embedded in Bayer's mission and employee values, employees at the German company headquarters protested the purchase of CropScience. Employees there argued that because of their mission statement, Bayer must sell CropScience. On the other hand, using child labor was an age-old practice on Indian farms in most communities and was a means to supplement income of small Indian farmers.

Bayer executives were faced with a seemingly either-or dilemma: either sell CropScience (and let the new buyer continue the age-old practice of using child labor) or go along with this practice on the Indian farms in order to get the hybrid seeds, ignoring their own mission statement but also not insulting Indian social practices that had been in place for centuries.

Bayer did neither. Thinking "out of the box" creatively, that is, engaging in moral imagination, they did the following. They did not sell CropScience, *but* in fighting child labor without insulting Indian practices, they paid farmers a premium for not using child labor and for sending their children back to school, with sanctions for continuing the child labor practice. Then they engaged an Indian nonprofit organization, Learning for Life, and employed Indian tutors for the unschooled children to bring them back to their school-age level so that these children would be accepted in their proper classrooms (see Dhanaraj et al., 2011a, 2011b).

When Bayer managers were asked why they did this rather than simply going along with Indian practices, one manager responded,

> Why should Bayer *not* do this? Here is an issue where we as a company have a professed value of zero tolerance to child labor. We are an agricultural company, and India is one of the largest agricultural markets. It is an opportunity for us to mean what we say and walk the talk.
>
> (Dhanaraj and Khanna, 2011, 697)

MORAL IMAGINATION

In *Aiming Higher* (1996), David Bollier cites companies "in which creative, socially committed business managers have enhanced their long-term profitability by instilling the best of their humanity into the nitty-gritty operations of their organizations" (Bollier, 1996, 1). According to Bollier, these companies have a "questing spirit... [or] moral imagination" (Bollier, 1996, 2). In this chapter we examine the question of moral imagination. While we do not claim that all moral reasoning is grounded in the imagination, we conclude that moral imagination is a necessary ingredient in responsible moral judgment. Only through imagination can one project alternate ways to frame experience and thus broaden, evaluate, and even change one's moral point of view.

Let us begin with some stipulative definitions of imagination and moral imagination. Philosophers have long been interested in the phenomenon of imagination. Many philosophers once thought that imagination was a particular psychological faculty that accounts not merely for our abilities to represent or create mental images but also for our creation and appreciation of aesthetic objects. Later, Adam Smith ([1759] 1976) believed imagination to be a faculty that enables us to understand the sentiments of others. Immanuel Kant ([1790] 1951) opined that imagination accounts for the ways in which the mind synthesizes sensations and perceptions to form experiences and relates experiences to the understanding. Imagination can be usually distinguished from reason, for – according to Kant's architectonic theorization – to be imaginative one need not be restricted by reason. But – outside of Kant – imagination is not necessarily merely subjective: We each share some appreciation of imaginative works, such as works of art or music. Nor, we suggest, is imagination necessarily or intrinsically irrational. One can create imaginative representations of possible worlds that, though unreal, nevertheless have logic and consistency.

At its most basic level, imagination is the ability to form mental images of real or unreal phenomena or events and to develop different scenarios or different perspectives on those phenomena or events. Part of being imaginative is being creatively projective, creating new images or scenarios with known conceptual analogs. Imagination includes creating fantasies or myths. Paul Ricoeur once observed that "to imagine is to make oneself absent from the whole of things" (Ricoeur, 1979, 152), to become disengaged, fragmented, focused on the fantastic, distanced from reality and ordinary experience. Imagination, then, can involve creating a fresh phenomenon, situation, or series of events (Beidelman, 1986, 1–10).

Moral imagination is a more slippery term, sometimes used in management literature by writers such as Bollier to signal a morally courageous or unique activity or decision of a particular manager or company. Yet Bollier fails to define moral imagination except obliquely. Moreover, Bollier does not clearly distinguish moral imagination from other forms of management decision-making except for his conclusion that morally imaginative managers and companies take on activities that extend the ordinary expectations for economic enterprises.

Edward Tivnan in *The Moral Imagination* (Tivnan, 1995) uses the term to argue that controversial moral debates in our society, such as abortion, capital punishment, and racial justice, can be understood and even transcended if we, as an open democratic society, develop moral imagination. Relying on John Dewey, for whom " imagination is the chief instrument of the good" (Dewey, 1958, 348), Tivnan defines moral imagination as "imaginative sympathy" (253), "moral creativity" (250), or the ability to take an "imaginative leap" (252), allowing one to be "a decent, compassionate, good person in a diverse community" (249). Yet these definitions are not fully developed in Tivnan's book, and it is unclear from reading Tivnan how moral imagination is distinctively *moral* or how one develops moral imagination, either as an individual or as a society.

Dewey offers an array of insights on imagination that connect it to architecture, sculpture, painting, music, literature. consciousness, creativity, to our apperceptions, and to the human mind. He offers context for everything from navigating our local environment to understanding the universe.

> Imagination shares with beauty the doubtful honor of being the chief theme in aesthetic writings of enthusiastic ignorance. More perhaps than any other phase of human contribution, it has been treated as a special and self-contained faculty, differing from others in possession of mysterious potencies. Yet if we judge its nature from the creation of works of art, it designates a quality that animates and pervades all processes of making and observation. It is a way of seeing and feeling things as they compose an integral whole.
> *(Dewey, [1932] 2005, 267)*

Such a claim challenges a traditional (i.e., Kantian) and non-processual understanding of imagination which is as a synthetic faculty. Imagination is not a dexterity which can straightforwardly associate, predict, or prompt. Rather, and processually, "an imaginative experience is what happens when varied materials of sense quality, emotion, and meaning come together in a union that marks a new birth in the world" (Dewey, [1932] 2005, 267).

Dewey also neologizes the term "imaginary" to give greater nuance:

> Time is the test that discriminates the imaginative from the imaginary. The latter passes because it is arbitrary. The imaginative endures because, while at first strange with respect to us, it is enduringly familiar with regard to the nature of things.
> *(Dewey, [1932] 2005, 269)*

In *Experience and Nature* (1929), Dewey emphatically connects his take on imagination to our, to the mind, and to our perceptions:

> Imagination as mere reverie is one thing, a natural and additive event, complete in itself, a terminal object rich and consoling, or trivial and silly as it may be. Imagination which terminates in a modification of the objective order, in the institution of a new

object is other than a merely added occurrence. It involves
a dissolution of old objects and a forming of new ones in a medium
which, since it is beyond the old object and not yet a new one, can
properly be termed subjective.

(Dewey, 1920, 220)

In *Reconstruction in Philosophy* (Dewey, 1920), he writes:

As imagination becomes freer and less controlled by concrete
actualities, the idealizing tendency takes further flights
unrestrained by the rein of the prosaic world. The things most
emphasized in imagination as it reshapes experience are things
which are absent in reality. In the degree in which life is placid and
easy, imagination is sluggish and bovine. In the degree in which life
is uneasy and troubled, fancy is stirred to frame pictures of
a contrary state of things. By reading the characteristic features of
any man's castles in the air you can make a shrewd guess as to his
underlying desires which are frustrated. What is difficulty and
disappointment in real life becomes conspicuous achievement and
triumph in revery; what is negative in fact will be positive in the
image drawn by fancy; what is vexation in conduct will be
compensated for in high relief in idealizing imagination.

(104–105)

Moral imagination is a term widely used in literature and literary theory to talk about works that exemplify "paradigm[s] of moral activity" (Nussbaum 1990, 148) or that "draw analogies between the imaginary world [of the work of literature] and the world in which we live" (Guroian, 1996, 6). Moral imagination sometimes describes the approach an artist or novelist takes in developing material. For example, in *Forms of Life: Character and Moral Imagination in the Novel* (1983), Martin Price argues that "moral imagination ... is the depth and adequacy of the novelist's conception of experience: the degree to which he recognizes the complexities of decision or action or inaction and the effort or release involved in solving or ignoring or evading problems" (Price, 1983, xii).

A work of literature may exhibit a depth of moral imagination, its characters may exemplify moral imagination, or the work may stimulate the moral imagination of its reader. Yet, surprisingly, while "moral imagination" is widely circulated in literary theory, it is seldom defined with the clarity required for a good philosophical analysis.

Surprisingly, too, "moral imagination" is not well developed by many moral philosophers. However, in a recent fine book, *Moral Imagination* (1993), Mark Johnson defines moral imagination as "an ability to imaginatively discern various possibilities for acting within a given situation and to envision the potential help and harm that are likely to result from a given action" (Johnson, 1993, 202).

Concerned with the limits of moral reasoning and moral judgment, in a recent article, the philosopher Charles Larmore defines moral imagination as "our ability to elaborate and appraise different courses of action which are only partially determined by the given content of moral rules, in order to learn what in a particular situation is the morally best thing to do.... Moral imagination belongs to ... the exercise of moral judgment" (Larmore, 1981, 284–285). Larmore questions the ability of moral rules, by themselves, to function adequately in particular contexts, and he explicitly links moral imagination to situational moral judgments. Unfortunately, Larmore is less explicit about why and how situational moral judgments are imaginative.

Elaborating further on moral imagination, Martha Nussbaum claims that "the work of the moral imagination is in some manner like the work of the creative imagination" (Nussbaum, 1990, 148). Moral imagination enables one

> to see more deeply into the relationship between fine-tuned perception of particulars and a rule-governed concern for general obligations: how each, taken by itself, is insufficient for moral accuracy, how (and why) the particular, if insufficient, is nonetheless prior; and how a dialogue between the two ... can find a common "basis" for moral judgment.
>
> *(Nussbaum, 1990, 157)*

Nussbaum's thoughts on moral imagination recall our arguments in Chapter 2 that moral awareness and moral judgment begin with the particular – with a particular situation, temptation, or dilemma, because it is in the context of social, particular situations that the thick self is embedded. Yet as critical thin selves we make rule-based judgments that enlighten, reshape, and sometimes resolve situational issues, temptations, and dilemmas.

Bayer's decision in the CropScience case exemplified a company that was able to break out of a mindset or "rule-governed concern" that places profitability over a long-standing mission not to engage in child labor, founded in the principle that child labor is wrong because of what it does to the futures of children. Bayer's managers took a creative and imaginative moral risk in banning child labor in Indian farms, questioning age-old customs on these farms. Its creative decision to tutor children in their "back-to-school" program was a successful attempt to both uphold their corporate mission and work withing Indian culture in employing Indian tutors. One will recall from Chapter 1 that Carroll defines moral imagination as "the ability to perceive that a web of competing economic relationships is, at the same time, a web of moral or ethical relationships" (Carroll, 1987, 13). Bayer's managers engaged in doing both.

Moral imagination, then, is the capability in particular circumstances to discover and evaluate possibilities not merely determined by that circumstance, or limited by its operative mental models, or merely framed by a set of rules or rule-governed concerns. In managerial decision-making, moral imagination entails perceiving norms, social roles, and relationships entwined in any situation. Developing moral imagination involves heightened awareness of Contextual moral dilemmas and their mental models, the ability to envision and evaluate new mental models that create new possibilities, and the capability to reframe the dilemma and create new solutions in ways that are novel, economically viable, and morally justifiable.

SOME ROOTS OF THE CONCEPT OF MORAL IMAGINATION

One early proponent of the concept of moral imagination was the eighteenth-century philosopher and economist Adam Smith. In the first chapter of *Theory of Moral Sentiments* (TMS) ([1759] 1976), Smith argues that "how selfish soever man may be supposed, there are evidently some principles in his nature, which interest him in the fortune of others" (I.i.1.1). One of these "principles" is sympathy. At the same time, Smith says that "as we have no immediate experience of what other men feel, we can form no idea of the manner in which they are affected, but by conceiving what we ourselves should feel in the like situation" (I.i.2).

In Smith's technical use of the term, sympathy is neither empathy nor any other sentiment or passion. Rather, it designates an agreement to or an understanding of the sentiments of another (Smith, [1759] 1976, I.i.1.5). When each of us sympathizes, we are placing ourselves in another's situation, not because of how that situation feels to us or how it might affect us, but rather as if we were that person. We project ourselves into another's experience, according to Smith, in order to understand, although not vicariously experience, what another person is feeling, rather than merely to relate that situation to our own. Sympathy, then, is the recognition and comprehension of what another feels or might feel in a situation, but it is not an experiential, emotionally empathetic, or sentimental identification with that feeling. Thus, through sympathy we can cognitively understand, or have insights into, the emotions of others without actually feeling them.

The role of imagination is crucial in understanding Smith's concept of sympathy and, indeed, his whole moral psychology. Smith claims that each of us has an active imagination, which enables us mentally to recreate another's feelings, passions, and point of view. In this imaginative process of sympathy, one does not literally feel the passion of another; rather, one understands what another is experiencing from that person's perspective.

Imagination is also useful in self-evaluation; it enables each of us to look at ourselves from the point of view of another person.

Imagination plays another important role. In the beginning of TMS Smith says that sympathy is a general principle of "fellow-understanding" that enables us to understand another's passions and interests even if we were to resent or even abhor those passions or that person. Imagination is important in this scheme, perhaps more important than Smith admits, because it allows one to project oneself and understand what another is feeling even when one is revolted by that feeling. We might, then, understand how someone like Ivan Boesky felt when he was engaged in insider trading, even though we may disapprove of the object of his feelings and passions.

Like his teacher David Hume, Smith breaks with a rationalist tradition by linking moral judgment to moral sentiment. According to Smith, sympathy and imagination are necessary for moral judgment because in judging intentions or actions one must first understand what another feels, or, in the case of oneself, engage in imaginative self-evaluation of one's own emotions that accompany the intention, or action. From this understanding one has a series of second-order emotions deriving from sympathy. Smith calls these moral sentiments of agreement, approval, or disapproval of the intention, activity, and its accompanying emotion. Having understood the sentiments of another, we may then determine whether those sentiments agree with our own and approve or disapprove on the basis of societally espoused moral rules, that is, what most agree ought to be the case. Finally, we determine what and who will benefit or be harmed by the character or action in question.

Moral judgments are not purely subjective personal reactions, however. Sympathy and imagination are the basis of Smith's impartial spectator theory, which, in turn, accounts for the social nature of moral rules and moral judgments. Sympathy, along with imagination, allows us to disengage ourselves and evaluate a situation or person more dispassionately, judiciously, or impartially. The spectator is that element of human judgment within us that step back from particular situations to evaluate in terms of a general socially espoused moral rule. Alliteratively, in one's mode as an impartial spectator, one may also revise a particular rule to fit a new kind of situation more appropriately. The impartial spectator phenomenon explains how we cannot merely understand, judge, approve, or disapprove of one another and our activities but also decide whether a certain character, person, intention, or action is one we ought to approve. The basis for the "ought" is what we and others judge, in these impartial moments, to be right or correct. These judgments, both our own and those of others in society, form the basis of moral rules that impartial people would adopt as normative measures of human behavior.

Moral rules, in turn, become the basis for impartial moral judgments. According to Smith, moral rules are not predetermined principles written in stone. Rather, they develop out of, are used to evaluate, and are altered because of particular judgments of particular situations. The impartial spectator also is the source of one's own conscience, the element within us able to disengage from oneself, in order to engage in critical self-evaluation, self-criticism, or approval. The impartial spectator within explains our sense of duty, our desire to do what is honorable, noble, and morally correct (Smith, [1759] 1976, III.3.4; Werhane, 1991a).

Smith's impartial spectator is an early version of the idea of the moral thin self we developed in Chapter 2. Smith's spectator is embedded in a web of social relationships out of which he or she develops the realization that one is more than those relationships. The impartial spectator is the thin self stepping back to evaluate and critique oneself and others and then developing or reiterating moral rules that apply to a social and personal situation.

According to Smith, no one is ever a totally disengaged, completely disinterested, ideal spectator. Rather, Smith's idea of an impartial spectator is that element within each of us, functioning on an individual and social level, that accounts for our ability to distinguish what we do, what we approve of, and what we judge we ought to do and approve of – the social ideals any individual or society sets for itself.

Smith's idea adds to the discussion in Chapter 2 because it introduces the role of imagination. Functioning adequately as a judicious spectator depends on imagination, moral imagination, to make the interconnections between human character and action, and between sentiments, moral rules, and moral judgments. As a spectator one goes back and forth between a particular situation and its context, between one's moral sentiments and those of others, and then applies general moral rules to evaluate that situation or character. Never does Smith suggest that an impartial spectator merely generates abstract moral rules outside a social context or simply applies the rules without first beginning with the particular – the situational context out of which moral sensibilities and moral judgments arise. Moreover, sometimes, to fit a new kind of situation, this process calls for a reform of general moral rules that depends on an imaginative projection of what individuals agree *should* be approved.

Smith's analysis is prescient, because it forms the basis for much of the contemporary discussion of moral imagination as the ability to empathize, to understand another point of view, and to be creative in ethical decision-making. Moral imagination, along with sympathy, shapes our moral judgments as we impartial spectators discern what society ought to approve, affirming community rather than individual values. Smith does not think that moral judgments are merely a result of general or universal principles that one applies, ad hoc, to all human situations. Rather, he believes moral judgments to result from interactions between persons, situations, and general, revisable rules. This interest in the particular as well as the general in morality and moral judgments, one will recall from earlier discussions, continues later in moral psychologists (e.g., Rest, 1988) and by writers such as Nussbaum, who use literature as a catalyst for development of moral imagination (Nussbaum, 1990, 338–346).

But Smith's work is limited by his assumption that each of us deals with the world in much the same way – through the conceptual scheme of an eighteenth-century Scottish gentleman. Assuming that human nature is homogeneous, one can more easily project and sympathize with another person, or make self-evaluations, and often actually be correct. But, as we argued in Chapter 3, each of us functions from a set of mental models, schemas of which most of us are only vaguely aware, not identical even in Scotland, or even among Scottish gentlemen of the same generation. Smith's analysis introduces the idea of moral imagination, but it does not describe how one sympathizes with non-Scots, or account for how we reshape our own mental models and moral rules.

The late eighteenth-century German philosopher Immanuel Kant further develops the concept of imagination. Kant is credited with the idea that all our sensations are structured through conceptual categories of the understanding that originate in the mind of the perceiver but are universally the same in the minds of each of us. Kant claims that imagination is essential for organizing one's sensations into perceptions, which become representations of experience from which we derive knowledge. Kant distinguishes at least three kinds of imagination: reproductive, productive, and reflective, or free play. What they are and how they are related are subject to some interpretation, but, relying on the work of Rudolf Makkreel, one can summarize these concepts. Because the data of our experiences are nonrecurring, but similar, sensations, one has to account for the fact that we perceive recurring objects, not sense data. Kant argues that the reproductive imagination synthesizes nonrecurring sensations into representations in order to make perception and memory possible. Without reproductive imagination, according to Kant, we would merely be aware of nonrecurring sensations. The reproductive imagination works in at least three ways: (1) it forms images or representations from collections of sensations; (2) it connects these representations to reproduce those images in memory; and (3) it connects images with other similar images, thus enabling recognition (Makkreel, 1990, chapter 1; Werhane, 1984, 192–194).

The productive imagination is more active and has at least three functions. First, it structures, schematizes, and provides order to representations through the categories of understanding so that experience is possible. Its function, then, is "to construe things sensibly present as instantiating pure concepts of the understanding" (Young, 1988, 155). Second, it helps us to make sense out of the categories as pure categories of the understanding, so that, for example, we can think about the category "quantity" abstractly without having to recall a concrete representation of quantitative sensible things (Woods, 1983, 201–205). Third, it synthesizes all our experiences as "ours" from the locus of what Kant calls the "transcendental unity of apperception," the independent nonempirical self, the "I" that is the subject and unity of all that we call "my experiences."

In the *Critique of Judgment* ([1790] 1951) Kant extends his concept of imagination, arguing that in addition to its reproductive and productive functions, imagination engages in free reflection or free play. The imagination in this role, Kant argues, uses material from experience, but "in this process we feel our freedom from the law of association ... Although it is under that law that nature lends us material, yet we can process that material into something quite different, namely into something that surpasses nature" (§182). Representations created by the imagination are aesthetical rather than rational ideas, because they "play" with what we know from experience and also sometimes manipulate the categories of understanding. For example, we can create unicorns, images of gods, stories, myths, fantasies, and music, all of which play with experience. We can also imagine four-dimensional space, geometries in multidimensions, and mathematical number systems, and play with the logic of those systems without their experiential ground.

Aesthetic ideas go beyond reason, according to Kant; they have no adequate counterparts in actual experience or in the categories of the understanding. Thus, they are creative associations, both in content (how they manipulate experience) and form (how they manipulate universal categories of the understanding). According to Rudolf Makkreel, "aesthetic ideas add to our interpretation of experience by suggesting significant affinities even when direct conceptual connections are lacking" (Makkreel, 1990, 5). Imagination in this third sense, as free reflection, is then neither mimetic nor rationally productive. It does not merely re-present our sensations as perceptions or experience; neither does it just mimic or represent experience. It is not restricted to working within the categories of the understanding or the confines of reason as Kant defines those terms. Indeed, Kant calls the aesthetical idea an "inexponible presentation" ([1790] 1951, §343).

Kant claims that

> an aesthetical idea is a presentation of the imagination, which is conjoined with a given concept, and is connected, when we use imagination in its freedom, with such a multiplicity of partial presentations that no expression that stands for a determinate concept can be found for it. Hence it is a presentation that makes us add to a concept the thoughts of which that is ineffable.
>
> *([1790] 1951, §316)*

Aesthetic ideas are often the creative ideas of geniuses, and thus the source of great art. Because they are creations of the imagination rather than reason, aesthetical ideas and their counterpart representations in works of art can be appreciated as ideas apart from, and indeed at a distance from, their purpose, function, representational accuracy, or utility, as purely contemplative aesthetic objects.

Nevertheless, free reflection begins with and uses perceptions, experience, memories, and concepts of understanding as its material. It is not to be identified with the transcendental self in the act of creation. (See, for example, Coleridge, [1907] 1973, 21.) Kant simply does not make that sort of connection between free reflective imagination and the transcendental unity of apperception, and it will be important for my purposes that he did not.

Kant does not elaborate on an idea of moral imagination, and, given the role of rationality in his moral theory, this is not surprising. Makkreel points out that according to Kant, one can consider the intellectual beauty of the construction of moral laws, just as one can consider the beauty of a painting. We can appreciate formulations of the categorical imperative and admire the ideal of their purposiveness disengaged from actual purposiveness in practical reason and morality

(Makkreel, 1990, 125–127). But this is different from linking imagination directly to morality. In *Critique of Practical Reason* Kant ([1789] 1985) claims that the productive imagination (the second form of imagination according to our reading of Kant) cannot function in moral judgment because moral judgments entail the categorical imperative, the form of all moral laws that directs the transcendental subject; thus, the categorical imperative is not experienced, and, unlike aesthetic objects, is exempt from schematization by the categories of the understanding (Johnson, 1993, 70–72).

Mark Johnson contends, however, that the idea of moral imagination derives from Kant's concepts of natural law and free reflection. Kant's use of the term "law of nature" or "universal law of nature" in the first formulation of the categorical imperative ("Act as though the maxim of your action were by your will to be a universal law of nature," [Kant, (1784) 1959, f421] is a metaphorical bridge, so that Kant's universal law of nature is the practical analog of the categorical imperative. Moral judgment, then, "involves an act of imaginative envisionment of a nonexistent world (the kingdom of ends) as a means for judging a proposed maxim," Johnson, 1985, 273). This metaphorical dimension or imaginative envisionment is very much like Kant's description of free reflection in *Critique of Judgment* where the imagination makes reflective judgments about *possible* representations or concepts. More simply put, moral imagination might have a role in Kant's moral theory as "the ability to envision the pattern of human life and action which is embedded in one's decisions and actions" (Rossi, 1980, 157), or as the ability to envision how my decisions and actions embody, or fail to embody, Kant's ideal of the categorical imperative functioning in an ideal kingdom of ends.

Kant's analysis is helpful in sorting out various forms of imagination, and he initiates the idea that imagination is not merely mimetic. But if Kant views moral imagination at all, it is most likely as an aesthetical idea, not as part of the practice of acting in accordance with various formulations of the categorical imperative. Moreover, even if Johnson and Rossi are correct in their interpretations, there is still difficulty. We are left with Kant's assumption that ideally there is one universal moral law and a unified notion of the kingdom of ends. Those are the ideals of morality, the models to which all moral action and moral judgment should aspire. But if the arguments of Chapter 3 are correct, there could be other models in which another form of moral principle is embedded (e.g., the principle of utility) that is considered to be universal and adopting that principle might create different grounds for moral judgments than adopting the categorical imperative.

MORAL IMAGINATION

Given the thinking of Smith and Kant, we now turn to a more finely tuned definition of moral imagination. Mark Johnson describes moral imagination as

> [1] self-knowledge about the imaginative structure of our moral understanding, including its values, limitations, and blind spots ... [2] similar knowledge of other people ... [3] [the ability to] imagine how various actions open to us might alter our self-identity, modify our commitments, change our relationships, and affect the lives of others ... [4] what it might mean, in terms of possibilities for enhanced meaning and relationships, for us to perform this or that action ... [and 5] the ability to imagine and to enact transformations in our moral understanding, our character, and our behavior.
>
> (Johnson, 1993, 187)

The term "imaginatively" refers to what Johnson in another place calls "metaphoric understanding, [the] projective process in which we structure one domain by means of principles and material taken from a different kind of domain" (Johnson, 1985, 274–275). He also refers to moral imagination as *"imaginative rationality* that is at once insightful, critical, exploratory, and transformative" (Johnson, 1993, 202).

We will define the "projective process" as the ability to understand the nature of a conceptual scheme and mental models; the ability to distinguish various "structure[s] of our moral understanding," assuming that different mental models structure moral understanding differently; and the capacity to envision their implications in present and fresh contexts. This process is imaginative just because, given a nexus of mental models, one envisions them and how they affect one's interpretation of the situation. Given that, as Senge claims, mental models ordinarily "exist below the level of awareness" (Senge, 1990, 176), the process is also imaginative only if one distinguishes the operative or dominating script at hand; grasps its strengths, incompleteness, and its shortcomings; and envisions other applicable points of view or scripts that could similarly define, and apply to, this particular context.

Johnson ties his notion of moral imagination to his theory of metaphor. This leads him to conclude that

> moral reasoning is a constructive imaginative activity.... Our most fundamental moral concepts (e.g., will, freedom, law, right, duty, wellbeing, action) are defined metaphorically, typically by multiple metaphoric mappings for a single concept. The way we conceptualize a particular situation will depend on our use of systematic conceptual metaphors that make up the common understanding of members of our culture.
>
> (Johnson, 1993, 2)

We agree that "the way we conceptualize ... will depend on our use of ... conceptual metaphors." But as we argued in Chapter 3 that these metaphors, which we labeled conceptual schemes and mental models, are neither thoroughly systemic nor simply common cultural understandings. They are much more complex, partly idiosyncratic, partly ethnically, religiously, culturally, socially, and historically based. Each of us functions through a bundle of mental models that overlap with each other and with each other's schema. These schemata are partly, but not wholly, governed by "common cultural understanding" that includes a shared language or languages. Some of them are idiosyncratic, others broader, more universal in range and scope. Underlying is a common coordinate system that accounts for cross-schematic or cross-cultural understanding, evaluation, and revision of metaphors. "Our most fundamental moral concepts ... are defined metaphorically," but in the sense that each is embedded in a conceptual scheme and a set of mental models that frame and shape its meaning. Moreover, each is incomplete and revisable. However, as we argued in Chapter 3 and shall reinforce in Chapter 7, the universality of conceptual schemes and mental models or conceptual metaphors and the fact that all experience is constituted by a conceptual scheme do not result in obvious relativist implications.

Johnson is not altogether clear about the distinction between moral imagination and other forms of free reflection. We propose that moral imagination, unlike some other forms of free reflection, begins not with the general but with the particular, a particular person of moral or immoral character, an event, a situation, a dilemma, or a conflict. Second, moral imagination entails the ability to disengage. Third, moral imagination, as distinct from free reflection, deals not merely with fantasies but with possibilities or ideals that, if not practical, are at least theoretically viable and actualizable. Further, these possibilities have a normative or prescriptive character; they concern what one ought to do, with right or wrong, with virtue, with positive or negative consequences, or with what common morality calls "good" or "evil." This activity is imaginative when it explores a wide range of possibilities not merely explicit in the circumstance in question, or, on the other hand, fully explicated by moral abstractions such as the categorical imperative or the principle of utility.

Kant's concepts of productive imagination and free reflection are useful in thinking about another dimension of moral imagination. Moral imagination, if effective, not only fantasizes creatively about fresh options or new possibilities from a normative perspective. Bayer's managers could think creatively about CropScience and child labor because they were not trapped in only one perspective. From a neo-Kantian perspective, their productive imaginations understood the schema or "concepts of the understanding" ordinarily at work at

Bayer, at least in the CropScience case.[1] These managers were familiar with Bayer's anti-child labor mission that supposedly could or should not be overridden in any circumstance. Thus, Bayer's managers were able to find another perspective on the "normal managerial script" that governs much of management decision-making and choice of research direction. Part of the job of moral imagination is to perceive the ethical dimensions of a managerial or corporate situation. Further, moral imagination helps us disengage from situational or organizational perspectives and consider viable alternative possibilities based on reasonable moral standards. Bayer's strongly worded mission statement gave Bayer CropScience good reasons for their decision without disrespecting Indian custom, even though his reasons were not those commonly used to evaluate purchases and projects at for-profit organizations.

In clarifying moral imagination, John Kekes, in "Moral Imagination, Freedom, and the Humanities" (Kekes, 1991) and in *The Morality of Pluralism* (Kekes, 1993), distinguishes four kinds of imagination: imaging, problem-solving, fantasizing, and moral imagination, "the mental exploration of what it would be like to realize particular possibilities" (Kekes, 1991, 101) and "evaluating the possibilities ... as good or evil" (Kekes, 1993, 101). Kekes claims that moral imagination has two aspects. "Moral imagination is, first, the threefold imaginative re-creation of possibilities [including] those that were generally *available* in the agents' context, those that the agents could reasonably have been *expected* to believe themselves to have, and those that the agents *actually* believed themselves to have" (Kekes, 1991, 102, emphasis added). Moral imagination also includes a second element, the evaluation of these possibilities in terms of their moral worth, a process both exploratory and corrective. According to Kekes, one of the ways to develop moral imagination, that is, to expand the scope of one's beliefs and thus one's possibilities from the point of view of what a "reasonable

---

[1] Bayer recently bought the American chemical company, Monsanto, which makes genetically modified seeds and a lethal weed killer Roundup. This decision was not without controversy and Bayer is still involved in law suits against various Monsanto products.

agent" would do, is to engage in retrospection. This process, Kekes contends, gives one a better understanding of how one's belief structure operates and helps one to redirect that belief structure in the future.

Kekes claims that merely being aware of possibilities is not itself imaginative. We disagree, using as evidence the British Post Office case. Alan Bates was thoughtful and imaginative, but for years he was blocked by an intransigent post office bureaucracy. Bates was imaginative enough to see problems and realized the limits of his situation. But he was unable to go beyond this awareness, and thus his moral imagination was incomplete.

What, then, is moral imagination? Moral imagination begins with a particular case, scenario, or event in which we become engaged as thick social selves. In the particular, our moral sentiments begin to function, in Smith's sense, to understand the anguish and complexity in the dilemma at hand. Most important, one begins with the particular because ethical issues arise in specific real-life situations, not in abstract moral theory, although moral theory is about particular events. Simply considering principles such as the categorical imperative or the principle of utility divorced from a particular case or example interests philosophers working on metaethics. But such abstract analyses, if separated from examples, are not as relevant in applied ethics. Moreover, merely applying general principles to specific situations often creates a disconnect between moral theories and moral dilemmas, as we argued in Chapter 2, and as the Bayer CropScience case illustrates. In contrast, Boeing's marketing of the new 737 MAX illustrates a utilitarian perspective, forgetting or ignoring the fact that marketing strategies do not work in the same ways in different contexts and that the primary principle underlying airplane manufacture is or should be safety, not volume of sales.

Beginning with awareness of the particular, moral imagination, functioning analogously to Kant's notion of the reproductive imagination, includes (1) awareness of the character, context, situation, event, and dilemma at issue; (2) awareness of the script or schema function in that context and role relationships entailed in that context; and (3) awareness of possible moral conflicts or dilemmas that might arise in that situation, including dilemmas created at least in part by the dominating script or the situation itself.

However, the human mind seldom rests on the particular, so moral imagination entails a second factor, the productive imagination. Almost all of us always generalize from a particular case to other similar and dissimilar characters, situations, or experiences. The productive moral imagination is critical as we generalize, because one could argue that Volkswagen (VW) was extremely creative in redesigning the emissions measures on its diesel autos. Apparently, VW did not challenge and evaluate their activities from any other moral perspective, such as the perspective of common morality (assuming that in their personal lives they were decent people, as all evidence about these engineers and managers at VW indicates). Because they did not challenge the framing script or schema operative at VW, or at least the script they thought should be defining their activities and expectations, their activities became morally questionable. Mired in a particular context with a dominant operating script, one must confront and question the script to challenge one's perspective on an activity (e.g., that safety is the primary principle governing all engineers and their projects). This awareness of an incomplete, perhaps even limiting or distorting script and one's subsequent challenge to it require what Kant would call a productive moral imagination.

The productive moral imagination is usually triggered by the impartial spectator, the thin self in its critical mode. This element of moral imagination is essential to become aware of one's social roles and role relationships and to evaluate the demands and limits of role morality. The engineers at VW who redesigned the diesel autos were very creative, but only in their roles as VW employees whose primary overriding duty was to the company. Thus, most of them did not step back to evaluate the absurdity of their actions through their engineering values.

Moral imagination entails a third element, analogous to, but not exactly identical with, what Kant calls free reflection. Being imaginative entails not merely awareness of a moral conflict but also awareness of a different mental model. In the now historic *Challenger* case, on the night before the launch neither the engineers nor the managers at Thiokol were able to critique the conceptual schemes in which they were operating, a great deal to expect from any person in that stressful situation. But it illustrates how building certain habits can create a script that is very difficult to evaluate or escape from, even when doing so might, in retrospect, have changed the outcome. Creative moral imagination or free reflection, when operative, helps us to project beyond the constraints of particular scripts or biases. Creative imagination facilitates the ability to envision and actualize novel, morally justifiable possibilities through a fresh point of view or conceptual scheme. Thus, creative moral imagination helps us criticize our own and others' points of view and generate adequate alternatives.

That one can change the script or operative mental model is illustrated in the Bayer CropScience case. Bayer challenged the "tradition" of using profitability as the basis for choosing corporate buyouts. It placed child education ahead of its own criteria of profitability and shareholder returns.

What is distinctive about *moral* imagination in all these examples is that at each stage of decision-making the imagination enables critiquing the situation at hand and evaluation of newly formulated possibilities and justification of possibilities outside a given script or a defined role, such as giving away a drug or pulling a popular product off the market. The moral imagination resembles Smith's imaginative spectator, moving one's thinking from the status quo to new possibilities and then evaluating those possibilities by some norm, perhaps a company credo or statement of principle, or other more general principles of morality.

In this evaluative facilitation, moral imagination may play another role, that of enabling creative thinking about how to revise or revamp common precepts of morality set forth by a particular group, religious community, culture, or society behavior norms. Revising moral rules or moral standards may seem extreme, but one can give an obvious and very simple example. Given newly developed awareness of environmental degradation in the late twentieth century, we are now in the process of revising our theory of human rights to include the right to a viable environment and rights of future generations as part of common morality. We can then use these revised moral rules in criticizing individual, organizational, institutional, and societal habits of consumption, pollution, and waste. From particular evidence of environmental degradation and the limits of the ecosystem, we are altering our moral precepts, thus moving from the particular to the general, and then using revised moral standards or rules to evaluate specific environmental practices.

To illustrate,

> thirty years ago, the typical American paper mill spewed 40 million gallons of contaminated water a day into a nearby river or stream and belched fumes that stank like rotten eggs and corroded the metal of cars for miles around. Today, the Weyerhaeuser Company's mill in [Oglethorpe] Georgia releases just 11 million gallons of much cleaner effluent a day into the Flint River and emits a faint and not unpleasant scent resembling turpentine. And many other paper producers ... are following the same pristine path.
>
> (Holusha, 1996, A35)

Years ago and as framed in historic theories of the materials economy it was commonly assumed pollution and waste were inevitable byproducts of operating pulp and paper mills. Paper mills commonly discharged millions of gallons of polluted water and disgorged unpleasant polluting discharges into the air. The waste generated was thought of as just that – unusable garbage that had to be disposed of. The standard argument at that time was that this pollution was an inherent part of producing paper. To change these processes would be inordinately expensive, and indeed, some argued, virtually impossible technologically. Recycling paper was too costly, and recycled paper products were not acceptable to most consumers.

Today, the leading mills such as those owned by Weyerhaeuser, Champion International, and Louisiana Pacific, have revamped their processes, cutting pollution by up to 80 percent, developing new processes for recycling paper that are inexpensive and produce decent paper, and recovering for reuse chemicals formerly dumped into local streams. Technology has been developed that is cost effective, and pulp mills are becoming increasingly sound environmentally, and ecologically conservative. This is a revolution – a revolution not just in production but in thinking about production – a revolution in the mental model of pulp manufacture. This revolution is due, in part, to increased regulations on the industry. But it is also due to an imaginative realization that conservation saves money, that there are new profitable uses for what was once called waste, and that it is to the competitive advantage of pulp producers to respond, as customers become more demanding for "green" processes and products. It took great imagination to disengage a well-entrenched and profitable industry from the mental model mandating inevitable pollution and useless wastes. And it took moral imagination to develop critical self-evaluation of these traditional practices. Pulp manufacturers have learned, for example, that

> recycling has economic payoffs beyond just potential savings on water costs. For example, many mills have developed the technology for recovering and reusing the chemicals that separate the cellulose fibers in wood that are transformed into paper from the lignin glue that holds a tree together.... [According to one plant manager,] "We simply could not afford to run the plant unless we could recover the digesting chemicals."
>
> (Holusha, 1996, A37)

In 1975, no one could have imagined a pulp manufacturer uttering those words.

We see in this illustration a particular environmental problem with pulp manufacture coupled with increasingly alarming evidence of environmental degradation. Environmental regulation and a revision of environmental moral standards have resulted. Because of all these factors, pulp mills have transformed those regulations and standards into particular solutions that are advantageous to paper manufacture and to the environment and to creation of new technologies that become competitively transforming as well. In other words, they have engaged in morally imaginative solutions that focus on environmental sustainability and profitability.

CONCLUSION

Moral imagination is both creative and applied. As reproductive imagination, it enables us to become aware of the moral demands of particular events and the conceptual schemes or mental models operating in specific contexts. As productive imagination, moral imagination accounts for our ability to reframe our experiences in different terms, so that we can evaluate our operative mental models and critique role demands. As free reflection, moral imagination helps in developing fresh interpretations of particular scenarios and creating new perspectives.

But moral imagination is not merely creative or exploratory. Moral imagination enables us to integrate common morality into decision processes and moral judgments, anticipate untoward consequences, and project new practical solutions that take into account a variety of points of view and respond to or even create moral demands. Finally, moral imagination accounts for the possibility of interaction between similar cases, new data, and moral rules, so that we can rethink traditional solutions to similar problems and revise the moral rules that justify evaluative judgments. Moral imagination thus is an enabling mechanism for the ongoing process of moral deliberation and moral judgment that is not merely reactive, sentimental, or absolutist.

Have we asked too much of moral imagination? Is it doing all the work of, or displacing, moral reasoning? Is there not a role for the impartial reasonable spectator as well as the imaginative one? Is there only a minor role for moral principles? In the next chapter we address these questions.

6 Moral Reasoning and Moral Imagination

In Chapter 5 we argued that moral imagination is essential for creative moral decision-making that was not merely contextual, role-driven, or institutionally constrained. In this chapter we will link moral imagination and moral judgment to a limited notion of moral objectivity in the following arguments.

- Moral imagination is a necessary but not a sufficient condition for moral decision-making.
- The contention that "moral understanding is *fundamentally* imaginative in character" (Johnson, 1993, 217) is a questionable thesis. Without moral imagination one can remain mired in a particular situation or within a particular mental model; without moral reasoning one may slip into moral fantasy.
- A particular moral judgment derives from "a specific kind of reflective, exploratory, and critical process of evaluation carried out through communal discourse and practice" (Johnson, 1993, 217). But moral judgments are not merely a result of communal discourse and practice. They depend on, and form the basis of, moral rules and moral standards that are not merely traditionally, culturally, or communally grounded, and moral judgments appeal to standards that do not merely arise from, or depend on, communal discourse.

Given that all experience is conceptually framed, "*moral objectivity consists, not in having an absolute 'God's eye point of view'*" (Johnson, 1993, 217, emphasis Johnson's). Nevertheless, we shall question Mark Johnson's thesis that "moral reasoning is a constructive imaginative activity that is based, not primarily on universal moral laws, but principally on metaphoric concepts" (Johnson, 1993, 2). We shall argue instead that:

- The concept of moral imagination, by itself, does not entail bringing into question all forms of moral objectivity, particularly the view that moral objectivity is an (albeit unreachable) goal and the ground of moral decision-making and moral judgment. Therefore,
- One can make a case for limited moral objectivity that does not rely on an "absolute 'God's-eye point of view.'"

A DISENGAGED VIEW FROM SOMEWHERE

As we argued in Chapter 5, moral imagination enables each of us to develop a discourse between the particular (a particular case or event) and the general, between "communal discourse and practice" and a less engaged, more "critical process of evaluation," or "between fine-tuned perception of particulars and a rule-governed concern for general obligations" (Nussbaum, 1990, 157). Moral imagination enables the development of a critical, thin, spectator self. Without moral imagination one has difficulty distancing oneself from mental models operative in a particular context. In those instances, one often fails to evaluate that conceptual scheme, its limiting perspective, and the consequences it produces, from another point of view. On the other hand, as demonstrated in Chapter 5, an over-preoccupation with imagination, coupled with a simplistic narrative approach, may lead to distortions or even creations of fact, as we saw in reports from and about the British Post Offices. The internalization or acceptance of a particular narrative account may result in discounting scientifically verified (positionally objective) data, or, alternately, treating emotional reactions as irrational, as illustrated in the treatment of British Post Office employees by their superiors. Merely stimulating one's imagination may lead one to accept an interpretation of a series of events, such as SBF's "hype" of cryptocurrencies. Or imagination may create a set of explanatory narratives that, while coherent and reasonable, tell stories that may or may not describe actual events, as the British Post Offices scandals illustrate. Imagination, alone, then, as free play, can create fantasies or justify a parochial set of values consistent with a particular narrative just because it is imaginative and creative.

The narrative story in which an event or a person is a part contributes to the event and cannot be ignored. Nevertheless, merely recounting narratives may not allow one to perceive the relevant operative mental models and thus reinforces the problem and accounts, in part, for its iteration.

Similarly, if one's imagination creates a causal connection between, say, cryptocurrencies and wealth, it is difficult to accept other explanations, and that connection becomes the explicatory frame for these who invest in those currencies and imagine that Bankman-Fried is able always to increase one's wealth even when sometimes the Bankman-Fried story was a fraud. Being moral imaginative involves challenging very basic assumptions, for example, interpreting correlations as cause-and-effect relationships. At the same time, one has to replace those assumptions with other reasonable, and in some sense corroborated, explanations. To replace the cause-and-effect stories of Bankman-Fried as a genius investor with a contention that he was simply a gamer and a fraud and that his alleged genius was misplaced, for example, simply replaces a questionable causal connection with another.

Still, because reality is framed by a conceptual scheme and sets of mental models, apparently each of us lives in a set of narratives created by a scheme or mental model wherein there are only narratives or texts and no possibility for objective challenges, appeals to more general moral principles, or truly impartial moral tests. If all our experiences and thus our reasoning processes and knowledge are embedded in a conceptual scheme, how can we learn how a particular schema functions? How can we evaluate a prototypical interpretation or scripted series of events? How can we be discriminating or imaginative except through a conceptual scheme and the set of mental models in which we are imagining, schemes and scripts that control the direction of that discrimination and imagination? Nothing short of a very active free-playing imagination will enable us to distance ourselves from our scripts, roles, or narratives to envision new possible scripts. To be truly imaginative, we must be disengaged, yet even "at a distance" we will be operating within a scheme.

These conceptual constraints, however, are not as regressive or circular as they appear. In the process of analyzing the limits of roles and role obligations, in Chapter 2 we argued that one cannot perceive the self except in its roles and other social relationships. Nevertheless, it is necessary to postulate a thin notion of the self as an explanatory mechanism to account for the differences between role obligations and one's moral responsibility for roles and role acts and to explain the phenomena of self-identity and human choice. In Chapter 4 we distinguished language, conceptual schemes, narratives, and mental models or scripts from Davidson's "common coordinate system," the bedrock of human activity. There we argued that, just because we are always operating within a scheme or framework, and even if what we call "reality" is always contextualized, does not imply either subjectivism or most forms of conceptual relativism.

Chapter 5 introduced Amartya Sen's positional objectivity, qualifying it to take into account the disparity of conceptual schemes and mental models. There we concluded that position-dependency defines the way in which the object appears "from a delineated somewhere" so that any person in that position sharing the same conceptual scheme (or, on a smaller scale, the same or similar mental model) is able to make similar observations or draw similar conclusions. Sen argues that no positionally objective view is complete; almost every position has alternatives generated either from ignored data or, as we argued, from different ways of construing the object or event in question. In almost every instance, other data or alternative ways of framing events are available that one could adapt to challenge a positionally objective conclusion. We shall argue further that challenges are possible only when, minimally, one is able to become at least partially distanced from the view, the data, or situation. While a "God's-eye point of view" or transpositional view from nowhere is impossible except as a constructed critique of a particular event or conceptual scheme, no positionally objective view is merely relative or immune from challenge, even within the parameters of a particular set of narratives. Clearly, when there are contradictory narratives or frameworks, there is even more opportunity for raising questions about the operative mental models. We can now turn that argument into a more positive analysis of how we can imaginatively disengage from operative conceptual schemes.

Sen introduces the notion of a "constructed view from nowhere" to account for our ability to compare various positionally objective points of view to make coherent sense of them and, in this process, develop other general theses about what is being observed or experienced. Such transpositional assessments are crucial when there are clashes of narratives. These assessments, however, depend on a well-developed moral imagination in order to begin the disengagement and assessment processes, and these were missing at Boeing when developing the new 737 MAX.

Transpositional assessments are *constructed* views, because they depend on trans-positional conceptual schemes shared by the assessors. There are a number of reasons why we can disengage ourselves from a particular point of view, understand various perspectives, and make trans-positional assessments. First, we all share a common coordinate system that grounds our differences. Therefore, there is a common ground out of which the myriads of mental models develop, accounting for their overlap. Second, a thin theory of the self, developed in Chapter 2, accounts for our ability to understand the limits and incompleteness of the mental models we employ. Because we are not merely the sum of our roles, our history, our social relationships, and our practices, we are at once involved in the nexus of narratives and social relationships that make up who we are, and at the same time we can function as a critic and evaluator of those relationships and narratives. Third, no mental model is complete; hence, we can accommodate fresh ones. Fourth, we are, or can be, imaginative, morally imaginative. Thus, we can critique and change our mental models. Transpositional schemes, then, are shared or shareable, and they too can be questioned on the basis of their coherence or explanatory scope. These questions, while disengaged from a particular narrative or positional objective point of view, could be asked only from another conceptual scheme or mental model, and revisions of the scheme or schema in question, will, of course produce another schema. Sometimes, however, these assessments and questions are revolutionary, leading to paradigm shifts or dramatic revisions of a conceptual scheme, as Thomas Kuhn argued so well (Kuhn, [1962] 1970).

We call these transpositional assessments disengaged views from somewhere rather than constructed views from nowhere. Although they involve disengagement from a particular narrative and set of mental models, they can never entail either complete impartiality or absolute disengagement from some place. They are always grounded in a conceptual scheme and operate from a set of mental models even while challenging those schemata.

We may now conclude that none of us is necessarily embedded in a blindly situated, socially constructed perspective so that one cannot be imaginatively reflective, evaluative, and critical. As various cases we have examined suggest, it is critical to disengage from the operating narratives or communal discourses and from the perspectives of colleagues, constituents, personal and professional roles, and from one's organizational, institutional, or regulatory framework. Examining extant narrative is helpful; moral imagination is essential for extrication. For example, as we noted in Chapter 2, Boeing has been cited for many violations of air safety and currently faces the challenge of bring back to earth its rogue satellite. This is likely not an anomaly. Rather, these occurrences suggest repeated decision-making based on assumptions that have not been adequately challenged or replaced within Boeing (Englehardt et al., 2021).

How does one distance oneself from one's current operative mental models? How does one become imaginatively reflective and develop a disengaged view from somewhere? Interestingly, Adam Smith is helpful in sorting out a concept of self-reflective impartiality that, coupled with an active imagination, can help to develop habits of creative moral decision-making. Whereas Smith claimed that humans are intrinsically social beings and "can subsist only in society," he also argued that it is possible imaginatively to step back from one's situation within society and view it from another perspective. The impartial spectator, one will remember, explains how we are when we are engaged in acts of evaluation, self-reflection, and moral judgment when we try to step out of a context and take another perspective that is as disengaged, disinterested, or unbiased as possible. This new perspective is neither idealized (a God's-eye view) nor opaque or behind a Rawlsian "veil of ignorance." This is a psychologically distanced view from somewhere that is not disengaged from our personal, historical, cultural, institutional, and social background. In taking such perspective a person tries to disengage from the exigencies of the situation to look at the world and oneself from a more dispassionate point of view, from the point of view of another person, or from the perspective of another narrative or conceptual scheme. In our roles as imaginative impartial spectators, Smith suggests, from a particular character or situation we move to more general moral rules and engage our sympathy in reactive moral sentiments of approval and disapproval. In this way we make moral judgments about the particular person, character, situation, or set of events that are not merely about the particular, and sometimes we alter the rules in question. But we begin, always, with the particular, and it is because of that starting place that imagination is essential to enable disengagement. Being imaginative and at the same time acting as a disengaged spectator allows one not only to get a critical and evaluative perspective on a script or mental model but also to be self-reflective: to step back from one's situation and view the event or oneself from another vantage point, but never a view from nowhere.

An impartial spectator theory such as Smith's helps explain how, ordinarily, each of us is a product of and engaged in a set of communities and narratives linked by imaginative sympathy, mutual interests, and interdependence. Still, the phenomenon of the core thin self enables us to act as spectators and critics of the very mental models in which we are engaged. Thus, we are able to step back from our engagements to become a critic and initiator of change.

Additionally, our analysis of moral imagination in the preceding chapter provides an outline for moral imaginative judgment that at least implicitly includes a role for a reasonable, impartial, or judicious spectator. In every aspect of moral imagination, reasonable limited impartiality plays a role. Accompanying creative moral imagination, then, are three control elements: a disengaged view from somewhere, reasonability, and appeals to common morality. Reproductive imagination, entailing the process of disengagement and discernment of moral dilemmas and the operative framing scripts, is both imaginative, and, in discernment, at least not irrational. For even in this mode, one is comparing one set of scenarios to others and evaluating what is at stake. Productive imagination challenges and often reformulates the event and its script in different terms. As free reflection, moral imagination is not spontaneous or unbridled free play. It creates possible scenarios that, often unique and risky, must be morally justifiable and practicably viable. Moral imagination is thus distinguished from fantasy and from mere creative imaginability such as Bankman-Fried's game-like thinking.

The Bayer CropScience case illustrates the integration of moral imagination and moral reasoning. It was enormously imaginative to think that one could operate successfully in a culture that used child labor without appearing to be neo-colonialist in its Indian-based solution.

This case illustrates how imagination provides the means to challenge one's perspective through "pushes" to impartiality that jar one from a particular point of view. Moral imagination involves developing less partial and self-critical perspectives. But this is obviously a dynamic, two-way relationship, for being self-critical and at the same time cognizant of one's schema requires lots of imagination on one particular situation. On the other hand, this process is not just imaginative. To be morally imaginative, one needs to appeal to good reasons as the basis for evaluation and moral judgments, good reasons supplied by the ideal of an impartial spectator, social moral rules, expectations of common morality, and moral standards.

MORAL REASONING AND MORAL IMAGINATION

Herein lies a temptation – to allow an appeal to a disinterested or impartial spectator to do all the moral work. It is tempting to link impartiality to rationality, and then to argue that an impartial, rational perspective in the moral reasoning process is necessary and sufficient for moral decision-making. (See, for example, Gert, 1987.) But an impartial, rational perspective is still a perspective from someplace within some conceptual scheme. Nestlé thought it was taking an impartial, rational perspective when it marketed infant formula in East Africa, and from one positionally objective point of view, this was true. And Dow Corning Corporation took a scientific positionally objective perceptive when it failed to take into account emotional reports from ill women with implants. In both cases, the company in question failed to imagine another point of view, another way of looking at the set of events which, it turned out, affected the outcome of the issues in question.

There is a second reason why an impartial, rational perspective is not sufficient for moral decision-making. In Chapter 2 we argued that moral theory tends to start with the general – general moral principles – and then applies those principles or modes of reasoning to particular cases. The result is often a disconnect between theory and practice, a failure of application due to a failure to comprehend how moral theory relates to the relevant practice. Analogously, an impartial, rational perspective by itself may separate the moral from the practically realizable, or the ethical from the economic.

Moral imagination helps each of us to perceive and frame the normative core embedded in all human enterprises including commerce and economics without dividing it from its subject matter and particularities of its practices. Therefore, an idea of a disengaged, reasonable perspective cannot be separated from the idea of moral imagination. Otherwise, one becomes mired in moral theory or in situational economics. That connection between a disengaged, reasonable perspective and moral imagination entails the following:

(1) an awareness of the particular: the character, context, situation, event and dilemma at issue;
(2) awareness of the script or conceptual scheme functioning in that context;
(3) awareness of possible moral conflicts or dilemmas that might arise in that situation, including dilemmas created at least in part by the dominating script, as well as others created by the situation itself;
(4) envisioning possibilities that other reasonable but disengaged persons could envision too, given that situation and the protagonists' roles in that situation.

In a more productive mode, the imaginative reasonable impartial spectator might begin to ask questions such as:

(1) Is this dilemma solvable given the parameters of the context, and extant "scripts"?
(2) What are the possibilities that are not context-dependent?
(3) Might we have to revamp the operative script to take into account new possibilities not within the scope of one's particular situation or within one's role in that situation?

And last, creative moral imagination or normative free reflection includes evaluation and revision:

(1) evaluating both the status quo and newly formulated possibilities;
(2) envisioning how morally to justify actualizing new possibilities, appealing now in both cases to moral rules or general principles of morality;
(3) revising operative scripts or even a conceptual scheme that affects particular interpretations of this situation and other similar particular situations; and sometimes
(4) revising social norms, moral rules, or standards themselves in light of new facts or reinterpretations of past and present events.

Every stage of this process involves imagination, disengagement, and evaluation. This process includes appeals to, or alterations of, standards or moral rules while at the same time grounding the decision in what is morally possible and practically achievable.

MORAL MINIMUMS

But we are still left with a question. Are these processes merely constructivist or relativist? One evaluates an event through moral rules that themselves arise out of, depend on, or are reformulated by a particular community or practice. One reformulates mental models or revises a conceptual scheme; still these are context dependent. A disengaged or constructed view from somewhere is still that-a view from somewhere, that is, at best, created from a background of historical context, tradition, and social narratives that cannot be eliminated.

Appealing again to Michael Walzer's work, we shall now introduce another element that will partly respond to this problem. In his well-known book *Spheres of Justice* (1983), Walzer develops a pluralistic and relativistic theory of the good. Walzer argues that who we are and what we value are defined in terms of social goods. Even though social goods may overlap, each social good has its own definition and "sphere" of application, values, and distributive criteria. Because different societies or different groups within a society could have quite disparate social goods, one can define "basic goods, or the human good" only contextually (Walzer, 1983, chapter 1).

In a later book, *Thick and Thin*, Walzer qualifies the relativistic notion of spheres of social goods. He argues that running through the thickness of each sphere of social goods – and on a larger scale, running through each culture – is a "thin theory of the good," or what Walzer also calls "moral minimums." Walzer is arguing that throughout history and in different cultures spins a thin thread of coherence and agreement. The agreement is less about what is *good*, but rather on at least a partial universal recognition of "bads." For example, Walzer argues, although there is wide disagreement about definitions or theories of justice, there is mutual recognition of *injustice*. We are uncertain about the constitution of the "good life," but there is widespread agreement about deficient or despicable living conditions, indecencies, violations of human rights, mistreatment, and other harms. We all agree that child labor, particularly with children under the age of twelve, is wrong. We are less certain about how to prevent these practices globally. Walzer does not spell out the content of these minimums. We suggest that moral minimums are best understood as negative standards, universally agreed upon "bottom lines" beyond which it is morally questionable to act. For example, it is almost always wrong to deliberately harm or contribute to harming another person or persons; to deliberately violate their rights to freedom, life, or property; to treat individuals or classes of individuals with disrespect; to compete or cooperate unfairly; not to honor promises or contract; or to be dishonest or deceitful. Whereas these moral minimums do not define goodness, fairness, or benefit, or define the positive content of rights, they set minimum guidelines for behavior that most people everywhere might agree on, and the idea of moral minimums gives a strong counterargument to those who find values merely context-dependent (Walzer, 1994).

In a similar vein and applying Walzer's notion of moral minimums to business, Tom Donaldson has developed "moral minimums for multinationals." Donaldson develops a list of basic rights minimally required in any humane society or on any minimally morally decent context. These rights include rights to freedom of movement, speech, political participation, and association; rights to ownership to freedom from torture; rights to a fair trial, nondiscrimination, physical security, minimal education, and subsistence. Donaldson then argues that multinational corporations have duties to avoid depriving any person of these rights. For some of these rights – those of physical security, freedom of speech, minimal education, political participation, and subsistence – Donaldson contends, multinationals have duties to help protect people from deprivation. Although one may debate Donaldson's particular list of rights and duties, his general argument that there are some recognizable and universally acceptable moral minimums for behavior, the violation of which is an agreed-upon wrong, seems sound (Donaldson, 1989b).

The idea of a set of moral minimums presents another temptation, the temptation to declare moral minimums as absolutes. But the idea that the content of these moral minimums is subject to historical change is consistent with Walzer's thinking. They are not fixed absolutes; rather, they are revisable negative ideals. A moral minimum is a candidate for a universal principle but never elected for eternity or even for life. In Chapter 5 we gave the example of how we have revised moral minimums to include environmental standards as a new moral minimum. Moral minimums explain how we appeal to general principles – but from a context, from a tradition, or as a challenge to a tradition, and never from "nowhere" – and thus how we revise or change the standards.

The thread of moral minimums is an appeal to standards that are not merely products of a particular tradition or a specific historical moment. They provide a limited objectivity so that the process of decision-making and moral judgment is just that, a process, but not a circular one (Brink, 1989, 139–143). The appeal to moral minimums, to these common "threads" of principles that reappear in different historical periods and in disparate cultures is an appeal to impartial standards, albeit impartial within limits of human understanding and imagination. Moreover, moral minimums provide standards with which to judge not merely Boeing, Bayer CropScience, the British Post Office, Volkswagen and the diesel crisis, or other similar scenarios but also the background narrative and tradition of each of these cases, commonsense morality, one's allegedly impartial perspective, and even the minimums themselves.

MORAL IMAGINATION, MORAL REASONING, AND MORAL MINIMUMS

The idea of moral imagination, the background of tradition and custom in which a narrative or situation is embedded, a disengaged view from somewhere, and a thin theory of moral minimums are all central elements of a viable moral decision-making process when that process begins with the specific and particular. One begins with the particular, a particular event or series of events embedded in a culturally, socially, and sometimes institutionally defined context within traditions, laws, customs, narratives, language, and practices that define and help to determine the event. Recognizing that an event poses moral problems is also in part determined by the practice in which the event occurs.

Part of the process of taking a disengaged view is to test and evaluate the dilemma and possible solutions. This process entails testing moral judgments in particular contexts against moral minimums in the context of traditions, practices, narratives, conceptual schemes, and other presuppositions out of which decision-making takes place. One begins with a decision, to buy CropScience, an Indian company, because of its fine linseeds. One tests alternatives first against the background tradition and practice in Indian small farms to use child labor to harvest these crops. Taking a more impartial perspective, one tests alternatives against the wider background of culture, tradition, and relationships of those affected by the harvest, in particular, children who drop out of (mandatory) school to work on these farms versus the Bayer mission of never condoning child labor anywhere in its facilities. Third, one tests the decision possibilities against negative moral minimums.

Who is harmed? What if Bayer does not buy Crop Science? Who will protect these children if Bayer does not step in? Does the loss of these linseeds affect Bayer's bottom line? In these processes, moral imagination, the ability to conceive of, envision, evaluate, and actualize new possibilities, plays a key role.

Finally, given a particular set of recurring events and a very active disengaged imagination, one begins to examine and sometimes revise the moral rules or precepts of common morality themselves. In Chapter 5 we offered the example of how we have revised our moral standards, adding responsibilities to the environment. Let us give an example from politics. It took many centuries of political dialogue to arrive at what developed into the American Constitution. One of the rights proposed by the Constitution is the right of every adult to vote. Originally interpreted, this was interpreted as the right of every adult white, non-Catholic, property-owning male to vote. Gradually, however, practices changed, and today, with the help of the fifteenth, nineteenth, and twenty-sixth amendments, this right is guaranteed to all adult citizens of all races, genders, ethnic origins, and religious commitments who are eighteen or older. This interpretation of the right to vote has reached an equilibrium; that is, we no longer challenge it, and almost no one conceives of reverting to property rights or gender as defining a right to vote. What we have done, over time, is to redefine the content of the right to vote to make it more inclusive, and this right, as presently interpreted, has become a model to which other nations appeal in setting their own standards. This does not mean that sometime in the future we will not again revisit this right and reinterpret it further; indeed, we are in the process of extending that right to the homeless. This is a tentative universal standard, a candidate, but, momentarily at least, this right is no longer morally challenged.

In the case of constitutional rights to vote, in many Western democracies we have reached a stage of equilibrium, no longer challenging this right. According to *Websters Collegiate Dictionary* equilibrium is "a state of balance, poise, a state of adjustment between opposing or divergent influences or elements, a state of balance between opposing forces or actions that is either static or dynamic." Occasionally, one does reach a state of moral equilibrium wherein succeeding events do not present a challenge but rather are solvable because of past moral judgments. It is a process, the aim of which is not unlike what John Rawls and Norman Daniels call wide reflective equilibrium. Rawls summarizes this process:

> By going back and forth [between the particular and principles], sometimes altering the conditions of the contractual circumstances, at others withdrawing our judgments and conforming them to principle, I assume that eventually we shall

find a description of the initial situation [solution or set of solutions to the decision process] that both expresses reasonable conditions and yields principles which match our considered judgments duly pruned and adjusted.

(Rawls, 1971, 48; see also Daniels, 1979)

This process of moral decision-making we have just described that takes into account context and tradition, impartiality, and minimum moral standards, is just that: a dynamic process, in which one challenges the presuppositions of tradition, tests one's impartiality against context, and continues to shape one's decisions and refine one's moral minimums. Moral judgments are a result of a delicate balance of context, evaluation, the projection of moral minimums, and the presence or absence of imagination. Such a process is seldom complete, pure objectivity is impossible, but infallibility of judgment is not part of the goal. Indeed, moral judgments are at best partial solutions. Still, they should be solutions that serve as the starting place or models for new series of decisions, as the Bayer CropScience case illustrates, even though these, too, are always at risk of being morally challenged. The linchpin of this process is a highly developed and attentive moral imagination that perceives the nuances of a situation, challenges the framework or scheme in which the event is embedded, and imagines how that situation and other similar situations might be different. The ideal is not absolute agreement but rather a temporary and contextual equilibrium, a dynamic consensus that provides the ground and impetus for moral progress.

7 Systems Thinking, Process Philosophy, and Moral Imagination[1]

Taking up a lead from Susan Wolf's and Linda Emanuel's work on systems thinking, and developing ideas from Moberg's, Seabright's, and Werhane's work on mental models and moral imagination, in this chapter we shall argue that what is often missing in management decision-making is a systems approach. Systems thinking requires conceiving of management dilemmas as arising from within a system with interdependent elements, subsystems, and networks of relationships and patterns of interaction; this sort of thinking may also be considered as processes. Processes continue and evolve: They evade reduction to any kind of singularity (Bevan, 2024). Taking a systems and process approach and coupling this with moral imagination, now engaged on the organizational and systemic as well as individual levels of decision-making, we shall conclude, is a methodology that encourages managers and companies to think more imaginatively and to engage in integrating moral decision-making into ordinary business decisions. More importantly this sort of thinking is a means to circumvent what often appear to be intractable problems created by systemic constraints for which no individual appears to be responsible.

MORAL IMAGINATION

Dennis Moberg and Mark Seabright define moral imagination as "a reasoning process thought to counter the organizational factors that corrupt ethical judgment" (Moberg and Seabright, 2000, 845). According to Mark Johnson (1993), moral imagination requires envisioning a full range of possibilities in a specific context in order to

---

[1] An earlier version of this chapter was published as "Moral Imagination and Systems Thinking." *Journal of Business Ethics*, 38 (2002), 33–42.

resolve some ethical challenge. Johnson insists that acting morally requires more than a strength of character. For Johnson, moral action requires empathy and the imaginative awareness of discerning what is morally relevant and just. For Minette Drumwright and Patrick Murphy (2004), it is the ability to be simultaneously ethical and successful by imagining new and/or creative alternate outcomes.

In earlier work and in Chapter 6 of this revised edition, we delink moral imagination from moral reasoning, defining the former as "the ability in particular circumstances to discover and evaluate possibilities not merely determined by that circumstance, or limited by its operative mental models, or merely framed by a set of rules or rule-governed concerns" (Werhane, 1999, 93). To reiterate what we argued at length in Chapters 5 and 6, moral imagination is by and large an affective facilitating process that influences, but is not identical to, reasoning, even moral reasoning. Moral judgments require cognitive reasoning processes and a measure of impartiality that are not merely imaginative. Moral imagination helps one to disengage from a particular process, evaluate that and the mindsets which it incorporates, and think more creatively within the constraints of what is morally possible. Without moral imagination one might remain mired in a particular situation, but without moral reasoning one could slip into moral fantasy. To reiterate again, on the individual level, being morally imaginative includes:

SELF-REFLECTION ABOUT ONESELF AND ONE'S SITUATION

Self-reflection entails disengaging from and becoming aware of one's situation, understanding the mental model or script dominating that situation, and envisioning possible moral conflicts or dilemmas that might arise in that context or as outcomes of the dominating scheme. Moral imagination entails the ability to imagine new possibilities. These possibilities include those that are not context-dependent and that might involve another mental model. Moral imagination further requires that one evaluates from a moral point of view both the original context and its dominating mental models and the new possibilities one has envisioned (Werhane, 1999).

Notice that this analysis focuses on the individual decision-maker, and in their writings, Moberg, Seabright, and Werhane have focused primarily on individuals and individual moral judgments. But, we shall now suggest, this is an oversight. Moral imagination is not merely a function of the individual imagination. Rather, moral imagination operates on organizational and systemic levels as well, again as a facilitative mechanism that may encourage sounder moral thinking and moral judgment. It is these latter phases that we will elaborate in this chapter.

SOME INTRACTABLE PROBLEMS

Let us begin by enumerating a series of problems, moral problems, that occur on the organizational or systemic level, problems that appear either to be no one's fault, or are not solvable given the structure of the system in question. First, to recall the British Post Office case (see Chapter 5), one the reasons that that set of crises seemed intractable, and thus these cases of sub-postmaster fraud kept appearing, was because management decisions were based on software – a nonhuman, seemingly objective judgmental mechanism that appeared hard to dispute.

A second example comes from Bangladesh. The Bangladesh Bank (the national government-owned bank of Bangladesh) controls the inflow of money into that country and, until recently, the kinds of loans available to Bangladeshis. Taking its lead from sound Western financial education, advice from the International Monetary Fund and the World Bank, the Bangladesh Bank lends money only to those who have good credit ratings, property, capital, or other collateral, or other demonstrated assurances that the loan will either be paid back or can be collected in some fashion. All of this seems sensible to the Western mind. However, because most of the population of Bangladesh has no money, no ability to borrow any money, nor any form of recognizable property or other collateral, loans are available only to the wealthy. The population is too large and the country is too poor to instigate a welfare system. So the poor and the poorest of the poor remain so, because of financial systemic requirements of the system (Alam, 2024).

Henk van Luijk (2001) argues that these problems are structural or systemic problems not created by, nor, by implication, solvable by an individual ethical actor even with the tools of moral or financial reasoning or even with the help of individual moral imagination. Thus, a more systemic approach must be used to frame these issues. In what follows we shall develop van Luijk's thesis. We want to argue that these are not irresolvable problems, but the resolution has to take place in process through the tool of systems thinking, and a more systemic approach to moral imagination. Still, we will conclude, there remains a critical role for the ethical actor and individual moral decision-making without which change would not take place at all.

PROCESS PHILOSOPHY

Since the time of Aristotle, traditional Western philosophy has largely focused on static entities. What we can call substance positivism suggests a world made up of substances and non-substances that endure over time (Whitehead, 1929). Process philosophy, by contradistinction, emphasizes change, becoming, and evolving as the fundamental aspects of reality. Everything is continuously in lively flux and events or processes take precedence over ay fixed substances or non-substances (Rescher, 1996). This processual view offers a more flexible and accurate way of understanding phenomena such as evolution, growth, and transformation, which are central to science and life.

Process philosophy aligns closely with modern scientific understanding, particularly in the fields like quantum physics and evolutionary biology, where change, uncertainty, and relational processes are key. Philosophers such as Henri Bergson (1889) and Alfred North Whitehead ([1929] 1978) propose a phenomenological setting for a world that is relational and dynamic, rather than one based on immutable materials. Instead of seeing entities as independent, process philosophy views them as interconnected always-changing events or moments of experience. This relational ontological approach has profound implications, particularly for ethics and ecology. It supports apperceptions such as deep ecology in which humans and nature are interdependently entangled, and any process actions ripple effects throughout a broader web of existing.

Because process philosophy focuses on processes rather than static events and substance objectivism, it is significant in understanding complex systems. Processes accommodate interdependence and emergent properties of systems better than more inflexible ontologies, making this approach invaluable in systems thinking and organizational behavior. For ethics, process philosophy's take on reality suggests a mental model of a dynamic and evolving morality that is sensitive to context and any change of circumstances. Instead of rigid moral rules, this approach emphasizes the continuous evolving nature of ethical decisions, making it highly relevant for "real" social, economic, environmental, and political problems where rigid categories – as we shall see – so often fails. But let us first define what we mean by systems and systems thinking.

SYSTEMS AND SYSTEMS THINKING

A system is "a set or arrangement of things so related or connected as to form a unity or organic whole" (Neufeldt, 1997, 1359), "assemblages of interactions within an organization or between organizations" (Emanuel, 2000, 152), and/or "a complex of interacting components together with the relationships among them that permit the identification of a boundary-maintaining entity or process" (Laszlo and Krippner, 1998, 51).

What is characteristic of processes and all types of systems is that any phenomenon or set of phenomena that are defined as a system has properties or characteristics that are lost or, at best, obscured, when the process or system is broken up into components. For example, in studying organizations, if one focuses simply on its organizational structure, or merely on its mission statement, or only on its employees or managers, one loses the interconnections and interrelationships that characterize that system or subsystem. In studying organizations one cannot forget that they are embedded in a political economy or economies that affect their operations and well-being. The kinds of processes and systems on which we are concentrating have another characteristic. Each type of process, system or subsystem is purposive or goal oriented. Organizations and institutions have goals that are usually reflected in their mission statements or other statements of purpose. Other processes or systems such as political economies are ascribed goals based on their constitutions, laws, public statements, or habits of behavior.

The goal-orientation of any process or system accounts for its normative dimensions. As has been argued extensively elsewhere, organizations and individuals have purposes and goals that carry with them moral obligations, and we hold organizations and institutions, as well as individuals, morally accountable (French, 1979; Werhane, 1985). While it is less transparent that processes or systems are moral agents of some sort, it is arguable (through the acceptability of cause and effect arguing) that the structure, interrelationships, and goals of a particular system produce outcomes that have normative consequences. Any alteration of a particular system or parts of that system will produce different kinds of outcomes. As networks of relationships between individuals, groups, and institutions systems are relationships between people.

For example, the resolution of the Post Office scandal changed the dynamics of this organization and the Royal Mail to which it is accountable. Thus, how the system is construed – how its processes operate – affects and is affected by multiple individuals. The character and operations of a particular system or set of systems affects those of us who come in contact with the system, whether we are individuals, the community, professionals, managers, companies, or government agencies. Equally, moral responsibility is incurred by the nature and characteristics of the system in question (Emanuel, 2000). For example, we blame the Post Office as an organization, even though we cannot pinpoint all the individuals involved in developing and maintaining its software and those who agreed with its accusations. We blame the political economists and banks in the Bangladeshi government for the country's endemic poverty even though it appears to be no one set of individuals we can single out, given what is taken to be sound the financial philosophy such that apparently there is nothing they can do about it.

Systemic arrangements and organization networks create roles and role responsibilities, rights, and opportunities that affect individuals and individual activities and performance. What is less obvious is that one can take a single organization or a single individual functioning within that organization or system and apply different systems matrices and/or processes to that organization with differing outcomes. What subsystems and individuals functioning within these systems focus on and the ways values and stakeholders are prioritized affects the goals, procedures, and outcomes of the system or subsystem in question. On every level, the way we frame the goals, the procedures and what networks we take into account makes a difference in what we discover and what we neglect. These framing mechanisms will turn out to be important normative influences of processes and systems thinking, as we shall illustrate later in this chapter in describing the Grameen Bank of Bangladesh.

> A truly systemic view thus considers how ... [a phenomenon] ... operates in a system with certain characteristics. The system involves interactions extending over time, a complex set of interrelated decision points, an array of actors with conflicting interests ... and a number of feedback loops ... Progress in analyzing [ethical issues] ... can only be made with a full understanding of the systemic issues.
>
> *(Wolf, 1999, 144)*

In the examples we have cited in this chapter, each of the situations revealed a complex network of relationships embedded in a complex set of systems and subsystems. To deal with ethical issues in these cases either from an individual or even from an organizational perspective often belies what is really at issue and thus ignores a number of elements that are related to the issue in question. To evaluate a system (and thus begin to change it) requires what the organizational and scientific literature call "systems thinking" or a systems approach.

What do we mean by "systems thinking" or a "systems approach?" Systems thinking has different definitions, depending on the discipline. For our purposes systems thinking presupposes that most of our thinking, experiencing, practices and institutions are interrelated and interconnected processes (Bevan 2019). Almost everything we can experience or think about is in a network of interrelationships such that each element of a particular set of interrelationships affects the other components of that set and the system itself, and almost no phenomenon can be studied in isolation from all relationships with at least some other phenomenon. Systems thinking, then, involves two kinds of analysis. In a systems approach, "concentration is on the analysis and design of the whole, as distinct from ... the components or parts" (Ramos, 1969, 11–12). Systems thinking requires conceiving of the system as a whole with interdependent elements, subsystems, and networks of relationships and patterns of interaction. Studying a particular component of a system or a particular relationship is valuable only if one recognizes that that study is an abstraction from a more systemic consideration.

Secondly, few systems are merely linear, and few are closed systems that are not constantly in dynamic processes of changing and reinventing themselves. Therefore, systems thinking involves multiple-perspective analyses of any subject matter because "the fundamental notion of interconnectedness or nonseparability, forms the basis of what has come to be known as the Systems Approach ... every problem humans face is complicated [and] must be perceived as such" (Mitroff and Linstone, 1993, 95). So, each system or subsystem, because it is complex, because it entails a multitude of various individual, empirical, social, and political relationships, and because it is always a dynamic process, needs to be analyzed from multiple perspectives.

Mitroff and Linstone argue that any phenomenon, subsystem or system needs to be analyzed from what they call a multiple perspective method. Such a method postulates that any phenomenon, organization, or system or problems arising for or within that phenomenon of system should be dealt with from least three perspectives, each of which involves different world views where each challenges the others in dynamic exchanges of questions and ideas. Mitroff and Linstone suggest that in business, economic, and public policy contexts one needs to look at problems from a technical, or factfinding point of view, from an organizational or social relationships perspective, and from an individual perspective, ranking problems, perspectives, and alternate solutions, and evaluating the problem and its possible resolution from these multiple perspectives (Mitroff and Linstone, 1993, chapter 6). A multiple perspectives approach also takes into account the fact that each of us individually, or as groups, organizations, or systems, creates and frames the world through a series of mental models, each of which. by itself, is incomplete. While it is probably never possible to take account all the networks of relationships involved in a particular system, and surely never so given these systems interact over time, a multiple perspectives approach forces us to think more broadly, and to look at particular systems or problems from different points of view. This is crucial in trying to avoid problems such as Bangladesh's, because each perspective usually "reveals insights ... that are not obtainable in principle from others" (Mitroff and Linstone, 1993, 98). It is also invaluable in trying to understand other points of view, even if, eventually one disagrees or agrees to disagree. A multiple perspectives approach is essential if, for example, one is able to develop new thinking about banking in poor countries or electrification where the return on investment may be negative.

A MULTIPLE PERSPECTIVES APPROACH

In examining ethical issues in systems, subsystems, and organizations, a multiple perspectives approach requires developing an overlapping set of two grids, the elements of which we shall initially label descriptive and normative. We shall see, however, that these are provisional labels, because the two elements overlap considerably and because they are always in flux (or in process).

The first, a descriptive or "technical" approach, includes the following. First, one describes the system in question from a sociological point of view. Included in the description are networks of interrelationships between individuals, groups, organizations, and systems, and the number, nature, and scope of subsystems in the system.

Second, one outlines the boundaries and boundary-creating activities so that it is clear what is not included in the system. Stakeholder theory is useful in this context. By enumerating the various stakeholders involved in or affected by the system, their interrelationships and accountabilities one can get clearer on the networks of interrelationships entailed in a particular system and who or what has been left out of previous calculations (see Werhane, 2002). However, this is problematic. Different stakeholders will outline the boundary conditions differently because of the way each prioritizes stakeholders. For example, a Western-trained Bangladeshi banker will calculate loans to the poor differently than, say, someone working for an NGO. This illustrates how prioritization of stakeholders and values (including economic values) affects the perception of boundary conditions and affects decision-making. But it also illustrates that a reevaluation of that prioritization may shed light on new ways to think about fairly traditional problems (see Werhane and Painter-Morland, 2011).

Linked to the boundary conditions and stakeholder prioritization are the accountability relationships between each stakeholder and element of the system in question. It is tempting to conceive those dyadically, as Figure 7.1 illustrates.

And from an organizational approach a dyadic description of accountability may be adequate. But organizations are parts of more complex systems, and these relationships are much more overlapping and interlocking. See Figure 7.2 for a partial graphic depiction of some of these. More importantly, being clear about these relationships, and how each individual and each element of the system are or should be accountable to each other helps to clarify where decisions go wrong.

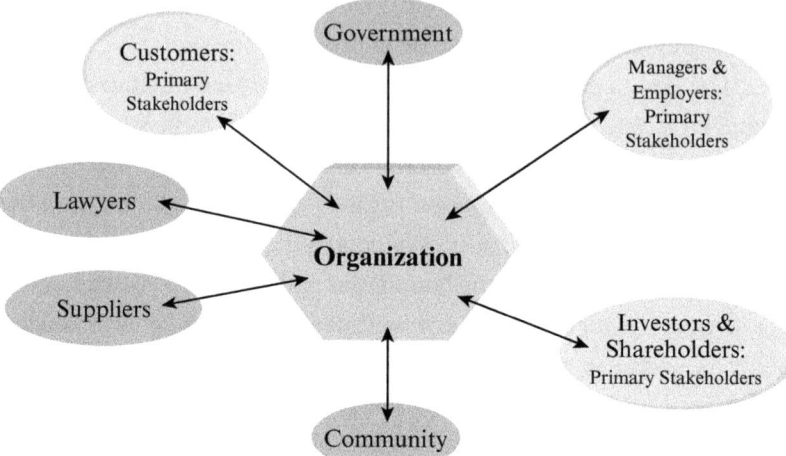

FIGURE 7.1 Standard stakeholder map.

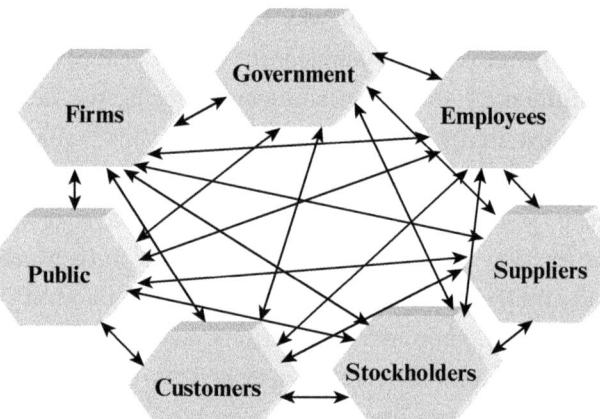

FIGURE 7.2 Stakeholder networks.

Finally, one needs to determine what goals or purposes the system has, or what goals it should have, and how these are prioritized, since the goals a system has will affect its structure and interrelationships. These prioritized goals then become the evaluative elements overlaid on the descriptive grid.

The descriptive grid imports normative/evaluative components in evaluating the shortcomings of the boundary perceptions, accountability relationships, and goal prioritization. But there are other elements a normative dimension introduces as well. From the normative perspective, one investigates or should investigate how a particular configuration of a system or subsystem affects individuals. in the Post Office case, after so many convictions, the management should have investigated the accusing software, but they did not. One evaluates or should evaluate, the boundary-creating processes, to be clear about what is left out, as well as accountability relationships, as we illustrated earlier. Then one evaluates both by prioritizing the goals of the system and indeed, by evaluating those goals (including the professional, organizational, economic and political norms) implicit in the system.

SYSTEMS THINKING, BOUNDARY CONDITIONS, AND MORAL IMAGINATION

We have left underdetermined what we mean by "boundary conditions" and how they are limiting. One way in which they are limiting is because of the operative mental models or mindsets of any particular system, organization, or subsystem. Although the term is not always clearly defined, "mental model," as we have used the term, connotes the idea that human beings have mental representations, cognitive frames, or mental pictures of their experiences, representations that model the stimuli or data with which they are interacting, and these are frameworks that set up parameters though which experience or a certain set of experiences, is organized or filtered (see Gorman, 1992, Gentner and Whitley, 1997, Senge, 1990, Werhane, 1999).

As we have argued in Chapter 5, mental models might be hypothetical constructs of the experience in question or scientific theories, they might be schema which frame the experience, through which individuals process information, conduct experiments, and formulate theories. Mental models function as selective mechanisms and filters for dealing with experience. In focusing, framing, organizing, and ordering what we experience, mental models bracket and leave out data, and emotional and motivational foci taint or color experience. Nevertheless, because schema we employ are socially learned and altered through religion, socialization, culture, educational upbringing, and other experiences, they are shared ways of perceiving, organizing, and learning.

Because of the variety and diversity of mental models, none is complete, and "there are multiple possible framings of any given situation" (Johnson, 1993; Werhane, 1999), as process philosophy delineates. By that we mean that each of us can frame any situation, event, or phenomenon in more than one way, and that same phenomenon can also be socially constructed in a variety of ways by others. It will turn out that the way one frames a situation is critical to its outcome, because "there are ... different moral consequences depending on the way we frame the situation" (Johnson, 1993; Werhane, 1999).

Mental models, as Peter Senge carefully reminds us (Senge, 1990), function on the organizational and systemic levels as well as in individual cognition. So often we are trapped within an organizational culture that creates mental habits that function as boundary conditions, precluding creative thinking. Similarly, a political economy can be trapped in its vision of itself and the world in ways that preclude change on this more systemic level. The Western finance mindset that precludes lending to the poor functions to block such exchanges in Bangladesh. Thus, moral imagination, the ability to get out of these models and traps, is critical at all levels. To change or break out of a particular mindset requires a well-functioning moral imagination.

But how do we do all of that while at the same time taking into account situational peculiarities, social context, and the processes and systems in which we are embedded? How do we act in a morally reasonable manner and trigger moral imagination? Mitroff and Linstone emphasize that systems thinking requires individual as well as systemic input. But, importantly for this paper, how does moral imagination work on the organizational and systemic levels?

An example of this is the Grameen Bank of Bangladesh has operated in that country since 1976 and is still working to reduce poverty through microlending. A Bangladeshi, Muhammad Yunus, a US-trained economist and former employee of Bangladesh Bank, is its founder (and currently the chief advisor to the government of that country!). Early on in the early 1970s Yunus was struck with the realization that his country received a great deal of foreign aid; yet most of his people remained in abject poverty. He and his students discovered that part of the problem, in a country with high unemployment and little opportunity for job creation, was the inability of those without capital and property to borrow enough money to develop even micro-entrepreneurial enterprises and thus work themselves out of poverty. Except for loans available at up to 200 percent interest from fairly questionable sources, there were no resources available for the poor.

So, with the permission of the Bangladesh Bank, Yunus started the Grameen Bank with the philosophy of lending money only to those without capital or property, the exact inverse of what he had learned in school. Today, in 2024, the Grameen Bank serves over 18,000 villages, the bank has more than 10 million member/borrowers, 97 percent of whom are women. It lends about $40 to $60 million a month, and its rate of loan loss is under 2 percent. Each of their offices are profitable. The bank has subsequently expanded into other industries, developed cell phone services in rural communities, and is planning training and job development in the new economy of wireless networking and internet services in a number of rural communities. Almost half of Grameen members are now economically above the poverty line, infant mortality rates have been drastically reduced, and at least 40 percent of children of Grameen members complete primary education.

In this process, Yunus has revolted against both traditional banking practices and the systemic subjugation of women in his country. This was enormously risky both financially and morally; yet he has succeeded and set a model that is now being copied in at least sixty-five other underdeveloped countries around the world and in Bangladesh by an even larger non-profit organization, Bangladesh Rehabilitation Assistance Committee (BRAC) (https://grameenbank.org.bd/about/gb-now). This required a great deal of moral courage and moral imagination to step out of an entrenched banking system and work toward constructive change. In 2006 Yunus received the Nobel Peace Prize.

From a process and systems approach, moral imagination involves a systemic multiple perspectives approach. This includes the following.

- Concentration on the network of relationships and patterns of interaction, rather than on individual components of particular relationships, spelling out the networks of relationships from different perspectives.
- A multi-perspective analysis.
- Understanding the various perspectives of the manager, the citizen, the firm, community, state, law, tradition, background institutions, history, and other networks of relationships.
- Taking an evaluative perspective, asking:

    Who are the stakeholders we have not prioritized?
    What values are at stake?
    Which stakeholders or values take priority, or should take priority?
    What are the practical constraints and which ones can be circumvented and how?

- Involve pro-active leadership both within the system and in initiating structural change.

In these processes one needs to describe the system and the processes and networks of interrelationships to grasp the interconnectedness of the system. One needs to investigate what is not included in the system (its boundaries and boundary-creating activities) and what mindsets are predominant, asking who the stakeholders are (e.g., individuals, associations, organizations, networks, agencies) and what are the core values of each set of stakeholders. Additionally, one needs to outline the core values of the system and speculate as to what these should be. Finally, one should think about whether and which organizations or individuals within the system might be capable and willing to risk challenging bits of the system that are the most vulnerable or amenable to change. In this set of processes moral imagination and systems thinking encourage networked systems analyses that are engaged and critical, creative and evaluative, and values grounded and encourage constructive change within a network of relationships.

INDIVIDUAL RESPONSIBILITY

> He who would do good to another must do it in minute particulars;
> General good is the plea of the scoundrel hypocrite, and flatterer.
>
> (Blake, [1832] 1877, Plate #55)

There is one more consideration, that of individual responsibility, the responsibilities of politicians, professionals, managers, and of individual citizens. A process and systems approach should not be confused with any form of abdicating individual responsibility. As individuals we are not merely the sum of, or identified with, these relationships and roles, we can evaluate and change our relationships, roles, and role obligations, and we are thus responsible for them. That is, each of us is at once a byproduct of, character in, and author of our own experiences. So each of us is responsible for examining, evaluating, critiquing and finding means to change organizations and systems in which we find ourselves.

All of this sounds much too idealistic and impossible, in fact, to achieve, and it belies the existence of sometimes-impossible systems constraints. So let us conclude with a counterexample, the resolution of the British Post Office scandal. One person, Alan Bates, persevered to finally unearth the source of this fraud: the allegedly invincible software the Post Office had employed to uncover what turned out to be false accusations of fraud. Bates persevered for more than fifteen years before finally winning his cases against the Post Office and the software company's admission of faulty software.

CONCLUSION

Understanding systems thinking and process philosophy are essential of we are to understand, evaluate, and institute structural, organizational and individual change. Alan Bates – a champion of British sub-postmasters – understood that. Nevertheless, despite the importance of such thinking, no organization, system or subsystem is, or need be, thought of as close static system in which change is impossible to achieve. Organizations, institutions, and political economies are dynamic processes: revisable phenomena, created and changed by individuals or groups of individuals. But until we comprehend the complexity of the systemic interrelationships within and across systems and the ongoing processes of change, we cannot successfully evaluate the system or subsystem in question and begin to make changes that are critical if we are to make moral progress. This chapter is an initiation of that set of thinking processes for each of us, focusing still on our opening epigraph from Iris Murdoch.

8 Next Stages
Reformulating the Paradigm of Western Industrial Global Capitalism through Moral Imagination[1]

In this chapter we step back from our analyses of individual, managerial, and organizational moral imagination to look more broadly at the role of moral imagination in analyzing and critiquing contemporary global capitalism and multinational corporations (MNCs) with their seemingly ubiquitous roles in expanding this phenomenon. We will engage in morally imaginative thinking to disengage howsoever from the processes of a Western capitalist mindset and so to look more broadly at the various cultures and "social imaginaries" that inhabit our world.

Capitalism remains an efficient and effective producer of human wealth. Competing with such necessarily thin, portmanteau definitions, a systems thinking approach suggests that capitalism is alternately a complex adaptive system itself fully integrated with – if not structural to – global, contemporary human society. As such, it is susceptible to criticism on account of increasing and disparate income inequalities; an array of unaddressed crises in climate change attributed to "free" industrialization; a one-size-fits-all to commercial organizations; and institutionalized racism, sexism, multiple additional forms of categorical discrimination, and widespread corruption. In the face of such polemical processes, a question arises as to what the future of this global capitalism is as it spreads throughout the planet.

---

[1] An earlier version of this paper was published in Bevan, D. and Werhane P., 2024. "Reformulating the Western Paradigm of Global Capitalism" in Pava and Dion, *Justifying Next Stage Capitalism*. Dordrecht NL: Springer. Reprinted by permission of the editors and publisher.

In what follows we discuss three possible scenarios for the future of global political economies. We will argue that the future of viable forms of free enterprise rests in the reformulation of this model as a set of social *imaginaries* lodged specifically within, and operating in conjunction with, local mores, norms, and social frameworks, each of which might produce a unique form of enterprise. To contextualize this discussion, we begin with a foreword offering a review of the structural significance and agency of the imaginaries that tend to dominate the discourses on this topic in the field of business ethics and by advancing a summary of conditions that we consider as indicative, significant, and structural for any possible analysis or paradigmatic reformulation exercise.

CONTEXTUAL FOREWORD

The paradigm of capitalism, along with its justifications and rationales, is a social construction produced by the Western, post-Enlightenment. Such a claim may be characterized as already predicated by imaginaries, that is, mental models (Werhane, 2008) dialogically abstracted from reality/experience. They are one among many possible paradigms underlying what we take to be our points of view, our arguments, and our values. More precisely, imaginaries are "the creative and symbolic dimension of the social world, the dimension through which human beings create their ways of living together and their ways of representing their collective life" (Thompson, 1984, 6). Alternately, the imaginary is "something broader and deeper than the intellectual schemes people may entertain when they think about social reality in a disengaged mode" (Taylor, 2004, 23). To this extent, and our rationale for drawing on them here, imaginaries are loosely under-determined, or incompletely ontologized (by comparison with tightly defined themes like the opening characterization of capitalism as a paradigm). In this way, imaginaries are useful – as we shall further show – in exploring the indeterminate future(s) of complex adaptive systems such as capitalism.

To some extent we live in a post-Enlightenment, Western world. Yet – and carefully avoiding any tendency to complacent self-congratulation for the relative security and privilege of our positions – this is a Western world where under one-third of the population inhabits the industrial or postindustrial countries usually identified with capitalism. Thus, any post-Enlightenment futuristic thinking require that we acknowledge the parochialism of the term "capitalism" and explore other ways – other paradigms, other imaginaries by which "next stages of capitalism" emerge in viable, but local and pluricentric formats.

As we have argued elsewhere (Bevan and Werhane, 2021), the term "globalization" remains contested but is usually defined in Western thinking as follows:

> In a general sense, the increasing worldwide integration of economic, cultural, political, religious, and social systems. Economic globalization is the process by which the whole world becomes a single market. This means that goods and services, capital, and labor are traded on a worldwide basis, and information and the results of research flow readily between countries.
> *(Hashimzade et al., 2017)*

Other and alternative definitions follow a pattern of identifying "globalization" as referring to widely unexplained conflations of free markets, trade, and basically various forms of capitalism (see for example, Friedman,1999; Piketty, 2014; Scherer and Palazzo, 2011, 2016; Stiglitz, 2002). They present these forms of globalized capitalism as what passes allegedly for democratic capitalism in the spirit of the twenty-first century (Boltanski and Chiapello, 2006). Thus the definitions of globalization appear as narrowly focused neo-Enlightenment definitions of what is basically Western free enterprise.

As a dimension of systemic globalization, and as a number of commentators have pointed out, in the last forty years there has been a massive spread of multinational companies, most of which are located in industrialized countries and spreading in emerging economies where there is often little development of infrastructure, basic transportation, social services, or even rule of law. Many of these organizations have become:

> providers of public goods in cases where public authorities are unable or unwilling to fulfil this role. This includes, but is not limited to, corporate contributions to different areas of governance, such as public health, education, public infrastructure, the enforcement of social and environmental standards along supply chains or the fight against corruption, discrimination or inequality. These public goods are provided to resolve public issues with the aim of enhancing social welfare.
>
> *(Scherer et al., 2016, 4)*

Further and in Joseph Stiglitz's words: "Globalization ... helped hundreds of millions of people attain higher standards of living, beyond what they, or most economists, thought imaginable but a short while ago [irrespective of whether or not these are forms of neo-colonialism]" (Stiglitz, 2002, 248–249).[2]

These interpretations seem to suggest good positive outcomes, at least from a utilitarian perspective. But let us step back from that parochial perspective. From another point of view, that of the principles of respect for diversity and alien cultures, as a number of critics such as Banerjee (2002, 2018), Banerjee and colleagues (2009), Mignolo (2011), Mignolo and Walsh (2018), Quinaro (2007), and others have argued, these interventions are forms of neo-colonialism. Neo-colonialism is here considered as "a continuation of colonialism without the traditional mechanism of expanding frontiers and territorial control but with elements of political, economic and cultural control" (Banerjee et al., 2009, 8). Whether or not this is the case, we are accepting of Kwame Anthony Appiah's (2007) caution to avoid any unintended, complacent or smug superiority, as this imaginary nevertheless supports or confirms a Western-oriented imaginary of globalization that is

---

[2] In his 2019 revision of this book, Stiglitz is more cautious of his praise of this phenomenon.

not universal, but in actuality parochial and partial, if not in intention, then most surely in practice.

A distinguishing character of capitalism as an economic *imaginary* is that this characteristic allows capitalism to change or to be emergent. By way of impartial illustration – we are not trained in economics – history shows that it has quite evidently changed contextually through the eyes of and as recorded successively in the accounts of Adam Smith ([1776] 1976), David Ricardo ([1817] 1992), Karl Marx ([1867] 1992), Vifredo Pareto ([1906] 2014), Milton Friedman ([1962] 2002), and Thomas Piketty (2014). Each of these accounts provides the basis for evolving, possible imaginaries in its historical context with roughly half-century intervals.

As last considerations here, we cannot neglect to mention the contingent disruption for global capitalism of the impact of the 2020–2022 pandemic, persistent Russian aggression in Ukraine since 2014, leading to stark energy and food resource constraints, and, before that, the financial crisis of 2008. The management of Covid-19 may come to be seen as an inflection point for generational attitudes toward anthropogenic climate change (see Extinction Rebellion, 2021). Beyond inflaming already-developing international disharmonies, the progress of globalization has been shaken by the disruption of its extensive supply chains. Further there has been a growing confrontation with the legacy of externalities from decades of carefree exploitation, for which a majority of industrialist CEOs have continued avoiding responsibility since at least 1905 (Tarbell, 1905).

Taking the above as a clearer articulation of the potentially imaginary character of global capitalism that is our starting point, what can we imagine for the future of global political economies in three indicative scenarios? These scenarios represent conventional, if not common hypotheses which are in current circulation.

SCENARIO I: CONSERVATIVE STATUS QUO

In the first of these three scenarios we postulate that global capitalism will continue and proceed at the pace at which it has operated in in the past. It will promote and facilitate the establishment of more or less democratic free enterprise globally. Recovering from the pandemic, overcoming advanced political enmities, and greenwashing away environmental concerns is not beyond the scope of well-funded propaganda. If this can be achieved, the global capital project might expand its interests around the world, providing jobs where expedient to the needs of the market; and, when necessary, working to improve the infrastructure and public services in the territories where they operate including and contingently embedding a structurally Western mental model in the course of performing their operations.

This continuation of the spread of global capitalism as a quasi-conservative reproduction of the status quo has at least two potential and overlapping flaws: (1) It does not respect a basic informal tenet of complex adaptive systems, (nor of imaginaries) that all things change – indeed this scenario seeks to deny that eventuality or prevent it from uncontrollably emerging; and (2) in that it does not respect the disparity of local cultures, habits and mores. In other words, despite the ubiquity of this particular "normalized" neoliberal mindset, once we move to the mode of imaginaries, there are deeply grounded issues that are endemic or presupposed in all the foregoing variety.

These issues begin with the use of the term "globalization" itself. Most post-Enlightenment industrialized political economies, with their multinational corporate economic engines, behave as though they are particularized forms of Western industrial neo-colonialism. These firms are/remain practically neo-colonial because of a widespread belief among industrialized nations and the management and ownership of these corporations that their engagements are almost natural, indeed, universal in their premises and values. Often, and allegedly democratically, this version of capitalism seems to have become a universal norm, which justifies its legitimate reproduction and proliferation around the world. In addition to allegedly improving the economy of any particular nation in which they operate, their engagements in the social and political activities of the nations and territories where they operate often involve in what they consider reforming the status quo in that country, and sometimes even regime change.

While such ultra-commercial activities may be worthwhile for an industrialized nation, they are not always accepted or acceptable when held up to the prevailing cultural and/or social regional norms in emerging economies. And notice how the imaginary of "emerging economy" itself implies that economic development (and subliminally, a hint that capitalistic economic development will allow an economy to emerge economically and thus thrive). These activities are meanwhile held up as beneficial, conservational, and even exemplary in the contexts in which they operate. Moreover, the power and economic largesse of these companies combine to embrace, or even subdue or replace local norms and practices. And, rather than imagining what might be a means to appropriate these norms and accommodate local customs, these companies engage in a project of justifying and reproducing a Western culture whose orthodox mindset may be vastly different from the one it seeks to efface. This is often without a thought for the possibility that a so-called Western democratic mindset may be neither universal nor always desirable.

What some critics of these forms of effective neo-colonialism worry about most is the complacent nonrecognition of divergent cultural and religious values that are grounded and considered basic in every culture. These are not identical in every community, and often these are not even of acknowledging differences in how one defines a human being (see Jackson and Carter, 1991; Mignolo and Walsh, 2018). Such differences are overlooked by globalized MNCs, usually because (1) they are simply unaware of and fail to acknowledge any differences in the countries where they operate away from home, or (2) they imagine that a Western capitalist view of what it means to be a human being, of the value of individual rights, and other revered Western points of view are universal. We will argue that this is not entirely the case.

Worse, arguably, some of these critics decry, there is sometimes a movement with these engagements to introduce forms of democracy or even deliberative democracy. Notice how we often substitute "free enterprise" for the term, "capitalism," as if the latter economic model was implicitly a democratic form of political economy. Moreover,

> Exporting deliberative democracy to societies with deep structural inequalities does not make the process more democratic, especially if the structural inequalities restrict or deny access to marginalized populations to deliberative processes. In other words, processes might be deliberative without being democratic, which brings into question the types of legitimacy that deliberative processes can provide. Deliberative processes may be seen as democratic by market and state actors but can be undemocratic from the perspective of marginalized and dissenting minorities.
>
> (Banerjee, 2018: 802)

Indeed, the outcomes are not always desirable even from a Western perspective. This is because the multitude of diverse stakeholders in many emerging economies who are not included in "our" Western global capitalized movement are marginalized from this so-called economic development while at the same time their indigenous culture and values are undermined or threatened. The result is often both economic inequality and value discrimination.

In her already "post-global" imaginary, Rana Foroohar articulates this cosmopolitan fallacy clearly: "One of the most pernicious neoliberal myths was that unfettered globalization was always a good thing, always the best way forward, for everyone everywhere" (Foroohar, 2022, 20). In reality it was *sometimes* a good thing; and only for *some*, rather than for all.

SCENARIO II: ANARCHIC REVOLUTION

Given the difficulties we outlined with Western-dominated global free enterprise there are some that propose the revival an interest in a command economy, a neo-Marxist, or a somehow socialized state, albeit based on economic ideals and formulations which have, in the past, been overturned in favor of capitalism. Alternately, extreme ecologists – Extinction Rebellion as an example – present an as yet inchoate prospectus for doing things quite differently either without, or with less, carbon. The planet and its atmosphere seem likely to remain, for the time being, an inseparable global commons. Environmental issues are increasingly a question at every new move by commerce or government.

Whether or not any new formulations of Marxism or pure socialism could be in the future more successful economically (as well as democratically), each is, like global capitalism, a Western-formulated imaginary that seldom takes into account the requisite diversity of human ideas and needs. More pragmatically, there is little evidence that the present system has lost any of the severe robustness. With the enduring successes of Western-modeled free enterprise that could be dated from the formation of the East India Company in 1600, there has to be doubt that there will be a return to any historically unpopular form of political economy: And, additionally, any innovations in anarchism may need to bear in mind Douglass's premonition that "Power concedes nothing without a demand. It never did and never will" (Douglass, 1857). On the basis of no empirical evidence from which to draw, the nonetheless often invoked possibility of revolutionary change cannot be illustrated with a case. It remains provisionally as a persistent but inoperable cypher among the field of all possible futures.

SCENARIO III: EVOLUTIONARY CHANGE

Here, let us engage in moral imagination with the imaginaries while allowing or assuming that the spread of Western-styled global capitalism continues to evolve the prevailing economic trend worldwide. Given the current ubiquitous spread of forms of this economic trend and the financial power of large corporations, this is not an unreasonable assumption.

The challenge then, persists to either decolonialize – or leave to self-organize – these post-Enlightenment allegedly "global" mindsets that are embedded in the spread of what the West calls global capitalism.

As Mignolo and Walsh argue, "A starting point for a decolonial praxis is to imagine radically different perspectives that can dislodge Western rationality as the only basis of reality" (Mignolo and Walsh, 2018, 120). But can we do that with the ubiquitous spread of global capitalism?

In line with this thinking, there is a respectful and economically viable alternative. At the same time, however, this trend need not be identified with a global spread of what seems to be a prevailing mindset extoling Western capitalism and/or Western democratic capitalism as correct, or *the best*, or what most reflects all mindsets in diverse cultures. Moreover, there is much to be learned from indigenous communities, as we learned in Chapter 7 that outlined Bayer's purchase of CropScience and subsequent operations in rural India.

One viable multidimensional approach to rethinking globalization is to consider how marginalized stakeholders are framed both through an Enlightenment mindset and alternately through the concept of a pluriverse. This idea, proposed by Mignolo (2011) and Maria Ehrnström-Fuentes (2016) is best summarized as follows.

> The integration of marginalized stakeholders [MSs] into the stakeholder and entrepreneurship streams of literature is imperative because current trends show that, in today's globalized world, it is harder for firms to ignore the impact of marginalization of stakeholders that often results in inequality and wellbeing issues for businesses... These factors negatively affect the financial and social performances of firms These issues also pose barriers to breakthrough innovations, as many MSs' valuable ideas are untapped due to organizational and social constraints, biases, and ignorance.
>
> *(Mignolo, 2011, 135)*

Previously (Bevan and Werhane, 2021) we proposed that cultural differences were because of varying mindsets from which each perceives and interprets the world, although with limited vision. Escobar and Mignolo describe these differences as being accessible through different social imaginaries.

The word pluriverse signals that the world we live in is not made up of one single history or worldview but is a constantly changing world that comprises many different worlds with different histories, different worldviews, and different ways of knowing, sensing, and being. This pluriverse is inhabited by different place-based life trajectories, different ontologies and epistemologies that define the contours of different historical processes, lived realities and future imaginations that sustain people's capacity to reproduce life in the places that they inhabit (Escobar 2008; Mignolo 2011). Thus, place is important both as a site of material and cultural reproduction. The place-based component of the pluriverse signals that societies (and the identities within these societies) are a production of historical processes simultaneously restricted and enabled by their geographic location.

(Escobar 2001; 2008, 1)

According to Ehrenstrom-Fuentes (2016) and Escobar (2008) there are radically different social imaginaries in different parts of the world. Differing assumptions about the history of place, meaning of subsistence, political structures, relationship to nature, human rights, and narratives of the future (see Escobar, 2001 on these distinctions). Thus Ehrenstrom-Fuentes calls for MNCs to recognize the existence of a "pluriversal" world of different social imaginaries.

Acknowledging the pluriversality of the world is not about engaging in cultural relativism but about exposing the interconnectedness of several social imaginaries, or cosmologies, previously occluded by one point of view. And Ehrenstrom-Fuentes argues convincingly that such an approach is not reduceable to moral relativism because of the overlapping nature of social imaginaries or mindsets, which recognizes the overlapping systems in which the human world operates.

As we outlined in Chapter 7, a systemic approach postulates that the total sum of reality is in actuality a set of complex adaptive systems: "a collection of individual [and organizational] agents ...

whose actions are interconnected such that one agent's actions change the context for other agents" (Plesk, 2001, 311–312). Human-constituted organizations and political economies are complex systems embedded in and interacting with this global complex and the multitude of cultural mindsets or "social imaginaries." Because of human or group choices and interactions, this set of systems is in constant flux and change (see, e.g., Miller and Page, 2007; see Chapter 8 in this volume).

Taking the use of cell phones as an example, we associate them with our own use in twenty-first century urban life while the Maasai tribes in central Africa, who wish to be left alone to raise their cattle (which they also use as currency), nevertheless enjoy using cell phones for locating cattle, social interaction, and entertainment. They cannot avoid interaction with curious tourists, nor governments who seek to appropriate their land in order to "improve" their way of life; but they do not wish to be urbanized. Because we are all continually bumping into each other, the Maasai cannot avoid these social exchanges. Nevertheless, respect for their way of life, which is unlike most others, should be part of the thinking of those who interact with these tribes. Often it is not (see Cunningham, 2019).

As part of an interrelated and interconnected global complex adaptive system or set of systems, our choices and interactions as humans in this set of systems are in constant flux and change (see, e.g., Miller and Page, 2007). Human-constituted organizations and political economies are complex systems embedded in and interacting with this global complex and the multitude of cultural mindsets or "social imaginaries." At the same time, as we were reminded by Huxley, each human individual is unique.

> In the course of evolution nature has gone to endless trouble to see that every individual is unlike every other individual. We reproduce our kind by bringing the father's genes into contact with the mother's. These hereditary factors may be combined in an almost infinite number of ways. Physically and mentally, each one of us is

unique. Any culture which, in the interests of efficiency or in the name of some political or religious dogma, seeks to standardize the human individual, commits an outrage against man's biological nature.

(Huxley, [1958] 1965, 21)

Huxley's efficiency nightmare encapsulates the harsh, efficiency of the cosmopolitanism of globalized trade referred to in Scenario I. Efficiency without built-in redundancy capacity and alternative suppliers on hand can easily become the victim of a market collapse, acts of war, extreme weather disruption, or pandemics. Any of these adversities can take efficiency from "just in time" to the collapse of a supply chain.

As Ehrenstrom-Fuentes argues, there are radically different social/cultural paradigms in different parts of the world. These include differing assumptions about the history of place, the meaning of subsistence, appropriate political structures, the relationship to nature, human rights, and narratives of the future. Thus, it is essential to recognize the existence of a "pluriversal" world of different social *imaginaries*. Because each of us is unique and each dwells in quite different cultures, we need to be able to get at and acknowledge the legitimacy of various mindsets or social imaginaries that are operative in different cultures and contexts. (See also, Bevan and Werhane, 2023.)

That is, each of us, as individuals or in a more collective social imaginary, as a social/cultural group, has the ability (not always exercised, to be sure), through the exercise of moral imagination, to step back from their own mindsets and engage in individual or social studies of how it is we as individuals or as a group perceive and frame our experiences. One value, in any culture, is the engagement with others, even those who are foreign and threatening. So, returning to the Maasai, their exposure to cell phone technology has helped them clarify and evaluate their own way of life and their aversion to "modernity," as they perceive it. The example of the Maasai here exemplifies the persistence of natural diversity in attitudes to things.

Recalling the Bayer CropScience case, Bayer's acknowledgment of cultural differences (different social imaginaries) enabled them to step out of their long-term commitment to child-labor prevention and find another approach that accommodated both the ancient, inbred farm cultures and Bayer's corporate-grounded principled approach to child labor. Here we see how a company can be sensitive to the operational context, rather than simply commanding an outcome. We would argue that this sort of approach, recognizing cultural differences and accommodating resources to function in alien communities, is a viable approach for global companies to operate in various communities that are often alien to their values and habits, while being both profitable and systemically acknowledging social difference. Adapting a vision of moral imagination as a tool of transition toward imagining of a pluriversal world, where multiple place-specific local legitimacies co-exist, all considered as equal alternatives for the future, also opens up the possibility for the co-construction of corporate/community legitimacies. The primary challenge of such vision lies in the leadership required from business leaders to rescale and reorganize corporate activities so that, rather than being a destructive feature of local livelihoods, they aim at constructing local economic alternatives that support the co-existence of different forms of life.

CONCLUSION

In this chapter we have speculated on three imaginary scenarios for the future of capitalism: First, a scenario envisaging the prolongation of the status quo – the continuing spread of global corporate ventures, many of which are neo-colonial in appearance if not in intent. While these ventures are not necessarily bad, they come from and perpetuate a cosmopolitan fallacy. They behave as though humanity has asked to be culturally homogenized and universally engaged in the Western dream of economic development. This procrustean nonrecognition of diversity, nor of how place, economic opportunity, and social context frame each individual's experiences differently and distinctly, is exacerbating the decadence of social coherence and accelerating the degradation of the planet.

We offer no objection to neoliberal ideologies, although we respectfully challenge what appear to be structural weaknesses in imagining that one person might know what is right for everyone else. Without opposing idealism we can conclude rather with an empirical observation for the forces of globalization. That is, to note that the multinational agencies that developed the present materials economy on free-trade principles seem not to have yet noticed the structural limitations to stability that arise from an over-extended supply chain across potentially divergent and distant territories. There is, after all, a known adverse correlation between the controllability of a process, and the number of links in the extent of the supply chain.[3]

In a second possible future, we considered briefly the possibility of a revolution of some kind as an alternative to simply carrying on with a system – globalized capitalism – that now appears severely compromised. We offered the recurrent fiction of revolution as a second option because it has culturally survived at least since the time of Marx, if not dating back to 1789. It is a scenario that requires repeated dismissal up to the point that it materializes. But there is little evidence at present that such movements have anything beyond disruptive agency. Without the necessary and realizable resources to back them, returning to the ideology of an earlier civilization which has not materialized and stabilized after 150 years seems like an act of romantic nostalgia.

We presented and defended a third scenario. Stepping back from a Western cultural and economic perspective in which both authors of this book grew up, we imagined a fully flexible imaginary for the future of capitalism, that of contextualizing and localizing each corporate venture to fit the place and cultural context. This would be an acknowledgement of the various different social imaginaries that make up what Mignolo terms a decolonial, or freely organizing,

---

[3] As pointed out some 250 years ago by Adam Smith ([1776] 1976).

approach (Mignolo, 2011), an approach that is locally situated with a recognition of the pluriverse we could identify with our world. "The primary challenge of business ethics lies in developing models to rescale and reorganize corporate activities so that ... they aim at constructing local economic alternatives that support the co-existence of different forms of life" (Ehrenström-Fuentes, 2016, 458).

This evolutionary renewal may well take decades – it is a challenge to imagine that neoliberalism, that took the best part of a half century to become systemic, will not be quickly replaced. The imaginary solution that is neither I nor II but some intelligent and well-considered response to III will by necessity emerge from a core of genuine compromise that is congenitally lacking in oligarchy or autocracy. Inevitably, too, there will be challenges, confrontations, and opportunities along the way.

The necessarily consensual and environmentally sensitive outcome toward which this chapter is drawn will have huge consequences for political, business, and professional life, for education and public service, for infrastructure, for transport, for housing and health. We openly encourage further research into all and any questions that arise from this review, which resources of space require us to determine at this point.

This move of elaborating capitalism as "capitalisms" – as sets of social/economic/political and ethical imaginaries – accounts for a pluriverse that recognizes dramatic cultural differences, particularly in emerging economies. This is not merely to acknowledge cultural, situational, historical, and moral differences, and work toward a morally respectful approach to global differences. At the same time we must not forget the interdependency created by various forms of capitalism that offer avenues for economic development, even in the most remote cultures that are completely different from the West. It is also worthwhile to provide access to these views that may rarely otherwise confront economists, because often much is to be learned from particular contexts that can contribute positively and broadly to economic well-being.

9 Moral Imagination in Technological Development

Amanda McCroskery[1] and Ben Zevenbergen[2]

INTRODUCTION

The day-to-day decisions of technologists have a profound role in shaping people's interactions with the world. As many philosophers of technology have argued, every technological decision can also be seen as an ethical one. The shape and affordances of technologies determine what people can do with them, and how social systems evolve around them. Most technologists generally have positive intentions and strive to do good, but the ethical outcomes of their work can be particularly complex and unpredictable. Adverse consequences can often arise not from malice but from failure to appreciate the full implications of technological advancements amidst the delicate interplay between technology, human behavior, and social dynamics.

In our roles at Google, we have heard a strong desire to reshape technology development processes to explicitly incorporate ethical and social considerations. As the ethics of technology has received increasing public attention, we frequently hear the question "How can our team set up a productive conversation about the ethics of our work?" Outside Google there are similar calls for elevating organizational

---

[1] Amanda McCroskery works at Google Deepmind as an applied ethics advisor and governance researcher. Her work focuses on bridging the gap between high level ethical principles and on the ground practice and policy. Previously, she led product design innovation teams in tech companies and studied philosophy and English literature at Columbia University.

[2] Ben Zevenbergen works at Google as a technology ethics advisor. His background is in law, policy, and philosophy. He holds an LLM in Information Law from the University of Amsterdam and an interdisciplinary PhD across philosophy, law, and computer science from the University of Oxford.

Reprinted by permission from Google.

cultures that shape technology production. But we have found that most common responsibility governance interventions that tech companies deploy do not yet directly address how group norms and operative scripts (understood as common mental frameworks, assumptions, and narratives) shape decision-making and action in technological design. In our experience, these cultural dynamics have a direct role in determining the trajectory of future technologies.

We saw promise in examining the role that social norms play in influencing technology teams' beliefs about the ethical dimensions of their work. It became clear that standard development practices and norms do not always lead to the most defensible outcomes. This may be due to a number of factors, but it certainly includes the issue that common industry practice and engineering education focus on technical values (e.g., speed, efficiency, latency, accuracy) and less on evaluating computational solutions for social and human values (e.g., autonomy, empowerment, justice, trust). To us, Werhane's "moral imagination" provided not only a clear articulation of an important problem set that technology industry cultures face but also the beginnings of a method we could adapt to the needs of this context.

Werhane's ideas have been central in shaping our approach at Google. In this chapter, we will sketch how we have adopted and adapted the moral imagination approach to suit the needs of our technical colleagues. In post-workshop evaluations, participants typically praised the moral imagination approach as important, lasting, and impactful. One senior product manager cited it as "the most important work I've done at Google," while another senior technologist maintained that it "helps us make better products," and another that "this work has really stayed with our team and influenced our approach." In this chapter, we position the importance of moral imagination in a technology industry setting, describe how we have built on Werhane's ideas to build capacity for moral imagination in this context, and share some of our learnings along the way.

TECH DEVELOPMENT CONTEXT

Common Conceptual Schemes among Technologists

We begin by describing some observations about common mindsets and organizational structures in our industry. Both descriptions are broad and of course, incomplete. This sketch is intended to set the scene for the approach we have taken in adapting moral imagination ideas to address the specific challenges of technology industry norms.

Innovation as a Moral Value

> All experience is interpreted or constituted by a conceptual scheme and an overlapping set of incomplete mental models through which we selectively frame, order, organize, and interpret the data of experience. Each of us functions through a set of mental models that are socially learned, culturally inculcated, educationally reinforced, and experientially altered. These mental models are necessarily incomplete and volatile: that is, they can be relearned and changed.
> *(Werhane, 1999, 11–12. Reprinted in this volume, Chapter 1)*

One major industry schema revolves around the opportunity and challenge of *innovation*. A data scientist at Google has described innovation as an "ambitious undertaking to invent, approach, and realize new products, processes or ideas in more helpful, and desirable ways." While those outside the technology industry may question its motives, innovation to many in the industry connotes novelty and genuine social betterment *at scale* by improving on the status quo. Technologists often speak to us about their desire to invent the future as part of a larger life project of leaving the world a better place. We also observe that those who occupy and recognize a privileged industry position (such as a job at an influential company like Google) feel a concrete onus to influence the broader industry in the general direction of "good." However, one downside of this emphasis on innovation can be overly simplistic or underspecified ideas about what constitutes "good" or "desirable" in a particular context. Among other interventions, we've seen our moral imagination methods successfully challenge and clarify previously under-interrogated views of innovation, and course-correct well-meaning teams toward building technologies that are more responsive to human and social needs.

Speed and Its Implications on Decision-Making

> They are neither universally, socially, institutionally, nor culturally the same in every individual, although they overlap and are socially, institutionally, and culturally shared or shareable with others. In some settings certain mental models function as scripts that focus our attention on a particular set of habits for dealing with that set of events in that context. In those cases these mental models serve as focusing mechanisms to bracket other points of view or other schema. Thus, I shall argue, the kinds of mental models operative in any setting create decision-making habits that may preclude taking into account some important data.
> (Werhane, 1999, 11–12. Reprinted in this volume, Chapter 1)

Another key driving mental model of the technology industry is its emphasis on *speed*, understood in terms of latency (i.e., the time delay between the cause and the effect) as well as speed-to-market. What counts as an innovation in the field of digital technology, and AI specifically, changes rapidly. As one Google technologist noted: "There's a base level of progress in the field that is actually quite swift. Any innovation has a shelf life that is brief, so keeping a steady stream of innovations is necessary in order to compete." The importance of speed has several downstream implications on decision-making norms. Firstly, entrepreneurial autonomy is seen as an important prerequisite for the ability to move quickly. To those involved in the herculean effort of building a technology from nothing, any potential ambiguity or loss of pace – for example, time to explore social impacts prior to building – has the potential to jeopardize momentum, employee commitment, and investment. Secondly, due to the rapidity of technological change, many companies tend to compete in similar domains, which creates a sense of technological inevitability. This perceived lack of agency can lead to foregone critical reflection among technologists and diligent exploration of alternative paths that deviate from the prevailing technology trends of the day.

Organizational Autonomy

And yet, like their peers in the broader "startup culture" of the industry, product and research teams at big companies like Google typically possess a high amount of autonomy. For example, they typically have the opportunity to set the vision for, define, and validate various technologies prior to seeking official sponsorship from corporate leadership. In this context, team culture and norms shape which ideas are considered "good" and should be brought to fruition, and which should be discarded. Design and technical decisions among these teams in the inception stages of a project generally determine the initial vision for a technology and how it will be built.

One motivation for introducing moral imagination ideas into practice at Google – along with other ethical interventions – stemmed from our impression that, despite this very real autonomy, technologists felt that ethical consideration was not central to their roles. As one colleague put it, considering social and ethical values was interesting and critically important but also "above their paygrade," and instead belonged in the domain of executives, ethics reviewers, and internal product policy authors. Indeed, the expertise and education that most technologists rely on day to day relates to technical goals. This often leads to an implicit assumption that social and ethical values are somehow separate from, or even secondary to, choices about what innovations to make. However, choices about what technologies to build, how to build them, and how to market them can have dramatic ethical and social impacts. Without explicit care, current industry norms and mindsets risk prioritizing technical progress over desirable social outcomes by failing to design for the intricate interplay between technology, society, and human values.

Elaborate and effective internal governance mechanisms typically do exist at large companies like Google, to ensure that products and research live up to social and ethical values stipulated by the organization. However, these processes do not typically focus on addressing the deeper cultural norms that shape technological trajectories, nor how these norms present among varied, autonomous groups within an organization.

TYPICAL ETHICS AND RESPONSIBILITY INITIATIVES AT TECH COMPANIES

Companies often employ a layered approach to internal governance, combining both hard and soft controls to address a range of concerns from compliance to responsible innovation. Soft controls include value statements, principles, codes of conduct, and formal training. They provide broad, high-level guidelines that ensure products work effectively for a wide variety of users. However, these controls require interpretation at the team level, particularly when it comes to technology-related decisions, as they do not typically address the specifics of technological content or its future implications.

In contrast, hard controls enforce the application of values and principles through technical and legal standards. Review boards often come in late in the decision-making process, offering high-level risk mitigation but may fail to anticipate emerging technological challenges or adjust the overall trajectory of technological development. Legal and compliance frameworks ensure adherence to current laws but often lag behind the pace of technological innovation. Internal policies set minimum standards for the responsible development and use of technology.

A central challenge for internal governance at tech companies is how to adapt and keep pace with rapid technological innovation. Effective governance interventions must address the right questions at the right moment, ensuring that decisions are both timely and contextually appropriate. If the nature of the intervention does not align with the needs of a project at a given time, then it risks irrelevance. If interventions are too early, they will lack concrete grounding. If too late, then they will miss the opportunity for maximal impact on project trajectory. Given the challenge of timing and context, perhaps the parties best positioned to incorporate ethical concerns are those that know the nature and stage of a project intimately: the project team itself.

Accordingly, many see the need for ethics education for technologists to convert them into proactive agents of responsible innovation. However, we find that traditional, didactic pedagogical approaches have limited efficacy in a technology context for several reasons. In our experience, ethics education typically starts with an overview of prominent Western moral frameworks. Without illuminating the relevant moral landscape of values and their trade-offs, technologists – who are extremely pressed for time – may quickly disengage as the practical relevance and usefulness of these frameworks is typically not immediately obvious. Relatedly, to apply ethics in technology practice requires skill to flexibly translate moral dimensions into concrete design and technical decisions, not mere awareness of moral frameworks. Finally, while individual ethics education can influence individuals' beliefs, this doesn't guarantee they can successfully convince others of similar beliefs or individually influence technological direction. To achieve these goals, teams need to learn to apply ethical methods to their own technology projects and reason through socially responsive solutions together, as a group.

HOW MORAL IMAGINATION WORKS AT GOOGLE

Over four years of research and experimentation, we created a program called "Moral Imagination" at Google to address the contextual challenges and gaps previously described. The program offers a workshop to any team at Google that requests it that creates a dialogic space for ethical reflection, deliberation, and translation into concrete action. Echoing Werhane, our approach is characterized by a focus on the particular. This section describes how it works on the ground, through goals, methods, and desired outcomes.

GOALS

Our methodology at Google aims to facilitate the development of moral imagination to the following ends:

(1) To facilitate a role obligation shift among teams of technologists. It aims to shift teams' shared mental schemas: from one in which their perceived responsibilities are separate from ethical considerations, to one in which their perceived responsibilities include ethical considerations as an inherent part of the research and development process. To do so, teammates must mutually develop a sense of self-reflective impartiality when evaluating their own work on a specific technology.

(2) To encourage technologists' social capacity for productive ethical discussion and decision-making, as part of their normal workflow. To do so, teammates must be introduced to shared ethical vocabulary, concepts and theories, and collectively gain experience in productive ethical discussion that transcends mere opinions and strongly held views.

(3) To enable proactive responsibility commitments, within a research development process, that are legitimate in the eyes of those involved. To do so, team members must have the opportunity to collaboratively define a set of responsibility objectives, which can instill a sense of shared ownership and even pride even if individuals do not agree on all aspects.

METHODS AND APPROACHES

Our methods aim to create a dialogic space that encourages open and critical engagement with moral considerations of a team's work by the team itself. An important prerequisite is that participants feel psychologically safe enough to express a wide range of perspectives, including those that may be potentially unpopular without fear of censure or reprisal. A facilitator plays a crucial role in cultivating this supportive atmosphere, ensuring equitable participation and respect for all viewpoints regardless of differences in seniority or formal role among the group. The emphasis is always on justifying and defending one's view, opening it up to challenges, and growing self-reflective impartiality toward their own work.

When teams undergo a workshop, most are in the early stages of defining their work on a technology. However, the nature of the technology and the particular attitudes of the team toward it tend to vary significantly. Accordingly, our approach is modular and adaptable. This adaptability allows facilitators to tailor the workshop's flow and activities to suit the specific needs and challenges of each team. This may involve focusing on salient ethical dilemmas, clarifying conceptual ambiguities, or articulating the tensions between competing values in the technology's design. Accounting for these contextual differences, we here describe several key characteristics of our baseline methods.

Priming Participants for Disengagement from Operative Scripts

Over the years we have developed several ways of preparing Google teams to disengage from their current schema, understanding of role responsibility, and cultural norms for the purpose of later reshaping them. A central strategy is to subvert participants' expectations of what a productive corporate workshop entails, and to replace them with new norms of interaction and engagement that are conducive to ethical inquiry.

Participants first notice that the aesthetics of our workshop materials bear no resemblance to Google corporate branding. This is a strong signal to temporarily and deliberately disengage with typical corporate or industry norms. Throughout the workshop we use imagery and graphic design to signal new norms and the quality of participation required for a given moment. For example, reflective exercises are furnished with large scale natural imagery to promote a reflective mood.

Participants also may expect rapid-fire ideation through the use of sticky notes, customary of a Google Design Sprint and similar industry workshops. Typically, in such workshops, quality is thought to emerge through sheer quantity of ideation. However, the early stages of the Moral Imagination workshop emphasize a slower pace, with deliberate time for productive reflection, signaling that quality of thought arises by asking "why?" and thinking deeply behind surface level considerations.

Participants typically expect encouragement to contribute from the standpoint of their professional discipline, not from their personal perspective. In the early stages of this workshop, however, facilitators ask questions such as "why work on this and not something else?" and "assume you're wildly successful, what characteristics would the new, emerging world have?" to signal the importance of the personal intuition on the professional practice, to provide facilitators the means of externalizing existing attitudes toward the work, and to provide participants with important insight into the motivations of their teammates that may influence decision-making.

Facilitators aim to mitigate any preconceived notions about ethicists only raising problems in a non-constructive manner by conveying diplomacy and humility while building epistemic authority (i.e., being a trusted source of knowledge and maintaining credibility as an expert). A successful affective strategy is to use humor to increase engagement and communicate expertise without egotism. Importantly, facilitators must display enough knowledge of technological systems and relevant philosophical discourse to demonstrate how technology design and development can concretely benefit from ethical consideration.

Awareness and Challenge to Prevailing Narratives

> What can we say about the role of narratives? Conditioned, but not determined by background narratives, each of us orders, selects, structures, and even censors all our experiences. These shaping mechanisms are mental models through which we experience the world, and we never see the world except through points of view, models, or framing mechanisms, some of which shape background and other more specific narratives. Indeed, narratives that shape our experience and influence how we think about the world are essential to the coherence of our experiences. As I have just illustrated, some narratives are more closely based on actual experiences; others are

taken from the narratives of others that we accepted as true; still others are closer to fiction. In any case, some narratives influence, dominate, or reshape our thinking about certain events.

(Werhane, 1999, 85)

Recognizing the influence of narratives on our perception of reality, we typically employ two methods to build awareness of and challenge default narratives. The first is a theoretical approach called conceptual analysis or conceptual engineering. The second is an experiential approach called the technomoral scenario or speculative fiction. Both create contexts in which participants are prompted to recognize and then challenge their current mindset and team norms.

Conceptual analysis is a process of making explicit and clarifying underlying values that a team uses to inform their technical design or communication decisions. We designed semi-structured conversations to elicit a diversity of participant attitudes about the underlying values in their work, without biasing responses toward what they may believe are socially sanctioned responses from facilitators or teammates. Facilitators take notes about participant responses. These are then used as a corpus of data from which the group spots the relevant values and determines which are most action-guiding in practice. With top values in hand, participants articulate their concrete meaning and importance in the context of the team's work, and the characteristics of the current technology path that either support or adversely impact these values. By engaging in this process, teams move beyond a minimum-viable approach (i.e., mitigating negative social consequences) and instead specify a positive vision for the technology, its benefits, and its effect on society.

Once existing attitudes are made explicit, a technomoral scenario is deployed to reshape participants' understanding of their work. For each workshop, we try to anticipate which values and attitudes teams are bringing to their work, their ethical blind spots, and the crucial conversations they need to have to meaningfully inform the trajectory of their work. Volunteers at Google work with facilitators to write a bespoke science fiction scenario for each team. Each scenario extrudes the underlying logic of the team's technology and complicates the interplay of technology and society five to ten years in the future. The aim of the scenario is to challenge the intuitions of the participating team, and prompt further information seeking to inform their work. The writing process proactively incorporates points that illustrate the values, needs, and interests of multiple stakeholder groups. We've found it essential that the stories use precise framing narratives to evoke the most critical ethical conversations among a team.

Once the scenario is read aloud, participants engage with the scenario through a mock debate. This activity structures an *experience* to challenge participants' attitudes. Participants role-play various stakeholder perspectives and in so doing, apply ethical vocabulary they've learned in the workshop and grapple with the values embedded within the technological design. The purpose is to a transformative and self-motivated realization about the limits of their own perspectives. This exercise thus builds a shared sense of agency to seek out and act on new information unlikely to have been considered before.

From Mental Acts to Proactive Actions

For an intervention to have practical import among a technology team, these mental acts must be accompanied by concrete implications for action. One useful approach, distinctive in ethics methodology, is to envision *possible worlds*. In the workshop, participants are prompted to engage in a series of thought experiments that imagine the world they are co-creating through the introduction of their technology. They learn to recognize that technologies are mere means and inherently transformative by reshaping human capabilities, their interactions, and how beliefs are formed. Participants are then proactively encouraged to consider the wider impact on this emergent world they are creating.

Once a desirable vision for a future world is articulated (with an awareness of the inherent limitations in predicting future outcomes) participants engage in retroactive reasoning sometimes referred to as "backcasting." This involves critically reflecting on the implications of this envisioned future for present-day responsibilities and technological choices. This is an exercise in creative moral decision-making that necessarily involves reasoning from the particulars of the technological context, and drawing on moral frameworks previously introduced in the workshop. By working backward from a justifiable and defensible possible world, the methodology aims to guide the development of technology in a manner that is aligned with positive ethical aspirations. Discussions are documented as they progress. The resulting artifact functions as a kind of new social contract among the teams, that they can reference again and again in the future.

Translating an abstract vision into a practical plan requires the help of a facilitator. By occupying a liminal state between the philosophical and technological worlds, facilitators flexibly apply knowledge of ethics and the philosophy of technology and effectively tailor discussion to be maximally productive. They also help the team surface relevant moral considerations and reason through them, while pointing out assumptions and areas where more information is needed.

DESIRED OUTCOMES

> Developing moral imagination involves heightened awareness of contextual moral dilemmas and their mental models, the ability to envision and evaluate new mental models that create new possibilities, and the capability to reframe the dilemma and create new solutions in ways that are novel, economically viable, and morally justifiable.
>
> (Werhane, 1999, x)

The Moral Imagination workshop is designed to flexibly achieve the following workshop outcomes. First, the team needs to externalize their current moral intuitions, beliefs, and convictions. By making these explicit, participants can challenge and alter them. Second, we challenge the team's general perspective on their technological artifact. This involves envisioning possibilities for acquiring additional ethically relevant information and incorporating that information into the team's approach and work. Third, we enable the team to reason through ethical perspectives about their work. Once the team has a better understanding of the ethical dimensions of their work, they can deliberate and reason through concrete ethical choice scenarios. Lastly, we empower the team to take action based on their learnings. This involves translating insights into concrete team practices, be it in the code, in the project governance, or in assembling valuable viewpoints that they might have not considered before. In doing so, participants reflect on prior related discussions and articulate ethical focus areas that can inform the technology concept and design in future work.

There is no one-size-fits-all approach to outcome artifacts. Teams are dealing with very specific ethical challenges and their resulting responsibilities will differ in myriad ways. Therefore, facilitators need to be mindful of working toward bespoke outcomes. Examples include elaborate value statements, slide decks to be presented in wider team meetings, new and adjusted objectives and key results (OKRs) for the team, updated user experience research questions, or revised product requirements documents (PRDs) to include the newly gained ethical and responsibility insights. Facilitators work with the team to think through what a valuable set of outcome artifacts might be and proactively work toward them.

After a workshop, the facilitators might work in parallel with the teams of technologists, supporting them over time. They can periodically check with the team during the workshop to see if they are on the right track. Overall, we've found that the Moral Imagination workshop is a valuable tool for helping teams to develop a culture of responsible innovation. By engaging in this process, teams can ensure that their work is aligned with positive ethical aspirations.

REFLECTIONS

Reception at Google

In the early days of developing the program, one prospective participant remarked "Have you been listening in on our team meetings? This is exactly what we've needed!" Over the years our approach has typically been immediately popular with those who only get to know its name ("Moral Imagination"). When they participate in a workshop, their enthusiasm tends to grow as they learn ways of using their agency to meaningfully explore their ethical choice environment with others on their team. One product manager working on Google's machine learning infrastructure remarked he had learned from the moral imagination method to "have great conversations with people needing to think through the ethics of decision making in their organizations." After a workshop, we often hear that various individuals have recommended the program to their colleagues on other teams.

One particularly well received attribute of the approach has been the facilitation of objectives for responsible development of technology. In keeping with the innovative spirit of technology culture, teams have found it useful and motivating to develop a concrete idea of what they are working toward as it relates to responsibility, not merely what they are working against. To our knowledge, this is a unique characteristic among existing responsibility governance interventions.

Perhaps most rewarding has been our consistent ability to convert skeptics. In each workshop, there are typically a few individuals who initially question the relevance of ethics to their work. Often these are technologists who have had prior exposure to ethics. However, as the workshop progresses, these individuals often experience a shift in perspective and become some of the most engaged participants, actively following up and seeking deeper understanding. This impact on individuals' mindsets has demonstrated, each time, that the moral imagination approach is effective in ways beyond improving individual products, but by catalyzing bottom-up culture change in technologists' mindsets at Google.

Approach to Program Development

Working on moral imagination in a context like Google has provided a unique and useful proving ground for repeated experimentation and learning. The scale of the company has enabled access to countless teams that might benefit from the program. With this in mind, we purposefully employed an iterative design process which enabled us to test new content, learn from each workshop, and continuously improve the methodology. Another benefit of the Google environment has been access to valuable multidisciplinary input. Moral Imagination has attracted like-minded collaborators from all over Google, who have been instrumental in fine-tuning the overall structure, content, strategy, and facilitation techniques to be responsive to a team's needs, the general strategy of the company, and the direction of the technology market as a whole. Our diverse team of contributors significantly broadened our capacity for designing content (written and visual), writing technomoral scenarios, adapting to evolving needs, co-facilitating workshops, writing academic papers, and building community of practice across the company. Their diverse expertise and perspectives enriched the program immeasurably and enabled us to scale our efforts more effectively.

Implementation Challenges the Team Faced

Like any initiative in a corporate setting, lack of time is a considerable challenge. Our process of experimentation and revision over the years at Google has largely been aimed at ensuring maximal meaningful progress for teams in minimal time.

Finding the right length of time to suit teams' needs has been a process of continuous refinement. At various times in its development, the workshop has been a twelve-hour experience scheduled across three consecutive days, an eight-hour sprint in a single day, and two-hour chunks across consecutive weeks. We find that too long on a single day and participants can get fatigued by extensive new ideas and ways of thinking. Too long of a total runtime, and teams will simply not be able to carve out the time. As of this writing, we've settled on a standard total length of six-and-a-half hours conducted over two days, with a day in between to allow new ideas to resonate with participants. Teams might also opt to take further modules after engaging in this initial workshop.

Over time we've tended to cut lecture content and instead demonstrate concepts interactively. For example, in the first year of the program's development, participants seemed to highly value lecture content which introduced them to the "why" and "what" of ethics and the philosophy of technology. As facilitators, we also valued it as a means of building epistemic trust with participants. Despite this, eventually we reduced the length, removed the lectures from the body of the workshop, and instead deliver them as a video prior to a workshop. We found that this change was well received, with almost all participants watching the videos with interest and formulating initial ideas for the workshop before it would start.

Much of the workshop proceeds through semi-structured discussion. While we find this format generally works well, its success does depend on the precision and sequence of structured questions, and the manner in which they are conducted. Minor changes to prompts can have dramatic effects on the nature of participants' thought processes and responses. If discussions and activities do not build on one another, participants may lose confidence in workshop structure or facilitators. Over time we've learned to hone our prompts to participants so that they are focused, clear, nuanced, evocative, and clearly built toward a desired and useful end state. We've also experimented with various social mechanisms for discussion and found that plenary discussions are most useful for sharing across a broad number of people, while smaller group discussions are most useful for making quick progress on a topic.

Strategic Challenges We Faced

On the ground we have also faced several challenges which relate to maximizing the impact of the workshop among teams. There appears to be an optimal range for moral imagination work within the early stage of technology development. One challenge is ensuring we are able to target teams that are within this optimal range. Of course, if it is too late in the process, then there are fewer development paths already available to teams and there may be little about the project trajectory that can be changed. However, a team must also have enough of a project idea to act as fodder for ethical deliberation. If the team engages in a workshop while they are still brainstorming options, they may be demotivated by spending too much time evaluating the ethics of an idea that they discard the next day. Ensuring that Google teams who are in the optimal range know about the workshop and are known to us is a difficulty for communications about the program across an extremely large organization. This has only become more challenging as the velocity of tech development has increased significantly since the introduction of AI to the general public in the last few years.

We have conducted variations of the workshop outside this optimal range, intended for educational rather than applied purposes. These have been offered to teams who are in the brainstorming stages of development, or for operational departments that are interested in building their capacity for ethics. The workshops in this context have been well received and useful. However, we also find that their concrete impact may be limited. Afterward, teams may then struggle to concretely apply their learnings to their research or products without further assistance from a facilitator. Individuals who attend from operational teams and later attempt to apply their learnings to a project may face challenges convincing others to broaden their moral imagination and incorporate explicit ethical considerations into their workflow.

Another challenge relates to offering the right format for a moral imagination intervention to the right groups in a changing decision-making context. As we have detailed elsewhere, in the technology industry broadly, development decisions are often negotiated within engineering, product, and research teams. These are largely autonomous, entrepreneurially driven groups that decide which problems are addressed through technology and how, before elevating recommendations to managers and executives. However, the industry's excitement about AI as a new technological medium has dramatically shifted the pace and level of competition in the industry. Organizational decision-making norms are also changing to meet this environment. Moral-imagination interventions should be applied to the locus of decision-making as that evolves. This likely means adapting what we have learned from team workshops to new formats.

LIMITATIONS AND CRITICISM

Limitations

Moral Imagination workshops are not a silver bullet for effective culture change in technology teams. Rather, they should be understood as an important complementary effort among existing organizational culture change mechanisms. For example, since it is aimed at early design stages of technology development teams, it should therefore not be considered as a replacement for ethics review boards that provide important due diligence at other stages of responsible technology development.

Moral Imagination workshops are not an optimal fit for projects whose trajectory is predetermined by others, or whose velocity is so fast that team members are not well positioned to engage with the ethical foundations of the project. In these cases, ethics review boards may be a more suitable mechanism for ethical risk mitigation prior to launch.

Lastly, proactive responsibility objectives generated during a workshop are contextual, which means that if a technology changes significantly, they should be rethought. In this event, the capacity for moral imagination developed during a workshop can aid teams in reevaluating future responsibility goals.

Limitations

Our moral imagination approach has faced several critiques. Some question whether or not moral imagination, and ethics, should be the domain of technologists: Does this really help technologists build better technologies? Shouldn't ethics be the responsibility of ethicists? To these questions, we respond that technologists are already making ethical decisions in their day-to-day work, but these decisions are often not labeled or understood as such. Moral imagination can therefore improve the nature of this decision-making by aligning on the ethical foundations of the work, the responsibilities involved, and driving toward more socially beneficial outcomes explicitly. Ethicists are useful collaborators in this effort and can provide guidance and support.

Others have questioned whether or not the desire to shift technologists' perceived role obligations conflicts with their existing incentives, which typically involve launching products and research quickly. The response to this criticism is that the workshop will lead to a smoother launch process by addressing potential ethical issues ahead of time. The workshop helps technologists build better technology and become more skilled at demonstrating the ethical soundness of their work to others, from ethics review boards to the public. In practice we have observed that teams who undergo moral imagination workshops have had more productive collaborations with ethics reviewers prior to launch.

Finally, some have asked whether the workshop, in particular the technomoral scenario role-play, is a replacement for stakeholder engagement. It is not. By role-playing stakeholder discussions, the intent and frequent outcome is that technologists understand the limits of their own worldview and how that impacts their approach. This would typically manifest in broader user experience research and wider stakeholder discussions.

NEXT CHALLENGE: SCALE AND ADAPTATION

Providing the Moral Imagination workshop for teams is a time and resource intensive exercise. While it is valuable for participating teams, it is difficult to offer this focused and bespoke approach to every single team at a company as large as Google which has hundreds of teams and perhaps thousands of projects. Over the course of developing this approach, we have been challenged various times about how to adapt Moral Imagination so that it is less time and resource intensive. While these are intuitively interesting ideas, the main benefit of the workshop is that facilitator-led deeper thinking and questioning that would be difficult to replicate without a human ethicist in the room.

One option would be to host these workshops at wider team offsites, where executives and possibly all technologists from a part of the company are present. We could focus a workshop not necessarily on their technology, but on their overall strategy and priorities regarding a set of technologies that are key to their organization. After all, strategy and decision-making processes are also, to some extent, mechanisms that can be scrutinized through moral imagination. Once the executives are convinced that this way of thinking and approaching their work is valuable, we discuss what the highest priority teams are that we should work with. This might be a team that develops the core technology, or a team that is particularly influential in setting the norms and governance of the wider organization's work. Focusing in this way increases the likelihood that new ethical insights will ripple across the organization.

A second approach would be an educational program for people who work across the company at the early stages. For example, privacy technologists work with many different teams through their design lifecycle, and lawyers also see the newest ideas emerging. There are various other groups that fall within this category. The training programs we develop are focused on spotting ethical values in the technology design that are, or should be, taken into account. Specifically, we train these colleagues to imagine and reason through human and social value tensions that might result after a technology is launched. By giving these groups the tools to spot when something needs a closer, ethical look, they know when to reach out to the Moral Imagination program at key moments to channel a team into the workshop.

A third approach is to leverage AI tools to guide technologists through a process of critical and constructive self-reflection. Such a process aims to broaden their worldview beyond purely technical considerations, fostering a more holistic approach that encompasses potential societal and human impacts. The use of AI is, of course, not only technically challenging but also requires careful framing to its users. It could be perceived as a replacement for diligent collaboration and discussion of the ethical dimensions of a new technology.

Overall, we think there is not a qualitatively similar replacement for time spent in human deliberation of the ethical dimensions and their resulting responsibilities that a technology team ought to go through. The end goal of a moral imagination approach in technology development is a mindset shift from optimizing for engineering values (speed, efficiency, elegance of code, etc.) to seeing technology more as a means to bring about a better world, where the optimized values are human and social in nature. This is likely hard to achieve with an approach that scales well, as it diminishes the multidisciplinary attention to individual dilemmas and considerations.

CONCLUSION

In this chapter, we demonstrated how we've adapted the idea and methods of moral imagination within the realm of technology development. Drawing inspiration from Werhane's insightful work, we illustrated how her conception of moral imagination can be effectively applied to navigate the unique ethical challenges presented by emerging technologies.

Werhane's influence is evident throughout our exploration of several key themes. For example, we emphasized how narratives shape our understanding of technology and its potential implications, stressing the need for critical reflection on the stories we tell ourselves about technological progress. This cannot be achieved without cultivating a sense of self-reflective impartiality in the individual technologist and the team as a whole, when evaluating ethical dilemmas, recognizing the limitations of our own perspectives and biases. As technologists progress through the workshop, they learn to appreciate what creative moral decision-making can bring to their own work. This empowers technologists to envision and evaluate alternative solutions that may not be immediately apparent.

A key lesson has been to develop the ability to critically evaluate the status quo mindset within which technology is built, and to explore new possibilities by developing a mindset that challenges assumptions and explores alternative paths. As technologists learn to use their ethical muscles, they appreciate the need to justify technical decisions with ethical arguments, ensuring that technological advancements are grounded in sound moral reasoning and justification. Finally, we recognized the power of the moral imagination methods to help revise operative scripts and norms that dominate technology cultures, and to promote a shift toward more responsible and ethical practices.

Overall, the Moral Imagination workshop has proven to be an effective approach for contributing to a culture of responsible innovation within Google. It is hard to overstate the degree of enthusiasm for this approach among technologists on the ground within the company. By engaging in this process, individuals and teams have found a way to connect their best intentions with their day-to-day decision-making.

Our success in implementing the Moral Imagination workshop at Google demonstrates the continued usefulness of Werhane's ideas in the twenty-first century in the rapidly evolving field of technology and AI. We are eager to continue refining and expanding this approach, exploring new modalities, affordances, and applications. As philosophers and technology ethicists, this work has profoundly influenced how we think about our own work, what we want to achieve, and our understanding of how philosophical inquiry can make a tangible impact in the world. We celebrate Werhane's contributions to the field and look forward to seeing her ideas continue to shape the development and deployment of AI for the betterment of all. We will, for sure, be an active part of that community.

References

Alam, A. 2024. "Everything You Need to Know about Poverty in Bangladesh." *The Borgen Project*. November 1. https://borgenproject.org/about-poverty-in-bangladesh/.

Allison, B. 2022. "FTX US Donated $1 Million to a Super-PAC Aligned with Mitch McConnell in October." *Bloomberg News*. November 25. www.bloomberg.com/news/articles/202211-25/ftx-mcconnell-bankman-fried-super-pac-donation.

Anderson, B. [1983] 2006. *Imagined Communities: Reflections on the Origin and Spread of Nationalism*, rev. ed. London: Verso.

Andre, J. 1991. "Role Morality as a Complex Instance of Ordinary Morality." *American Philosophical Quarterly*, 28: 73–80.

Anscombe. G. E. M. 1976. "The Question of Linguistic Idealism," in "Essays on Wittgenstein in Honour of G. H. Yon Wright," ed. J. Hintikka, special issue, *Acta Philosophica Fennica*, 28: 181–215.

AP News. 2024. "Key Events in the Troubled History of the Boeing 737 Max." July 8. https://apnews.com/article/boeing-plea-737-max-crashes-b34daa014406657e720bec4a990dcc.

Appiah, K. A. 2007. *Cosmopolitanism: Ethics in a World of Strangers*. London: Penguin.

Arendt, H. 1963. *Eichmann in Jerusalem*. New York: Viking Press.

Atiyeh, C. 2016. "Everything You Need to Know about the VW Emissions Diesel Scandal." *Car and Driver*. May 11. http://blog.caranddriver.com/everything-you-need-to-knowabout-the-vw-diesel-emissions-scandal/.

Averill, L., Durkin, B., Chu, M., Ougradar, U., and Reeves, A. 2022. "Deepwater Horizon Disaster." *Loss Prevention Bulletin (Institute of Chemical Engineers)*, 285: 7–12. www.icheme.org/media/18486/lpb285_pg07.pdf.

Bacon, K. H. and Salwen, K. 1991. "Summer of Financial Scandals Raises Question about the Abilities of Regulators to Police Markets." *Wall Street Journal*. August 28, A10.

Banerjee, S. B. 2018. "Transnational Power and Translocal Governance: The Politics of Corporate Responsibility." *Human Relations*, 71(6): 796–821.

Banerjee, S. B., Chio, V. C. M., and Mir, R., eds. 2009. *Organizations, Markets and Imperial Formations*. Cheltenham. Edward Elgar.

Bates, A. 2024. Post Office Horizon, Public Inquiry, London, England. https://postofficeinquiry.dracos.co.uk/phases-5-6/2024-04-09/#alan-bates.

Baumann, Z. 1993. *Postmodern Ethics*. Oxford: Blackwell.

Bayer. 2024. "Human Rights/Bayer Global." October 21. https://release.ace.bayer.com/sites/default/files/2020-04/bayer-human-rights-policy.pdf.

Bazerman, M., and Tenbrunsel, A. 2011. *Blind Spots*. Princeton, NJ: Princeton University Press.

Bebeau, M. 1994. "Influencing the Moral Dimensions of Dental Practice." In J. Rest and D. Narvaez, eds., *Moral Development in the Professions*. Hillsdale, NJ: Lawrence Erlbaum. 121–146.

Beidelman, T. O. 1986. *Moral Imagination in Kaguru Modes of Thought*. Bloomington: Indiana University Press.

Bell, T. E., and Esch, K. 1989. "The Fatal Flaw in Flight 51-L." *IEEE Spectrum*, 24: 36–51.

Belmont Report. 1979. Washington, DC: Department of Health, Education and Welfare. www.hhs.gov/ohrp/regulations-and-policy/belmontreport/read-the belmont-report/index.html.

Bentham, J. [1789] 1948. *An Introduction to the Principles of Morals and Legislation*. New York: Hafner.

Berger, P., and Luckmann, T. 1966. *The Social Construction of Reality*. New York: Doubleday & Co.

Bergson, H. [1889] 1910. *Time and Free Will: An Essay on the Immediate Data of Consciousness*, trans. F. L. Pogson. London: George Allen & Unwin.

Bettis, R., and Prahalad, C. K. 1995. "The Dominant Logic: Retrospective and Extension." *Strategic Management Journal*, 16: 5–14.

Bevan, D. 2019. "Systems Thinking." In D. Bevan, P. Werhane, and R. W. Wolfe, eds., *Systems Thinking and Moral Imagination: Rethinking Business Ethics with Patricia Werhane*. Dordrecht: Springer. 183–186. https://doi.org/10.1007/978-3-319-89797-4.

2024. *An Introduction to Secular Process Philosophy*. Valetta, Malta: Philosophy Sharing.

Bevan, D., and Werhane, P. H. 2015. "The Inexorable Sociality of Commerce: The Individual and Others in Adam Smith." *Journal of Business Ethics*, 127(2): 327–336.

2021. "Management, Political Philosophy, and Colonial Interference." *Journal of Philosophy of Management*. https://doi.org/10.1007/s40926-021-00187-9.

2022. "Adam Smith, the Enlightenment, and His Relevance for the 21st Century." *Dialogue and Universalism*, 32(1): 19–32.

2024. "Reformulating the Western Paradigm of Global Capitalism." In *Pava and Dion. Justifying Next Stage Capitalism*. Dordrecht: Springer.

Blake, W. [1832] 1877. *Jerusalem: The Emanation of the Giant Albion*. Pearson (Internet Archive). https://archive.org/details/jerusalememanati00blak/page/55/.

Bloomberg Intelligence. 2016. "VW Sees 10 Million Deliveries in 2014 on 100-Model Push." www.bloomberg.com/news/articles/2014-03-13/vw-sees-10-million-deliveries-in-2014-on-100-model-push.

Boeing.com. 2018. "Boeing Board Raises Dividend 20 Percent Increases Share Repurchase Authorization to 20 Billion," December 17. https://boeing.mediaroom.com/2018-12-17BoeingBoard-Raiss-Dividend-20-Percent-IncreasesShare-Repurchase-Authorization-to-20-Billion.

2019. "Lion's Share: Lion Air Orders 201 737 MAXs and 29 Next-Generation 737900s." www.boeing.com/commercial/customers/lionair/orders-lions-share-737-max.

2024. Annual Report. www.boeing.com/content/dam/boeing/boeingdotcom/company/annual-report/2024/2024-annual-report.pdf.

Boesky, I. 1986. Commencement Address, Haas School of Management, University of California. May 18.

Boffey, D. 2024. "Alan Bates Tells Post Office Inquiry Ministers Tried to Sabotage His Claim." *The Guardian*. April 9. www.theguardian.com/uk-news/2024/apr/09/alanbates-tells-inquiry-post-office-spent-decades-lying-and-trying-to-discredit-me.

Bollier, D. 1996. *Aiming Higher*. New York: American Management Association.

Boltanski, L., and Chiapello, E. 2006. *The New Spirit of Capitalism*, trans. G. Elliot. London: Verso.

Bornstein, D. 1996. *The Price of a Dream*. New York: Simon & Schuster.

Boston, W. 2015. "Volkswagen Emissions Investigation Zeroes in on Two Engineers." *Wall Street Journal*. October 5.

Bowler, T. 2015. "Volkswagen: From the Third Reich to Emissions Scandal." BBC. October 2. www.bbc.com/news/business-34358783.

Box, G. E. P. 1976. "Science and Statistics." *Journal of the American Statistical Association*, 1(356), 791–799.

Brann, E. T. H. 1991. *The World of the Imagination: Sum and Substance*. Totowa, i'U: Rowman and Littlefield.

Brink, D. 1989. *Moral Realism and the Foundations of Ethics*. Cambridge: Cambridge University Press.

Burger, J. 2007. "The Science of Evil." ABC Instincts. April 26.

2009. "Replicating Milgram: Would People Still Obey Today?" *American Psychologist*, 64(1): 1–1.

Byrne, J. A. 1995. "Informed Consent." *Business Week*. October 2, 104–116.

———. 1996. *Informed Consent: A Story of Personal Tragedy and Corporate Betrayal*. New York: McGraw-Hill.

Callahan, J., ed. 1988. *Ethical Issues in Professional Life*. New York: Oxford University Press.

Cameron, D., and Tangel, A. 2020. "Boeing Posts Full-Year Loss amid 737 MAX Setbacks." *Wall Street Journal*. January 29. www.wsj.com/articles/boeing-falls-to-fullyear-loss115803020912019.

Carroll, A. 1987. "In Search of the Moral Manager." *Business Horizons*, 30: 7–25.

Cassirer, E. 1932. *Die Philosophie der Aufklärung*, trans. F. C. A. Koelln and J. P. Pettegrove. Tübingen: Mohr Verlag.

Castoriadis, C. 1975. *L'institution imaginaire de la société*. Paris: Editions du Seuil.

Chambers, T. 1996. "From an Ethicist's Point of View: The Literary Nature of Ethical Inquiry." *Hastings Center Report*, 26: 25–33.

Chang, A. 2024. "Nearly All FTX Customers Are Getting Their Money Back: What to Know." *Los Angeles Times*. May 9. www.latimes.com/business/story/2024-05-09/ftx-cryto-moneyback.

Chappell, B. 2020. "Boeing 737 Max Completes 1st U.S. Commercial Flight since It Was Grounded." National Public Radio. December 29. www.npr.org/2020/12/29/951134212/boeing-737-maxcompletes-first-u-s-commercial-flight-since-it-was-grounded.

Chokshi, N. 2020. "Boeing 737 Max Is Cleared by F.A.A. to Fly Again." *New York Times*. www.nytimes.com/2020/11/18/business/boeing-737max-faa.html.

Chomsky, N. 1965. *Aspects of the Theory of Syntax*. Cambridge, MA: MIT Press.

Churchland, P. 1989. *A Neurocomputational Perspective*. Cambridge, MA: MIT Press.

Ciulla, J. 1998. "Imagination, Fantasy, Wishful Thinking and Truth." *Business Ethics Quarterly*, Ruffin series of the Society for Business Ethics, 1: 99–107.

Cohan, P. 2019. "Did Airbus Rivalry Drive Dangerous Tradeoffs for Boeing's 737 Max?" *New York Times*, March 28. www.forbes.com/sites/petercohan/2019/03/28/did-airbus-rivlry-drive-dangeroustradeoffs-for-boeings-737-max/?sh=7f0035462e18.

Coleridge, Samuel Taylor. [1907] 1973. *Biographia Literaria*, Volumes 1 and 2. Ed. J. Shawcross. London: Oxford University Press.

Cunningham, Brian. 1999. "Eskom and the South African Electrification Program" (University of Virginia Darden School Case Bank, Charlottesville), UVA E 0162.

Cunningham, T. 2019. Film interview of a Maasai tribe in Uganda with Tom Cunningham for a series, Big Questions. March. www.bqqnow.com.

Dancy, R.M. 1983. "Alien Concepts." *Syntheses*, 56: 283–300.

Daniels, Nonsan. 1979. "Wide Reflective Equilibrium and Theory Acceptance in Ethics." *Journal of Philosophy*. 76: 256–281.

Davidson, Donald. 1974. "On the Very Idea of a Conceptual Scheme." *Proceedings and Addresses of the American Philosophical Association*, 47: 5–20.

Davis, Michael. 1987. "Why Engineers Should Support Their Profession's Code." Speech to the Society of Hispanic Professional Engineers. June 10.

 1989. "Explaining Wrongdoing." *Journal of Social Philosophy*, 20: 74–90.

Deloitte. 2021. Fortune 1000 codes of ethics. www.deloitte.com/fortune1000codesofethics.

Derry, Robbin. 1989. "An Empirical Study of Moral Reasoning Among Managers." *Journal of Business Ethics*, 8: 855–862.

Dewey, John. 1920. *Reconstruction in Philosophy*. New York: Henry Holt and Company.

 1920. *Reconstruction in Philosophy*. New York: Henry Holt and Company.

 1922. *Human Nature and Conduct*. New York: Henry Holt and Company.

 [1932] 2005. *Art and Experience*. New York: Perigee Books.

Dhanaraj, C., Branzei, O., and Subamarian, S. 2010a. "Bayer CropScience I India (A): Against Child Labor." Richard Ivey School of Business Foundation Case # 910M61-PDF-ENG.

 2010b. "Bayer CropScience in India (B) Values and Strategy." Richard Ivey School of Business Foundation Case # 910M62-PDF-ENG.

Dhanaraj, C., and Khanna, T. 2011. "Transforming Mental Models in Emergence Markets." *Academy of Management Learning and Education*, 10: 684–701.

Diamond, Cora. 1991. "Missing the Adventure." *The Realistic Spirit*. Cambridge, MA: MIT Press. 309–318.

Doherty, Ben. July 20, 2021. "After 32 Years, Rio Tinto to Fund Study of the Environmental Damage Caused by Panguna Mine." *The Guardian*. www.theguardian.com/world/2021/jul/21/after-32-years-rio-tinto-to-fund-study-ofenvironmental-damage-caused-by-panguna-mine.

Donaldson, Thomas. 1989a. *The Ethics of International Business*. New York: Oxford University Press.

 1989b. "Moral Minimums for Multinationals." *Ethics and International Affairs*, 3: 163–182.

Douglass, F. 1857. "West India Emancipation." Speech given August 3, 1857. Canandaigua, NY.

Downie, R. S. 1971. *Roles and Values*. London: Methuen.

Drumwright, M. E., and Murphy, P. E. 2004. "How Advertising Practitioners View Ethics: Moral Muteness, Moral Myopia, and Moral Imagination." *Journal of Advertising*, 33(2): 7–24.

Earl, Peter. 1983. *The Economic Imagination*. Brighton, England: Wheatsheaf.

 1984. *The Corporate Imagination*. Armonk, NY: M. E. Sharpe.

Ehrnström-Fuentes, Maria. 2016. "Delinking Legitimacies: A Pluriversal Perspective on Political CSR." *Journal of Management Studies*, 53(3): 433–462.

Emanuel, Linda. 2000. "Ethics and the Structures of Health Care." *Cambridge Quarterly*, 9: 151–168.

Emmet, Dorothy. 1966. *Rules, Roles and Relation*. New York: St. Martin's Press.

Englehardt, E., Werhane, P., and Newton, L. 2021. "Leadership, Engineering and Ethical Clashes at Boeing." *Science and Engineering Ethics*, 27: 11–17.

Environmental Protection Agency. 2014. "Clean Act Overview." www.epa.gov/clean-air-act-overview/progress-cleaning-air-and-improving-peoples-health.

Ermarth, E. 1991. *Sequel to History*. Princeton, NJ: Princeton University Press.

Escobar, A. 2001. "Culture Sits in Places: Reflections on Globalism and Subaltern Strategies of Localization." *Political Geography*, 20: 139–174.

 2008. *Territories of Difference: Place Movements, Life, Redes*. Durham, NC: Duke University Press.

Espiner, T. 2024. "Alan Bates Says Post Office Was Run by 'Thugs in Suits.'" www.bbc.co.uk/news/business-68769090.

Ewing, J. 2016. "Volkswagen CEO Martin Winterkorn Resigns amid Emissions Scandal," *New York Times*, September 23. www.nytimes.com/2015/09/24/business/international/volkswagen-chief-martinwinterkorn-resigns-amid-emissions-scandal.html.

Ewing, J., and Bowley, G. 2015. "The Engineering of Volkswagen's Aggressive Ambition." *New York Times*. December 13. www.nytimes.com/2015/12/14/business/the-engineering-ofvolkswagens-aggressive-ambition.html.

Ewing, J., and Tabuchi, H. 2016. "VW's U.S. Diesel Settlement Clears Just One Financial Hurdle." *New York Times*. June 28. www.nytimes.com/2016/06/29/business/vw-dieselemissions-us-settlement.html.

Extinction Rebellion. 2021. "This Is an Emergency." https://rebellion.global/.

Fesmire, S. 2003. *John Dewey and Moral Imagination: Pragmatism in Ethics*. Bloomington, IN: Indiana University Press.

Feynman, R. 1988. *What Do You Care What Other People Think?* New York: W. W. Norton.

Fidelity Investments. 2024. "What Is Crypto?" Fidelity. https://tinyurl.com/5n8hemkv.

Fidelity. 2024. "What Is Crypto?" Fidelity. www.fidelity.com/learning-center/tradinginvesting/what-is-crypto.

Flinders, K. 2024. "Post Office Horizon Scandal Explained: Everything You Need to Know." *Computer Weekly*. November, 24. www.computerweekly.com/feature/PostOffice-Horizon-scandal-explained-everything-you-need-to-know.

Foroohar, R. 2022. *Homecoming: The Path to Prosperity in a Postglobal World*. New York, NY: Crown.

Freeman, R. Edward. 1994. "The Politics of Stakeholder Theory: Some Future Directions." *Business Ethics Quarterly*, 4: 409–422.

    1999, "Stakeholder Theory and the Modern Corporation." In T. Donaldson and P. Werhane, eds., *Ethical Issues in Business*, 6th ed. Upper Saddle River, NJ: Prentice-Hall. 247–257.

French, Peter. 1979. "The Corporation as a Moral Person." *American Philosophical Quarterly*. 16: 207–215.

Friedman, Marilyn. 1993. *What Are Friends For?* Ithaca, NY: Cornell University Press.

Friedman, Milton. [1962] 2002. *Capitalism and Freedom*. London: The University of Chicago Press.

Friedman, Tom. 1999. *The Lexus and the Olive Tree*. New York: Farrar, Straus and Giroux.

FTX Trading. 2022. Chapter 11. Case No. 22-11068. November 22.

Galston, William. 1991. *Liberal Purposes*. Cambridge: Cambridge University Press.

Gates, D. 2019. "Why Boeing's Emergency Directions May Have Failed to Save 737 MAX." *The Seattle Times*, April 3. www.seattletimes.com/business/boeing-aerospace/boeings-emergency-procedure-for-737max-may-have-failed-on-ethiopianflight/#:~:text=First%2C%20the%20original%20MCAS%20design,doomed%20the%20Ethiopian%20Airlines%20jet.

    2020. "Boeing Reports Worst Full-Year Loss in Its History, but CEO Calhoun Vows 'We'll Get through It'." *The Seattle Times*. January 29. www.seattletimes.com/business/boeing-aerospace/boeing-doubles-the-projected-costofthe-737-MAX-groundingto-18-4-billion/.

Gates, Gilbert, Ewing, Jack, Russell, Karl, and Watkins, Derek. 2016. "Explaining Volkswagen's Emissions Scandal." *New York Times*. June 1. www.nytimes.com/interactive/2015/business/international/vw-diesel-emissions-scandalexplained.html?_r=0.

Geertz, Clifford. 1973. *The Interpretation of Cultures*. New York: Basic Books.

    1983. *Local Knowledge*. New York: Basic Books.

Gelles, D. 2020. "Boeing's 737 Max Is a Saga of Capitalism Gone Awry." *New York Times*. November 24. www.nytimes.com/2020/11/24/sunday-review/boeing-737-max.html.

Gentner, Dedre, and Whitley, Eric W. 1997. "Mental Models of Population Growth." In Max H. Bazerman, David M. Messick, Ann E. Tenbrunsel, and Kimberley A. Wade-Benzoni, eds., *Environment, Ethics, and Behavior*. San Francisco: New Lexington Press.

Gert, Bernard. 1987. *Morality*. New York: Oxford University Press.

Gilligan, Carol. 1982. *In a Different Voice*. Cambridge, MA: Harvard University Press.

―――. 1986. "Symbols, Scripts, and Sensemaking." In H. P. Sims, Jr., and Dennis Gioia, eds., *The Thinking Organization*. San Francisco: Jossey-Bass. 49–74.

Gioia, Dennis. 1986. "Symbols, Scripts, and Sensemaking." In Sims, H. P., Jr., and Gioia, D. eds., *The Thinking Organization*. San Francisco: Jossey-Bass. 49–74.

―――. 1992. "Pinto Fires and Personal Ethics." *Journal of Business Ethics*, 34: 675–689.

Gioia, Dennis, and Pitre, Evelyn. 1990. "Multiparadigm Perspectives on Theory Building." *Academy of Management Review*, 15: 584–602.

Gioia, Dennis, and Poole, P. P. 1984. "Scripts in Organizational Behavior." *Academy of Management Review*. 9: 449–459.

Goffman, Erving. 1961. *Encounters: Two Studies in the Sociology of Interaction*. Indianapolis: Bobbs-Merrill.

Goldman, Alan. 1980. *The Moral Foundations of Professional Ethics*. Totowa, NJ: Rowman and Littlefield.

Goldstein, M., and Meier, B. 2014. "As Scandal Unfolds, G.M. Calls in the Lawyers." March 16. www.nytimes.com/2014/03/16/business/general-motors calls-the-lawyers.html.

Gombrich, E. H. 1961. *Art and Illusion*. Princeton, NJ: Princeton University Press.

Gorman, Michael. 1992. *Simulating Science*. Bloomington: Indiana University Press.

Greenwood, J. "How Would People Behave in Milgram's Experiment Today?" *Behavioral Scientist*. https://behavioralscientist.org/how-would-people-behave-in-milgrams-experiment-today/.

Griggs, R. A. 2016. "Milgram's Obedience Study: A Contentious Classic Reinterpreted." *Teaching of Psychology*, 44: 32–37.

Guroian, Vigen. 1996. "Awakening the Moral Imagination." *Intercollegiate Review*. 32: 3–13.

Hakim, D., Kessler, A., and Ewing, J. 2015. "As Volkswagen Pushed to Be No. 1, Ambitions Fueled a Scandal." *New York Times*. September 26. www.nytimes.com/2015/09/27/business/as-vw-pushed-to-be-no-1-ambitions-fueled-ascan dal.html.

Hardimon, Michael. 1994. "Role Obligations." *Journal of Philosophy*, 91: 333–363.
Hardyment, Richard. 2015. "CSR after Volkswagen Scandal." *TriplePundit*. October 28. www.triplepundit.com/2015/10/csr-volkswagen-scandal/.
Harre, Rom, ed. 1986. *The Social Construction of Emotions*. Oxford: Oxford University Press.
Harris, C. E., Pritchard, M., James, R., Englehardt, E., and Rabins, M. 2019. *Engineering Ethics: Concepts and Cases*. 6th ed. Boston, MA: Cengage.
Hashimzade, N., Myles, G., and J. Black. 2017. "Globalization." In Hashimzade, N., Myles, G., and J. Black, eds., *Oxford Dictionary of Economics*, 5th ed. Oxford: Oxford University Press.
Heisenberg, Werner. [1932] 1959. *Physics and Philosophy*. London: George Allen & Unwin.
Himmelfarb, Gertrude. 1991. *Poverty and Compassion: The Moral Imagination of the Late Victorians*. New York: Knopf.
Hobbes, T. [1651] 1968. *Leviathan*. London: Penguin Classics.
Holusha, J. 1996. "Pulp Mills Turn over a New Leaf." *New York Times*, March 9, A35–37.
Huang, V., Osipovich, A., and Kowsmann, P. 2022. "FTX Tapped Into Cintomer Accounts to Fund Risky Bets, Setting Up Its Downfall." *Wall Street Journal*. November 11. www.wsj.com/articles/ftx-tapped-into-customer-accounts-to-fund-risky-bets-setting-up-its-downfall-1166809373.
Huxley, A. [1958] 1965. *Brave New World Revisited*. New York: Harper and Row.
Irwin, Eleanor. 1974. *Colour Terms in Early Greek Poetry*. Toronto: A. M. Hakkert.
Isidore, C., and Goldman, D. 2016. "Volkswagen Agrees to Record $14.7 Billion Settlement over Emissions Cheating." *CNN Money*. June 28. http://money.cnn.com/2016/06/28/news/companies/volkswagen-fine/.
Jackson, Norman, and Carter, Pippa. 1991. "In Defense of Paradigm Incommensurability." *Organization Studies*, 12: 109–127.
James, Henry. 1934. *The Art of the Novel*. New York: Scribner's.
Janis, I. L. 1982. *Groupthink*. Boston: Houghton and Mifflin.
Johnson, Mark. 1985. "Imagination in Moral Judgment." *Philosophy and Phenomenological Research*, 46: 265–280.
    1993. *Moral Imagination*. Chicago: University of Chicago Press.
Johnsson, J., Beene, R., and Bloomberg News. 2020. "'Designed by Clowns … Supervised by Monkeys': Internal Boeing Messages Slam 737 MAX." *Fortune*. January 10. https://fortune.com/2020/01/10/designed-clowns-supervised-monkeys-internalboeing-messagesslam-737-MAX/.
Kamm, Judith. 1993. "Ethics Officers Gaining Acceptance at Many Firms, Survey Reveals." *Ethikos*. January/February, 7–12.

Kant, I. 1784. "Answering the Question: What Is Enlightenment? (Beantwortung der Frage: Was ist Aufklärung?)." *Berlinische Monatsschrift.* December: 36–43.

[1790] 1951. *Critique of Judgment,* trans. J. H. Bernard. New York: Hafner.

[1784] 1959. *The Foundations of the Metaphysics of Morals,* trans. Lewis White Beck. Indianapolis: Bobbs-Merrill.

[1781] 1970. *Critique of Pure Reason,* trans. Norman Kemp Smith. London: Macmillan.

[1789] 1985. *The Critique of Practical Reason,* trans. Lewis White Beck. New York: Macmillan.

Kedrosky, Paul. 2015. "An Engineering Theory of the Volkswagen Scandal." *New Yorker.* October. www.newyorker.com/business/currency/anengineering-theory-of-the-volkswagen-scandal.

Kekes, John. 1991. "Moral Imagination, Freedom, and the Humanities." *American Philosophical Quarterly,* 28: 101–111.

1993. *The Morality of Pluralism.* Princeton, NJ: Princeton University Press.

Kelly, G. A. 1955. *The Psychology of Personal Constructs.* New York: Norton.

Kitroeff, N. 2020. "Boeing Employees Mocked F.A.A. and 'Clowns' Who Designed 737 MAX." *New York Times.* January 10. www.nytimes.com/2020/01/09/business/boeing-737messages.html?searchResultPosition=1.

Kitroeff, N., and Gelles, D. 2020. "In Reversal, Boeing Recommends 737 MAX Simulator Training for Pilots." *New York Times.* January 7. www.nytimes.com/2020/01/07/business/boeing-737-MAX-simulator-training.html.

Kohlberg, Lawrence. 1969. "Stage and Sequence: The Cognitive-Development Approach to Socialization." In D. A. Goslin, ed., *Handbook of Socialization Theory and Research.* Chicago: Rand-McNally. 347–380.

1981. *Philosophy of Mural Development: Moral Stages and the Idea of Justice.* San Francisco: Harper & Row.

Kohlberg, Lawrence, Levine, Charles, and Hewer, Alexandra. 1983. "Moral Stages: A Current Formulation and a Response to Critics." *Human Development,* 10: 174.

Kuhn, Thomas. [1962] 1970. *The Structure of Scientific Revolutions.* Chicago: University of Chicago Press.

Kurosawa, A. 1950. *Rashômon.* In D. M. P. Company Production. Tokyo: Daiei Motion Picture Company/ RKO Radio Pictures.

Langer, Suzanne. [1942] 1951. *Philosophy in a New Key.* Cambridge, MA: Harvard University Press.

Langewiesche, W. 2019. "System Crash." *New York Times Magazine.* September 29, 36–45; 57–66.

Larmore, Charles. 1981. "Moral Judgment." *Review of Metaphysics,* 35: 275–296.

Laszlo, Alexander, and Krippner, Stanley. 1998, "Systems Theories: Their Origins, Foundations and Development." In J. Scott Jordan, ed., *Systems Theories and a Priori Aspects of Perception*. Amsterdam: Elsevier. 47–74.

Lawrence, D., Elgin, B., and Silver, V. 2015. "How Could Volkswagen's Top Engineers Not Have Known?" *Bloomberg Businessweek*. October 21. www.bloomberg.com/news/articles/2015-10-21/how-could-volkswagen-s-top-engineersnot-have-known-.

Leaning, J. 1993. "German Doctors and Their Secrets." *New York Times*. February 6. www.nytimes.com/1993/02/06/opinion/german-doctors-and-their-secrets.html.

Levin, B. 2019. "737 Report: Boeing Trained 737 MAX Pilots on IPADS to Save Cash." *Vanity Fair*. March 18. www.vanityfair.com/news/2019/03/boeing-trained737-MAX-pilotsonipads-to-save-cash.

Levin, D. 2015. "The Man who Created VW's Toxic Culture Still Looms Large." *Fortune*. October 16. http://fortune.com/2015/10/16/vw-ferdinand-piechculture/.

Levinas Immanuel. 1979. *Totality and Infinity*, trans. Alphonso Lingis. The Hague: Nijhoff.

Lewis, Michael. 1989. *Liar's Poker*. New York: W. W. Norton.

2023a. *Going Infinite*. New York. W. W. Norton.

2023b. "Play It Again, Sam." *The Washington Post*. October 1. www.washingtonpost.com/opinions/interactive/2023/michael-lewis-sam-bankman-friedftx-crypto/.

Li, A. H. 2022. "From Alien Land to Inalienable Parts of China: How Qing Imperial Possessions Became the Chinese Frontiers." *European Journal of International Relations*, 28(2): 237–262. https://doi.org/10.1177/13540661221086486.

Lovibond, Sabina. 1983. *Realism and Imagination in Ethics*. Oxford: Basil Blackwell.

Luban, David. 1988. *Lawyers and Justice*. Princeton, NJ: Princeton University Press.

Lucas, Amelia. 2022. "McDonald's Temporarily Closes 850 Restaurants in Russia, Nearly 2 Weeks after Putin's Forces Invaded Ukraine." CNBC. Englewood Cliffs, NJ: CNBC LCC (NBCUniversal). www.cnbc.com/2022/03/08/mcdonalds-will-temporarilyclose-850-restaurants-in-russia-nearly-2-weeks-after-putin-invaded-ukraine.html.

Lynch, Luann, Elizabeth Bird and Cameron Curto. 2018. "The Volkswagen Emissions Scandal." Darden Business Publishing Case UVA S-267. Charlottesville, Virginia.

Lyotard, J.-F. 1979. *La Condition postmoderne: rapport sur le savoir*. Paris: Les Editions de Minuit.

"The Maasai." http://maasaiwilderness.org/maasai/.

MacGillis, A. 2019. "The Case against Boeing: Since Samya Stumo's Death in a 737 MAX Crash, Her Parents and Her Great-Uncle, Ralph Nader, Have Devoted Themselves to Proving the Company Put Profit over Safety." *The New Yorker*. November 11. www.newyorker.com/magazine/2019/11/18/the-case-against-boeing.

Macintyre, Alasdair. 1981. *After Virtue*. Notre Dame, IN: Notre Dame University Press.

Makkreel, Rudolf. 1990. *Imagination and Interpretation in Kant*. Chicago: University of Chicago Press.

Marx, K. [1867] 1992. *Capital: A Critique of Political Economy*. London: Penguin.

May, Larry. 1996. *The Responsive Self*. Chicago: University of Chicago Press.

McCloskey, D. 2006. *The Bourgeois Virtues: Ethics for an Age of Commerce*. Chicago: University of Chicago Press.

2012. *Factual Free-Market Fairness*. http://bleedingheartlibertarians.com/2012/06/factual-free-market-fairness/.

McCollough, Thomas. 1991. *The Moral Imagination and the Public Life*. Chatham, NJ: Chatham House.

McCulloch, Adam. 2024. "The Post Office Horizon Scandal: An Explainer." *Personnel Today*, June 20. www.personneltoday.com/?s=post+office.

McHugh C. 2023. "Did Sam Bankman-Fried Just End the Era of the Boy Genius?" *Politico*, February 10. www.politico.com/news/.

Messick, David, and Bazerman, Max. 1996. "Ethical Leadership and the Psychology of Decision Making." *Sloan Management Review*, 37: 9–23.

Mignolo, W. 2011. *The Daker Side of Western Modernity*. Durham, NC: Duke University Press.

Mignolo, W., and Walsh, C., eds. 2018. "Introduction." *On Decoloniality: Concepts, Analytics, Praxis*. Durham NC: Duke University Press.

Milgram, Stanley. 1969. *Obedience to Authority*. New York: Harper & Row.

Miller, J., and Page, S. E., 2007. *Complex Adaptive Systems*. Princeton: Princeton University Press.

Mitchell, Russell, and O'Neal, Michael. 1994. "Managing by Values." *Business Week*. August 1, 46–52.

Mitroff, Ian I., and Linstone, Harold. 1993. *The Unbounded Mind*. New York: Oxford University Press.

Moberg, D. 2000. "Ethical Blind Spots in Organizations: How Systematic Errors in Person Perception Undermine Moral Agency." *Organizational Studies*, 27: 413–428.

Moberg, Dennis, and Seabright, Mark. 2000. "The Development of Moral Imagination." *Business Ethics Quarterly*, 10, 845–884.

More, T. [1516] 2020. *Utopia*. London: Penguin Classics.

Morrow, Allison. 2023. "Sam Bankman-Fried Found Guilty of Seven Counts of Fraud in Stunning Fall for Former Crypto Billionaire." CNN. November 2. www.cnn.com/2023/11/02/business/ftx-sbf-fraud-trial-verdict/index.html.

Morton. B. 2022 "McDonald's to Leave Russia for Good after 30 Years." BBC News. May 17. www.bbc.co.uk/news/business-61463876.

Murdoch, I. 1969. *The Nice and the Good*. London: Penguin Books.

1971. *The Sovereignty of Good*. London: Ark.

Mutter, Joann. 2013. "Volkswagen's Million to Dominate the Global Auto Industry Gets Noticeably Harder." *Forbes*. April 17. www.forbes.com/sites/joannmuller/2013/04/17/volkswagens-mission-to-dominate-globalauto-industry-gets-noticeably-harder/#52b13a501ab6.

Nagel, Thomas. 1986. *The View from Nowhere*. New York: Oxford University Press.

Neufeldt, Victoria. 1997. *Webster's New World College Dictionary*. New York: Macmillan.

Nguyen, B. 2022. "Sam Bankman-Fried Was Once Caught Playing the Video Game 'League of Legends' during a Pitch Meeting for FTX." *Business Insider*. November 10. www.businessinsider.com/ftx-sam-bankman-fried-league-of-legends-investor-pitch-meeting-2022-11.

Novitz, David. 1987. *Knowledge, Faction, and Imagination*. Philadelphia, PA: Temple University Press.

National Public Radio. 2015. "'It Was Installed for This Purpose,' VW's U.S. CEO Tells Congress About Defeat Device," NPR, October 8. www.npr.org/sections/thetwo-way/2015/10/08/446861855/volkswagen-u-s-ceo-faces-questions-on-capitol-hill.

Nussbaum, Martha. 1986. *The Fragility of Goodness*. Cambridge: Cambridge University Press.

1990. *Love's Knowledge*. New York: Oxford University Press.

Oliver, Joshua. 2022. "We Kind of Lost Track: How Sam Bankman-Fried Blurred Lines between FTX and Alameda Exchange's Former CEO Says He Was Close to Key Decisions at Nominally Separate Trading Firm." *Financial Times*. December 1. www.ft.com/content/a1df1d73-9932-4d1b-b63a-c0c82241a236/.

Osipovich, Alexander. 2024. "Bankman-Fried Is Returned to New York Jail after Abortive Cross-Country Trip." *Wall Street Journal*. May 30. www.wsj.com/livecoverage/stock-market-today-dow-jones-earnings-05-302024/card/bankman-fried-is-returned-to-new-york-jail-after-abortive-cross-country-trip-Gz1eekMVTq43oXK8BikG.

Pareto, V. [1906] 2014. *Manual of Political Economy* Oxford: Oxford University Press.

Parmar, B. 2017. "Disobedience of Immoral Orders from Authorities: An Issue Construction Perspective." *Organizational Studies*, 38: 1373–1396.

Parmar, B., Elms, H., and Werhane, P. 2016. Examining the women in the Milgram experiments. Working Paper.

Pasztor, A. 2020. "FAA, Boeing Blasted Over 737 MAX Failures in Democratic Report." *Wall Street Journal*. September 16. www.wsj.com/business/airlines/f aa-boeing-blasted-over-737-max-failures-in-democratic-report-11600246802.

Pasztor, A., Tangel, A., Wall, R., and Sider, A. 2019. "How Boeing's 737 MAX Failed: The Plane's Safety Systems, and How They Were Developed, Are at the Center of the Aerospace Giant's Unfolding Crisis." *Wall Street Journal*. March 27. www.wsj.com/articles/how-boeings-737-max-failed-11553699239? mod=hp_lead_pos9.

Perry, G. 2012. *Behind the Shock Machine: The Untold Story of the Notorious Milgram Psychology Experiments*. New York: The New Press.

Peters, Thomas J., and Waterman, Robert H., Jr. 1982. *In Search for Excellence*. New York: Harper & Row.

Piketty, T. 2014. *Capital in the Twenty-First Century*, trans. Goldhammer. Cambridge, MA: Harvard University Press.

Plato. [ca. 375 BCE] 2007. *The Republic*, trans. H. D. P. Lee with Introduction by M. Lane. London: Penguin Classic.

Plesk, P. 2001. "Redesigning Health Care with Insights from the Science of Complex Adaptive Systems." *Crossing the Quality Chasm*. Washington DC: National Academy Press. 309–317.

Plungis, J. 2015. "EPA Should Do More Road Emissions Tests, Critics Say." *Automotive News*. September 29. www.autonews.com/article/20150929/OE M11/150929807/epa-should-do-more-roademissions-tests-critics-say.

Pooler, M., & Croft, J. (2020, 11 September). Bankruptcy, jail, ruined lives: Inside the Post Office scandal. *Financial Times*. www.ft.com/content/0138cd7d-9673-436b-86a1-33704b29eb60.

Porter, Michael E., and Kamer, Mark R. 2011. "The Big Idea: Creating Shared Value." Harvard Business Review. January/February. https://hbr.org/2011/01/t he-big-idea-creatingshared-value.

Powers, Charles, and Vogel, David. 1980. *Ethics in the Education of Business Managers*. Hastings-on-Hudson, NY: The Hastings Center.

Prahalad, C. K., and Bettis, R. A. 1986. "The Dominant Logic: A New Linkage between Diversity and Performance." *Strategic Management*, 7: 485–501.

Price, Martin. 1983. *Forms of Life: Character and Moral Imagination in the Novel.* New Haven, CT: Yale University Press.

Putnam, Hilary. 1990. *Realism with a Human Face.* Cambridge, MA: Harvard University Press.

Quijano, A. 2007. "Coloniality and Modernity/Rationality." *Cultural Studies*, 21: 168–178.

Railton, Peter. 1986. "Moral Realism." *Philosophical Review*, 95: 168–175.

Ramo, Simon. 1969, *Cure for Chaos.* New York: D. Mackay Co.

Rawls, John. 1971. *A Theory of Justice.* Cambridge, MA: Harvard University Press.

Rendtorff, J. 2020. *Moral Blindness.* London: Palgrave MacMillan.

Rescher N. 1996. *Process Metaphysics: An Introduction to Process Philosophy.* New York: State University of New York Press.

Rest, James R. 1988. "Can Ethics Be Taught to Adults?" In Lisa H. Newton and Maureen M. Ford, eds., *Taking Sides.* Guilford, CT Dushkin Publishing Group. 22–26.

——— 1994. "Background: Theory and Research." *Moral Development in the Professions.* Hillside, NJ: Lawrence Erlbaum. 1–26.

Rest, James R., and Narváez, Darcia, eds. 1994. *Moral Development in the Professions.* Hillside, NJ: Lawrence Erlbaum.

Rhodes, C. and Fleming, P. 2020. "Forget Political Corporate Social Responsibility." *Organizations*, 27: 943–951.

Ricardo, D. [1817] 1992. *The Principles of Political Economy and Taxation.* Minneola, NY: Dover Books.

Ricoeur, Paul. 1979. "The Metaphysical Process as Cognition, Imagination and Feeling." In Sheldon Sacks, ed., *On Metaphor.* Chicago: University of Chicago Press. 141–157.

"Rio Tinto and Bougainville Community Residents Reach Agreement to Assess Legacy Impacts of Panguna Mine." July 11, 2021 *Business Wire.* www.businesswire.com/news/home/20210720006261/en/Rio-Tinto-and-Bougainvillecommunity-residents-reach-agreement-to-assess-legacy-impacts-of-Panguna-mine.

Roberts, J. 2022. "30-year-old Billionaire Sam Bankman-Fried Has Been Called the Next Warren Buffet." *Fortune.* August 1. https://fortune.com/2022/08/01/ftxcrypto-sam-bankman-fried-interview/.

Rorty, Amelie. 1980. *Explaining Emotions.* Berkeley: University of California Press.

Rorty, Richard. 1993. "Putnam and the Relativist Menace." *Journal of Philosophy*, 90: 443–561.

Rossi, Philip J. 1980. "Moral Interest and Moral Imagination in Kant." *Modern Schoolman*, 58: 149–158.

Rouse, William B., and Morris, Nancy M. 1986. "On Looking into the Black Box: Prospects and Limits in the Search for Mental Models." *Psychological Bulletin*, 100: 349–363.

Rowe, N. 2024. "Even in His Final Hour, Sam Bankman-Fried Insisted FTX Was a Crisis of Liquidity: Not Outright Fraud." *Fortune*. March 28. https://fortune.com/crypto/2024/03/28/sam-bankman-fried-sentencing-crisis-liquidity-fraud-ftx-crypto-exchange/.

Sampath, U. 2022. "McDondld's to Exit Russia after 30 Years amid Ukraine War." *Global News*. May 16. https://globalnews.ca/news/8838218/mcdonalds-russia-exit-ukraine-war/.

Sandel, Michael. 1982. *Liberalism and the Limits of Justice*. Cambridge: Cambridge University Press.

Sartre, Jean-Paul. 1940. *L'imaginaire: Psychologie phénoménologique de l'imagination*. Paris: Éditions Gallimard.

——— 1956. *Being and Nothingness*, trans. Hazel Barnes. New York: Philosophical Library.

Scherer, A. G. and Palazzo, G. 2011. "The New Political Role of Scherer." In "The New Political Role of Business in a Globalized World: A Review of a New Perspective on CSR and Its Implications for the Firm, Governance, and Democracy." *Journal of Management Studies*, 48: 899–931.

Scherer, A. G., Rasche, A., Palazzo, G., and Spicer, A. 2016. "Managing for Political Corporate Social Responsibility: New Challenges and Directions for PCSR 2.0." *Journal of Management Studies*, 53: 273–298.

Schwartz, H. 1987. *Narcissistic Process and Corporate Decay*. New York: New York University Press.

Sen, Amartya. 1993. "Positional Objectivity." *Philosophy and Public Affairs*, 22: 119–130.

Senge, Peter. 1990. *The Fifth Discipline*. New York: Doubleday.

Sethi, S. Prakash. 1994. *Multinational Corporations and the Impact of Public Advocacy on Corporate Strategy*. Dordrecht: Kluwer Academic Publishers.

Shackle, G. L. S. 1979. *Imagination and the Nature of Choice*. Edinburgh: Edinburgh University Press.

Shepardson, D. 2020. "Boeing, FAA Reviewing Wiring Issue on Grounded 737 Max." Reuters. January 5. www.reuters.com/article/us-boeing-737maxsafety/boeing-faa-reviewing-wiring-issue-on-grounded-737-max-idUSKBN1Z40U9 .

Shepardson, D., and Schectman, J. 2016. "VW Agrees to Buy Back Diesel Vehicles, Fund Clean Air Efforts." Reuters. June 28. www.reuters.com/article/usvolkswagen-emissions-settlement-idUSKCN0ZD2S5.

Shroff, N., and Reavis, C. 2024. "Sam Bankman-Fried's FTX." MIT Sloan School of Management Case # 23-210.

Sider, A., and Tangel, A. 2019. "Before 737 MAX, Boeing's Flight-Control System Included Key Safeguards." *Wall Street Journal*. September 29. www.wsj.com/articles/before-737-max-boeings-flight-control-system-included-key-safeguards-11569754800?mod=author_content_page_37_pos_8.

Smith, Adam. [1759] 1976. *The Theory of Moral Sentiments*, ed. A L. Macfie and D. D. Raphael. Oxford: Oxford University Press.

[1776] 1976. *The Wealth of Nations*, ed. R. H. Campbell and A. S. Skinner. Oxford: Oxford University Press.

[1763] 1978. *Lectures on Jurisprudence (A) and (B)*, ed. R. L. Meek, D. D. Raphael, and P. G. Stein. Oxford: Oxford University Press.

Solomon, R. 1992. *Ethics and Excellence*. New York: Oxford University Press.

Sorokanich, Bob. 2015. "Report: Bosch Warned VW About Diesel Emissions Cheating in 2007." *Car and Driver*. September 28. http://blog.caranddriver.com/report-bosch-warned-vw-aboutdiesel-emissions-cheating-in-2007/.

Soussi, Alasdair. 2024. "The Great British Post Office Scandal Explained." *Al Jazeera*. January 9. www.aljazeera.com/news/2024/1/9/the-great-british-postoffice-scandal-explained.

Starbuck, William H., and Milliken, Frances J. 1988. "Executives' Perceptual Filters: What They Notice and How They Make Sense." In Donald Hambrick, ed. *The Executive Effect: Concepts and Methods for Studying Top Executives*. Greenwich CT: JAI Press.

Stevens, R. 2022. "What Is an Exchange Token?" *CoinDesk*. November 8. www.coindesk.com/learn/what-is-an-exchange-token/.

Stigler, George. 1971. "Smith's Travels on the Ship of State." *History of Political Economy*. 3: 621–638.

Stiglitz, J. 2002. *Globalization and Its Discontents*. London: Penguin.

Stiglitz, J. 2018. *Globalization and Its Discontents Revisited*. New York: W. W. Norton & Co.

Strong, J. 2024. *Mr Bates vs The Post Office* [Miniseries]. UK ITV Studios.

Subramanian, Satyajeet, 2011. Bayer CropScience in India: Value Driven Strategy, Richard Ivey School of Business Foundation, University of Western Ontario, London, January.

Sweney, M. (2024, 7 January). What is the Post Office Horizon IT scandal all about? *The Guardian*. https://www.theguardian.com/business/2024/jan/07/what-is-the-post-office-horizon-it-scandal-all-about.

Tangel, A., Pasztor, A., and Wall, R. 2019. "Prosecutors, Transportation Department Scrutinize Development of Boeing's 737 Max. A Grand Jury's Subpoena Seeks Broad Documents Related to the Jetliner." *Wall Street Journal*, March 18. www.wsj.com/articles/faas-737-max-approval-isprobed-1155286840.

Tarbell, I. M. 1905. *The History of the Standard Oil Company*. New York, NY: McClure, Phillips & Co.

Taylor, C. 2004. *Modern Social Imaginaries*. Durham, NC: Duke University Press.

Than, Yi-Fu. 1989. *Morality and Imagination*. Madison: University of Wisconsin Press.

Thompson, J. 1984. *Studies in the Theory of Ideology*. London: Polity.

Tichy, Noel M., and Sherman, Stratford. 1993. *Control Your Destiny or Someone Else Will*. New York: HarperCollins.

Tierney, Nathan L. 1994. *Imagination and Ethical Ideals*. Albany: State University of New York Press.

Tivnan, Edward. 1995. *The Moral Imagination*. New York: Simon & Schuster.

Tkacik. M. 2019. "Crash Course: How Boeing's Managerial Culture Created the 737 MAX Disaster." *New Republic*. September 18. https://newrepublic.com/article/154944/boeing-737-max-investigation-indonesia-lion-air-ethiopian-airlines-managerial-revolution-737

Trilling, Lionel. 1972. *Sincerity and Authenticity*. Cambridge, MA: Harvard University Press.

1976. *The Liberal Imagination*. New York: Scribner.

Tronto, Joan. 1994. *Moral Boundaries*. New York: Routledge, Chapman, and Hall.

Tuan, Yi-Fu. 1989. *Morality and Imagination*. Madison: University of Wisconsin Press.

US Department of Energy. 2016. "U.S. HEV Sales by Model." Alternative Fuels Data Center. January. www.afdc.energy.gov/data/.

Useem, J. 2019. "The Long-Forgotten Flight That Sent Boeing Off Course: A Company Once Driven by Engineers Became a Company Driven by Finance." *The Atlantic*. November 20. www.theatlantic.com/ideas/archive/2019/11/how-boeing-lost-itsbearings/602188/.

Valukas, A. 2014. "Report to the Board of Directors of General Motors Company Regarding Ignition Switch Recalls." Jenner and Block White Paper.

Van Luijk, H. 2001. Extending Business Ethics Beyond the Ethical Actor. Georgetown University Unpublished Speech.

Vargish, Thomas. 1991. "The Value of Humanities in Executive Development." *Sloan Management Review*, 32: 84–89.

Velasquez, Manuel. 1988. *Business Ethics*, 2nd ed. Englewood Cliffs, NJ: Prentice-Hall.

Vidaver-Cohen, Deborah. 1997. "Moral Imagination in Organizational Problem Solving: An Institutional Perspective." *Business Ethics Quarterly*, 7: 1–26.

Vlasic, B. 2016. "G.M. Begins Prevailing in Lawsuits over Faulty Ignition Switches." *New York Times*. April 11. www.nytimes.com/2016/04/11/business/gmbegins-prevailing-in-lawsuits-over-faulty-ignition-switches.html.

Volkswagen. 2010. "The Volkswagen Group Code of Conduct, 2010." https://tinyurl.com/978dc7dj.

———. 2013. Annual Report. www.volkswagen-group.com/en/publications/corporate/annual-report-2013-2331.

———. 2014. Annual Report. https://annualreport2014.volkswagenag.com/collection.

———. 2015. "The Volkswagen Group Code of Conduct." September. https://tinyurl.com/p2feybf3.

———. 2016. Annual Report. https://annualreport2016.volkswagenag.com/.

Wallerstein, E. 2023. "FTX and Sam Bankman-Fried: Your Guide to the Crypto Crash." *Wall Street Journal.* January 19. www.wsj.com/articles/ftx-and-sam-bankman-fried-yourguide-to-the-crypto-crash-11669375609.

Walzer, Michael. 1983. *Spheres of Justice.* New York: Basic Books.

———. [1994] 2019. *Thick and Thin.* Notre Dame, IN: Notre Dame University Press.

Weaver, Gary, and Gioia, Dennis. 1994. "Paradigms Lost: Incommensurability vs. Structurationist Inquiry." *Organization Studies,* 15: 565–590.

Weick, K. 1995. *Sensemaking in Organizations.* Thousand Oaks, CA: Sage Publications.

Weil, S. [1947] 1952. *Gravity and Grace.* London: Routledge.

Werhane, Patricia H. 1984. *Philosophical Issues in Art.* Englewood Cliffs, NJ: Prentice-Hall.

———. 1985. *Persons, Rights, and Corporations.* Englewood Cliffs, NJ: Prentice Hall.

———. 1991. *Adam Smith and His Legacy for Modern Capitalism.* New York: Oxford University Press.

———. 1992. *Skepticism, Rules, and Private Languages.* Atlantic Highlands, NJ: Humanities Press.

———. 1997. "The Compatibility of Freedom, Equality, and a Communitarian Notion of the Self." In Jonathan Schonscheck and Larry May, eds., *Liberty, Equality, and Plurality.* Lawrence: University of Kansas Press.

———. 1998. "Moral Imagination and the Search for Ethical Decision Making in Management." *Business Ethics Quarterly 1998.* Ruffin Series Special Issue 1, 75–98.

———. 1999. *Moral Imagination and Management Decision-Making.* New York: Oxford University Press.

———. 2002. "Moral Imagination and Systems Thinking." *Journal of Business Ethics,* 38: 33–42.

———. 2008. "Mental Models, Moral Imagination and Systems Thinking in the Age of Globalization." *Journal of Business Ethics.* 78: 463–474.

———. 2023. "Silo Mentalities, Dominant Logics, and Their Ethical Challenges in the Defense Industry." In Daniel Schoeni and Tobias Vestner, eds., *Ethical*

Dilemmas in the Defense Industry. New York: Oxford University Press. 437–450.
Werhane, P. H., and D. Bevan. 2023. Unpublished paper. "Decolonializing the Political Responsibilities of Global Corporations: Cosmopolitanism and its Discontents."
Werhane, M., and Painter-Morland, M., eds. 2011. *Leadership, Gender, and Organization.* Dordrecht: Springer Verlag.
Werhane, P. H., Hartman, L., Archer, C., Englehardt, E., and Pritchard, M. 2013. *Obstacles To Ethical Decision-Making: Mental Models, Milgram and the Problem of Obedience.* Cambridge: Cambridge University Press.
Whitehead, A. N. 1929. *Science and the Modern World: Lowell Lectures, 1925.* Cambridge: Cambridge University Press.
Whitehead, A. N. [1929] 1978. *Process and Reality: An Essay in Cosmology (Gifford Lectures delivered in the University of Edinburgh 1927–28).* New York: The Free Press.
Wicks, Andrew, and Edward Freeman, R. 1990. "A Note on Obedience to Authority." University of Virginia Darden Graduate School Foundation, E-070. Charlottesville, VA: Darden School, University of Virginia.
Wieland, C. M. 1788. "Das Geheimniß des Kosmopolitenordens." *Der Teutscher Merkur*, 3 (August): 97–115.
Winterkorn, M. 2015. "Statement by Prof. Dr. Winterkorn," Volkswagen US Media Newsroom, September 23. http://media.vw.com/release/1070/.
Wittgenstein, Ludwig. 1953. *Philosophical Investigations*, trans. G. E. M. Anscombe. New York: Macmillan.
Wolf, S. 1999. "Toward a Systemic Theory of Informed Consent in Managed Care." *Houston Law Review* 35: 1631–1681.
Woods, Michael. 1983. "Kant's Transcendental Schematism." *Dialectica*, 70: 201–220.
Yale School of Management 2024. "Over 1,000 Companies Have Curtailed Operations in Russia: But Some Remain." Chief Executive Leadership Institute. October 22. https://som.yale.edu/story/2022/over-1000-companies-have-curtailedoperations-russia-some-remain.
Young, Michael J. 1988. "Kant's View of Imagination." *Kantstudien*, 79: 140–164.
Zhang, B. 2019. "Boeing's CEO Explains Why the Company Didn't Tell 737 MAX Pilots about the Software System That Contributed to 2 Fatal Crashes." *Business Insider*, 29. www.businessinsider.com/boeings-ceo-on-why-737-MAX-pilots-not-toldofmcas-20194.
Zimbardo, Philip. 1973. "A Pirandellian Prison." *New York Times Magazine*.

Index

Arendt, Hannah, 37, 38, 196
Aristotle, 20, 143

Banerjee, Bobby, 160, 164, 196, 197
Bangladesh Bank, The, 142, 153
Bankman-Fried, Sam, 6, 49, 96, 125, 126, 131, 207, 208, 210, 211, 214
Bates, Alan, 91, 92, 117, 155, 156, 197, 198
Bauman, Zygmunt, 3, 87
Bayer, 97, 98, 104, 115, 116, 117, 119, 131, 136, 137, 139, 166, 170, 197, 200, 212
Bentham, Jeremy, 47, 197
Bergson, Henri, 143, 197
Boeing, vi, 3, 5, 7, 8, 9, 10, 15, 16, 17, 18, 19, 20, 22, 24, 25, 28, 30, 31, 32, 35, 38, 45, 46, 47, 49, 63, 75, 117, 128, 129, 136, 198, 199, 201, 202, 204, 205, 206, 207, 209, 211, 212, 213, 215
boundary conditions, 149, 151, 152
Box, George, 70, 198, 211
BP, 3, 4, 5, 7, 35
British Post Office, 7, 12, 87, 88, 89, 90, 91, 92, 96, 117, 125, 136, 142, 145, 151, 155, 156, 197, 198, 202, 207, 212

capitalism, v, vi, 13, 157, 158, 159, 161, 162, 164, 165, 166, 170, 171, 172, 198, 202, 214
Carroll, Archie, 2, 104, 199
child labor, 97, 98, 104, 115, 116, 131, 135, 137, 170
Chomsky, Noam, 68, 199
conceptual scheme, v, 9, 11, 62, 63, 64, 65, 69, 78, 79, 80, 81, 85, 108, 113, 115, 119, 125, 126, 127, 128, 129, 130, 132, 133, 134, 175
CropScience, 97, 98, 104, 115, 117, 119, 131, 136, 137, 139, 166, 170, 200, 212

Davidson, Donald, 11, 64, 65, 76, 77, 78, 79, 80, 86, 127, 200
Dewey, John, 100, 101, 102, 200, 201
Donaldson, Tom, 135, 136, 200, 202

Ehrnström-Fuentes, Maria, 166, 201

Freeman, R. Edward, 38, 202, 215

Gilligan, Carol, 27, 28, 203
Google, vi, 13, 173, 174, 175, 176, 177, 178, 179, 180, 181, 183, 187, 188, 190, 192, 195
Grameen, 146, 153, 154

Halliburton, 3
Heisenberg, Werner, 81, 204
Hobbes, Thomas, 22, 23, 204
Huxley, Aldous, 168, 169, 204

imaginaries, 13, 157, 158, 159, 161, 162, 165, 166, 167, 168, 169, 170, 171, 172

Johnson, Mark, 68, 71, 75, 86, 103, 112, 113, 114, 115, 124, 140, 141, 152, 204

Kant, Immanuel, 63, 64, 65, 99, 109, 110, 111, 112, 113, 115, 117, 118, 119, 205, 207, 210, 215
Kohlberg, Lawrence, 7, 25, 26, 27, 28, 40, 205
Kuhn, Thomas, 76, 77, 129, 205

Levinas, Emmanuel, 43, 44, 206
Lewis, Michael, 50, 51, 52, 53, 205, 206
Lion Air, 17

MacIntyre, Alistair, 86
Mandeville, Bernard, 22
May, Larry, 41, 196, 199, 207, 208, 210, 211, 214
McDonald's, 1, 2, 3, 5, 13, 24, 29, 30, 45, 82, 206, 208
mental models, 6, 10, 11, 12, 62, 63, 65, 66, 67, 68, 70, 71, 72, 73, 74, 76, 77, 78, 79, 81, 82, 85, 86, 93, 94, 95, 96, 104, 109, 113, 114, 115, 122, 125, 126, 127, 128, 129, 131,

134, 140, 141, 148, 151, 152, 158, 175, 176, 182, 185
Milgram, Stanley, 37, 38, 75, 199, 203, 207, 209, 215
moral blindness, 5, 8, 20, 49, 53
moral imagination, i, iv, v, vi, 2, 9, 11, 12, 21, 28, 30, 54, 75, 82, 85, 95, 96, 97, 98, 99, 100, 102, 103, 104, 105, 108, 109, 111, 112, 113, 114, 115, 116, 117, 118, 119, 121, 122, 123, 124, 125, 128, 129, 131, 132, 133, 136, 137, 139, 140, 141, 142, 143, 151, 152, 154, 155, 157, 165, 169, 170, 173, 174, 175, 176, 177, 179, 180, 181, 185, 186, 187, 188, 189, 190, 191, 192, 193, 194, 195, 197, 201, 203, 204, 205, 207, 208, 210, 213, 214
moral reasoning, v, 2, 8, 9, 11, 12, 13, 21, 28, 29, 46, 78, 99, 103, 123, 124, 131, 132, 141, 195
Murdoch, Iris, 1, 14, 156, 208

Nagel, Thomas, 68
Nestle, 132
Nussbaum, Martha, 13, 48, 74, 102, 103, 104, 108, 125, 208

paradigm, v, 78, 102, 129, 158
perspectives, 2, 12, 29, 43, 62, 63, 68, 74, 76, 79, 81, 82, 84, 88, 95, 100, 116, 122, 128, 129, 131, 147, 148, 154, 166, 180, 184, 186, 188, 194, 203
process, v, 2, 3, 37, 41, 42, 43, 44, 46, 62, 66, 70, 71, 82, 85, 86, 89, 94, 96, 97, 105, 108, 110, 113, 114, 116, 117, 120, 122, 124, 125, 127, 128, 131, 132, 133, 136, 137, 138, 139, 140, 141, 143, 144, 145, 147, 149, 151, 152, 153, 154, 155, 156, 159, 164, 171, 178, 180, 183, 184, 186, 188, 190, 192, 194, 195
Putnam, Hilary, 68, 73, 76, 79, 210

Rashomon (movie), v, 53, 84, 85, 87, 92, 96
Rawls, John, 39, 40, 130, 138, 139, 210
relativism, 77, 78, 80, 115, 127, 134, 167
Rendtorff, Jacob, 21, 37, 66, 210
Ricoeur, Paul, 100, 210
Rorty, Richard, 64, 68, 73, 74, 76, 79, 210

Sandel, Michael, 39, 40, 47, 211
Sartre, Jean-Paul, 86, 211
Sen, Amartya, 94, 95, 127, 128, 211
Senge, Peter, 70, 71, 114, 151, 152, 198, 211
Smith, Adam, 22, 23, 24, 28, 67, 68, 99, 105, 106, 107, 108, 109, 113, 117, 119, 129, 130, 161, 171, 197, 198, 205, 212, 214
social construction, 65, 204
stakeholder theory, 149
Stiglitz, Joseph, 159, 160, 212
systems, (and system thinking), 2, 12, 52, 59, 64, 65, 69, 73, 76, 79, 110, 140, 143, 144, 145, 146, 147, 148, 149, 152, 154, 155, 156, 157, 158, 159, 162, 167, 168, 173, 182, 209

Taylor, Charles, 41, 158, 199, 213
Toyota, 58, 60
Transocean, 3, 4

Volkswagen, vi, 8, 36, 56, 57, 58, 59, 60, 61, 62, 63, 72, 73, 75, 76, 81, 82, 83, 118, 136, 196, 198, 201, 202, 203, 204, 205, 206, 208, 211, 212, 214, 215

Wall Street (movie), 6, 25, 50, 72, 198, 199, 208, 209, 212, 214
Walzer, Michael, 42, 43, 44, 134, 135, 136, 214
Weick, Karl, 66, 70, 71
Weil, Simone, 1, 14
Whitehead, Alfred North, 143, 215
Wittgenstein, Ludwig, 68, 69, 79, 81, 93, 196, 215

For EU product safety concerns, contact us at Calle de José Abascal, 56–1°,
28003 Madrid, Spain or eugpsr@cambridge.org.

www.ingramcontent.com/pod-product-compliance
Ingram Content Group UK Ltd.
Pitfield, Milton Keynes, MK11 3LW, UK
UKHW022140240226
468380UK00018B/404